UNCONDITIONAL SUCCESS

Loving the Work We Were Born to Do

www.**booksattransworld**.co.uk

Unconditional
SUCCESS

LOVING THE WORK WE WERE BORN TO DO

NICK WILLIAMS

BANTAM PRESS

LONDON · NEW YORK · TORONTO · SYDNEY · AUCKLAND

TRANSWORLD PUBLISHERS
61–63 Uxbridge Road, London W5 5SA
a division of The Random House Group Ltd

RANDOM HOUSE AUSTRALIA (PTY) LTD
20 Alfred Street, Milsons Point, Sydney,
New South Wales 2061, Australia

RANDOM HOUSE NEW ZEALAND LTD
18 Poland Road, Glenfield, Auckland 10, New Zealand

RANDOM HOUSE SOUTH AFRICA (PTY) LTD
Endulini, 5a Jubilee Road, Parktown 2193, South Africa

Published 2002 by Bantam Press
a division of Transworld Publishers

Geri Halliwell, *If Only*. Copyright © Geri Halliwell 1999. Extract used by permission.
George Herbert, 'Love'. From *The English Spirit*, by the Little Gidding Community.
Used with permission of the Little Gidding Community, Cambridge, UK.
Kabir, 'Clay Jug'. Reprinted from *The Kabir Book*, versions by Robert Bly, Beacon Press, Boston, 1977.
Copyright © 1977 Robert Bly. Used with his permission.
Machado, 'The Wind One Brilliant Day'. Reprinted from *Times Alone: Selected Poems of Antonio Machado*,
translated by Robert Bly, Wesleyan University Press, Middletown, CT, 1983. Copyright © 1983 Robert Bly.
Used with permission.
Oriah Mountain Dreamer, 'The Invitation'. Reprinted from *The Invitation* by Oriah Mountain Dreamer,
HarperCollins Publishers, London. Used with permission.
Rumi, 'This We Have Now'. Translated by Coleman Barks, from *The Essential Rumi* by
Coleman Barks and John Moyne. Used with permission of Coleman Barks.
William Stafford, 'A Ritual to Read to Each Other'. Reprinted from *The Way It Is: New & Selected Poems* with the
permission of Graywolf Press, Saint Paul, Minnesota. Copyright © 1960, 1998 by the Estate of William Stafford.
David Whyte, 'The Opening of Eyes'. From *Songs for Coming Home* by David Whyte.
Copyright © 1999 David Whyte. Many Rivers Press, Langley, WA.
The publishers have made every effort to contact copyright owners. In the few cases where they have been
unsuccessful they invite copyright holders to contact them direct.

A catalogue record for this book is available from the British Library.
ISBN 0593 048970

Typeset in 11/16 pt Sabon by Falcon Oast Graphic Art Ltd.

Printed in Great Britain by
Clays Ltd, Bungay, Suffolk

1 3 5 7 9 10 8 6 4 2

CONTENTS

ACKNOWLEDGEMENTS

For this book I have had continued support, encouragement and inspiration from old faithfuls, and some new inspirations.

As always, my partner Helen Bee has been my incredible love and support, and so accepting of me as I spent many long hours writing. To my mum and dad for providing me with love, space, encouragement and support to write at their home. To my sister Amanda. To Maurice Simons.

To the three guys with whom I have spent nearly ten years: we've watched each other grow, struggle and fly – Adam Stern, Matt Ingrams and Martin Wenner. To Juliette Pollitzer again for her continued insights and unfailing support, and to Peter, Jan, Linda and Catherine for our continuing journeying together. To Tom and Linda Carpenter for simply being in the world.

Great thanks to my editor Brenda Kimber and to Sadie Mayne at Transworld for their suggestions and support; to copy editor Beth Humphries and to my agent Andrew Lownie. Enormous thanks to The Heart at Work team – Kathy Doyle, Kathy Breidenbach, Niki Hignet, Sue Izzard, Maria Tramontana, Natalie Kennedy, Steve Jacab, Tom Cook. To Marsha Grothe, who died while I was writing this book. To everyone at Alternatives, my spiritual home. The trustees Steve Noble, Tom Cook, Richard Dunkerley, Mary Preist-Cobern, Amanda Denning, John Hunt, Chris Greaves and Malcolm Stern. To the rest of the team at Alternatives – Raphaelle Sadler, Jackie Butler, Priya Calay, Rachel Carroll, Samantha Marshall, Clive Hierons, Margaret Dempsey, Mujeeb Habab, Richard Ellison, Susannah Howe and Beatrice Ceccarelli. Thanks to all at St James's especially Charles Hedley, Mary Robins and Ashley Ashworth. Thanks to Kathy Doyle again for her friendship and support and for being the heart of Heart at Work. To Michael Daly for all the great organizing and grand times in Dublin, and to Linda Tuttiet for her hospitality. And to Patricia and Colin.

Thanks again to my Malvern family, Cally, Gordon, Alistair and Bethany, and to Edna. Thanks to Sharna, Anton and Sophie for love and friendship. To my Reading family, Chris Greaves and Peter Burton. My Littlehampton family – Ann Marie Woodall and Woody. Thanks to John Coyne for his generosity and being an inspiration to me. Thanks to Bill Pitcher for friendship and encouragement, and Phyllis for friendship, and everyone else involved in IACMP. Thanks to Celia Couchman and all the other couch people.

Thanks to Sally Morris, Patricia and Barry for friendship. Thanks still to Julia McCutchen for having faith and getting me started, and for our growing friendship. Thanks to William Bloom for continuing friendship.

To Robert and Miranda Holden for friendship, and to Ben Renshaw for daily check-ins, support and encouragement. To Jeff Allen who kindly agreed to give me substantial support, feedback and ideas while I was writing, and to the work of Chuck and Lency

Spezzano, whose work in Psychology of Vision continues to inspire me. Great thanks to David Peet for his insights. Thanks also to Julie Wookey, Su Allen and to all my other friends throughout POV, especially Jo, Pam, Debs and Anna, and special thanks to Jaki Harris and to Serenna Davies for being such great friends. To Barbara Winter, for fun, passion and enthusiasm and the sheer joy of meeting a kindred spirit, as well as for fixing up for me to come to the USA to work. Thanks to Karyn Ruth White for inspiration, and for showing me around Denver. Long live Electric Monks, and kicking 'ahss'.

To Gregg Levoy for his wonderful book *Callings*, and his London workshop, and our mutual admiration. To Marianne Williamson for being the wonderful and inspiring teacher of *A Course in Miracles*, and influencing me so deeply without even knowing it, and for introducing me to the Course. To Nancy Rosanoff and Carol Adrienne. Great thanks to soul friend Helen Burton for all her amazing work in Cape Town, and also to Gilly and Dave Shreeve. David Whyte for his work, and for helping me remember that I have a very poetic soul, and allowing me to honour that. To Lissie Evans for sorting my back out, Susannah Hall for Bowen and Karen Byrne for believing in me and keeping my energy high. To all involved in the New Warrior work, and especially Mike Jones for some crucial support. To Richard Olivier for doing such inspiring work in the corporate world. Thanks to Roxy and Karen for my accounting and bookkeeping, and many grateful thanks also to all the fellow travellers who have been at my talks and workshops, or who have sought coaching and support. They have all taught me so much.

Finally, once again I give heartfelt thanks for an amazing book called *A Course in Miracles*. It never ceases to illuminate my life and remind me of the unconditional love at the heart of creation. To the source and the scribe, thank you.

And again to Hergist, Hercule and the rest of our family.

The New Success Ethic

·

We have been told that the rat race is the road to success. Yet many of us today have an idea of success different from those of previous generations. For us, success is not defined exclusively in economic terms but includes the opportunity to express our innate talents and abilities, to be creatively engaged, to feel we are making a meaningful difference, and to integrate our spiritual values with the everyday business of working and making a living. This is unconditional success.

All of us have a calling to be true and authentic – it is up to us to create a channel for our love and passion to flow into the world, and our work and success are one great way we can make this happen. At the heart of each of us as a unique individual is the power to create unconditional success, right now. Within each of us are incredible creative contributions waiting to see the light of day. Fulfilment of our destiny helps so many people. As we discover the shape of our own soul, finding, following, and living our authentic calling, we create a beautiful match between who we are in essence and what we do in the world: our work becomes an expression of who we are, and a reflection of our essence. Our purpose in success is to bring the love that is deep within us into this world so that our spirits soar, we unleash our imagination and invoke our creative potential.

The call to follow our heart is eternal and universal, and can lead to deep fulfilment. We all want work that is a manifestation of our deepest values and the evolving notion of our life purpose. We need a sense of belonging, of connection, to belong to a family, team or organization, so that we can see and be seen, and create relationships that feed our spirit.

INTRODUCTION

We all have a blueprint for our personal success within us, right now. This is not necessarily the success that comes from competing and struggling to win wealth, fame and status; it is the success of happiness and fulfilment, the feeling of knowing that you are living your own authentic and natural life. It is the success of knowing, from deep inside, that you are OK, you are lovable, worthy and loving, that you are precious and valuable. Ultimately, it is knowing and finding the place in life that only you can uniquely fill, and knowing that you were created for that purpose. It is having your life unfold more easily on a day by day basis to greater love, abundance and creativity, and to essential joy. It is having whatever money and material things we need for the journey, but acknowledging that the journey isn't just about material success. It is a journey of discovery into who we really are, of abandoning the façades we have erected. It is the journey home. This is unconditional success, and its seeds are woven into our very soul.

In my early twenties, I set out to be successful; I thought that would make me happy. Success for me, at that time, meant money and all the material things it could buy me, like a house, a mortgage, a car. I could be grown up, work hard and push myself; I could play hard, and have a girlfriend. The world of sales and marketing appealed to me, and within a few years I had become pretty successful, in material terms. Increasingly, however, as my late twenties arrived, I began to question it all. Like so many successful people, I had all that I thought would make me happy, but it was dawning on me that I wasn't very happy at all.

Was there something wrong with me? I had, after all, achieved so much. I was confused, and began to feel a certain despair. Everything became a bit meaningless. What was the point of more of the same? If this much hadn't made me happy, how much more would? What should I do? I began to ask for and get help. I went into therapy, started to read about psychology, and then stumbled across some spiritual books. Then I had one of those insightful moments, an epiphany and revelation – there was no real spirit in my life!

I began to see that I was only *partly* living life. I was living the life I thought I should live, doing the things I thought you were supposed to do. It was then that I asked myself a life-changing question: what *would* I love to be doing? The answer that came to me was: teach, love, inspire, write, travel, be creative, be authentic, have fun, heal some of the pain I was now feeling, and grow. I thought I had the right answer – but for the wrong person! I was a computer salesman from Essex! How could I teach or inspire others; what spiritual ideas did I have to share with the world? What made *me* so special?

But this inner voice and intuition didn't go away, it remained strong. I realized how much I had prided myself on being able to talk down this voice. It wasn't going to get me! I was stronger than that. I could fight it! But gradually I saw that the inner voice calling me wasn't my enemy, it was my ally: it was trying to lead me to what would bring me happiness, to what would be my greatest joy. Slowly I began to listen to this inner voice, and the sense of rightness it offered me. As I started to choose to partner with it rather than fight it, my life began to click into place. I felt I was finding the path that had been there all the time, the one I'd missed when I was busy building my materially successful life. Quite suddenly, I literally felt that I was getting on track.

I discovered a new starting point. I had believed in and experienced a lack and an emptiness in myself and had thought that success would take this away – that it would fill the void. I now realized this was my ego at work and that there was another part of me – my spirit – that was telling me a different story. It told me that I was *already* a success and that my success was not dependent on outer achievements. My job was to delve deeper, and to discover this unconditional self. It is this self which exists within each of us.

What I want to share with you in this book is a journey to inner and outer success. Our *conditional* self or ego is the part of us that we have constructed and have come to believe. It is the story of our life – our beliefs and limitations, our achievements, and what we perceive to be our value and worth. And all too often this story leads us to feel inadequate, unworthy – even desperate – as we struggle to change what we feel is 'wrong' with us. What I want to show you is how to access your *unconditional* self. This is the part of you that isn't your history, it isn't your story, it isn't your beliefs. It is that part of you that was created whole, full and complete and wants for nothing. This is the *real* you. It is the love and spirit within you. This part of each of us is fearless and capable of miracles. It is powerful and creative. As we discover this innate, unconditional self we'll begin to feel more fulfilled, abundant, creative and energized. Our life will have a beautiful quality of authenticity to it and the boundaries and barriers which have contained us and limited our potential will begin to disappear. It works through laws known and unknown, natural and often miraculous. It can change the course of our destiny: and it is our destiny.

There is no one path or technique that will lead you to this unique self. There are many ways home to it, and here I will share some that I have found most powerful and most useful. I have been on many personal development courses; I have learned all the techniques. There are many attributes of success – positive thinking, dynamic will, self-analysis, initiative and self-control, which are all important. But these all fail to give credit to the most important factor of all – our unconditional self, the power of love and divinity within every one of us, right now. Attunement to our unconditional self is the key factor in creating and attracting true success in our life.

Part of our success is determined by inspiration, brilliant ideas and how we initiate them, and a major supporter of our success is our daily habits: what we do, how we think, what we tell ourselves, and what we focus on daily. Habits are consistent thoughts, actions and deeds. It's important to develop habits that nourish our unconditional self, our self-belief, our self-love. Good habits create opportunities. Unconditional success is freeing ourselves from unhelpful habits, and embracing new habits. I think we need constant reminders to keep us inspired.

Get yourself a journal, the best you can afford, so that you can capture insights and ideas as we travel together on our journey. You'll be gently challenged to see yourself as more than you think you are – more powerful, more creative, more loving, more worthy. Capture the limits, the resistance, as well as the insights and inspirations. Be willing to begin an adventure, to evolve, to shed skins and grow.

You are more than you think you are.

•

Unconditional success resides within you right now, in your unconditional self.

•

It is your very essence, your spirit, the you that you truly are, and is how you were created.

•

No outer success can ever give you more than you already are. As we remember the amazing beings that we are, our lives begin to work better and all we need begins to flow to us.

I

UNCONDITIONAL SUCCESS

*Success should therefore be measured by your yardstick of
happiness; by your ability to remain in peaceful harmony with
cosmic laws. Success is not rightly measured by the worldly
standards of wealth, prestige and power. None of these bestow
happiness unless they are rightly used.*

PARAMAHANSA YOGANANDA, author of *The Law of Success*

You are an unconditional success right now. There is nothing
wrong with you, in fact everything is right with you, although you
may not realize this. You were wonderfully and fearlessly made. If
you knew this truth, this book would be superfluous. If you believe
in a God, you are God's success story. If not, you are still an unconditional success, because there is a power beyond measure that
resides in you that is truly awesome. This is your unconditional
self, a being that was created in love and in beauty.

This book is about how you reveal the power of your

unconditional self in your life, and to the world, in order to have the things you want – but even more importantly, in order to experience the inner fulfilment that will make your life more complete.

One of our great challenges is not to let the practicalities of life overwhelm our joy, spirit and essential mystery, and to keep our sense of awe and wonder alive. This achievement will not come from what we do, but from who we are. The most important relationship in life is the relationship with our self, and in unconditional success we'll learn how to engage in meaningful conversations with the grander, more eternal and essential parts of ourselves. Unconditional success exists on another realm of consciousness from the one that dominates our everyday life. We need to develop a kind of X-ray vision if we are to gain the ability to see beyond the physical appearances of this world, to see with spiritual eyes as well as with the eyes of the body.

WAKING UP

Our life is a game of hide-and-seek. We hide the fact that we are powerful people, creative, abundant, loving, shining. We allow ourselves to believe that we are not good enough. We create the roles and duties in our life that make us unhappy, frustrated, bored and unfulfilled; it is only when we become steeped in dissatisfaction that we face the truth and admit to ourselves that there is something missing from our life. So we start seeking that something else that we think will fulfil us and make us happy. We look outside for things, for achievements. Think of the musk deer that spends its whole life seeking the source of the scent it adores, without realizing that it is itself the source of the fragrance. We too are seeking for ourselves, the true us that is hidden behind all the labels we carry. When we shift our seeking from outside us to inside us, we start to wake up. To awaken is to know that what we have been seeking has been with us all the time. The greatest blocks to our success are found within ourselves.

This is the journey of success. Something inside us is stirring, telling us there is more, but it's not more of the same. It's a *new* more, more of what truly matters, and it will truly fulfil us. Once this has started, we are on our way, and external effects cannot fail to happen. We're all capable of internal stirring, because we have been coded for it. It is our potential for greatness. This is the awakening of our incredible personal power, the power to create lives that are the true and authentic us.

THERE ARE TWO PARTS OF US TELLING TWO DIFFERENT STORIES ABOUT SUCCESS

Work is a place where the self meets the world and is made manifest, but the question is, which self? There are two parts of us, telling two stories of success. These parts are our ego, which is our conditional self, and our spirit, which is our unconditional self.

Our conditional self, or ego, is the part of us that we are familiar with; it's our personality and characteristics. It is an extraordinary concept because this knowledge of ourselves influences us enormously throughout our lives and often limits our potential. Underlying this knowledge is fear – fear that there is something missing. Consequently, we are always looking outside ourselves for success and happiness. Our conditional self has a worldview based on lack and scarcity, so sees life as a battle, a competition to get its share of the short supply; it is always striving, but never arrives. It's the part of us that is constantly judging ourselves and others and is always discovering that we're never quite good enough!

Our unconditional self is our true, magnificent and essential nature; it is our very being, who we *really* are. It is the part that has been created whole and complete, and was, is and always will be an unconditional success in the eyes of our creator. We can never lose our connection to our unconditional self. It is not of this world; we come, as William Wordsworth said, 'trailing clouds of glory'. It cannot cease to exist, and there is nothing we can do to alter it in any way at all. It is connected with the whole of creation, knows no fear, only safety; it needs to prove nothing, and its only goal is to extend itself. It is essentially creative, unlimited and abundant, existing eternally in a state of grace. When we connect with this unconditional self, we can truly experience joy and the success that we already are.

These two selves have very different stories to tell about success and what it means.

Our conditional self's version of success

•

Life is tough and unfriendly, and our happiness is largely dependent on our circumstances and achievements – success comes from outside. You aren't good enough, and there will always be someone better than you. There isn't enough to go around, you must compete, and indeed your self-worth is dependent upon competing and achieving. You cannot take your innate worth for granted: you continually have to prove yourself through hard work, effort and struggle. Around every corner could be failure, loss and scarcity, so life is a constant struggle against possible defeat. You can't relax, you can't trust. Life can be a competition to escape failure and defend against poverty. You always have to change, develop and learn new skills so that you don't end up redundant. Success is scarce, and needs to be guarded and fought for even when achieved. Life is full of stress, busyness, overwork and sacrifice, which is the price we must pay in order to minimize the risk of falling by the wayside or being abandoned. Survival is our great motivation.

Our unconditional self's version of success

•

The universe is essentially a friendly place, and we are born with many blessings. You have an incredible power within you, and are essentially happy, joyful and creative – independently of the circumstances, failures or achievements of life. You are already an unconditional success, and your success comes from within. You have intrinsic worth and value, and these attributes have little to do with material possessions or work status. You are not your work – who you are is bigger and more valuable than any work you will ever do. There is enough to go around, and everyone can win and can succeed. Within each person is the source of creativity and abundance, and success is about bringing out our own unique gifts and talents. When people join together, co-operate and form partnerships, they can all experience success. It can be a joy to learn, grow and develop. We know that we are divine beings, gods in embryo, and our motivation is not to prove ourselves but to create, to share our gifts and give expression to our divinity. Our motivation is not to struggle to survive, but to self-actualize and become who we truly are.

Most of us experience both voices within us, often in conflicting ways. Most of us have had a pretty good training in thinking we are our ego, that this is all we are, and tend to dismiss our unconditional self as a flight of fantasy or as something that may exist but is not a major factor in our lives. We are trained to think that the major purpose of work is to provide for our physical existence, rather than as a way of finding and expressing our innermost being. I want to help you understand that our unconditional self is the eternal truth of who we are, that it is within us right now, and is the most powerful and practical tool that we have in our life. One of the greatest disciplines in life is to remember what is truly important and precious to us in the midst of our busyness and business.

Success is our ego's offering of happiness, but our ego can't make us happy. Our unconditional self is already happy, right now. Our ego says: but if we are really successful we'll be safe, or at least safer. Our unconditional self is telling us that we are already safe. All we have to do is to learn to listen and trust this voice.

OUR UNCONDITIONAL SELF – OUR SPIRIT

Our unconditional self is our spirit, the essence of who we are. It is how we were created, and nothing has ever happened to it. Our unconditional self is our happiness, it is our joy, it is our peace and love. The key thing to remember is that our unconditional self is everything we ever wanted, right now. Yes, this very minute you have everything you could ever need inside you. Isn't that a wonderful thought? Our unconditional self has no off switch – it never goes anywhere. As we connect more to our unconditional self, our life can be an evolution towards experiencing new levels of inner and outer success. We can never be alone, we are never left without comfort, even though we may not be aware of it. Just as the sun shines whether there are clouds, rain, snow or hurricanes, so with our spirit. It is always there waiting for us to return to it.

The Eastern mystics call our unconditional self the uncarved block. Other concepts include the Zen term 'original face', the Buddhist idea of sacred happiness and the Christian mystic idea of inner Eden, the heaven within us. Others call it our higher mind, universal intelligence, our inner Presence, God, Goddess, and every other name that we have for God. It is our universal and eternal self. It is our original and most precious self, the answer to all our seeming problems in life. It contains everything we could ever want or need. It is the highest goal of all, but for many of us it is not how we identify ourselves. This concept of our unconditional self, and the conflict between ego and spirit, is not new, it is as old as humanity. In truth, our unconditional self does not fight or create conflict: our ego fights to keep us unaware of our unconditional self.

Our spiritual nature is often not found, because it is not looked for! Our spiritual nature can seem elusive because we spend 16 hours a day in a world that glorifies personality, not spirit. For example, we may need to take time out from the world to find it, so that we can return to the world and function better in it.

EXPERIENCING OUR GRANDEUR

A Course in Miracles is a wonderful book of spiritual psychotherapy. It teaches us that within us is both grandeur and grandiosity. Grandiosity relates to our conditional self, our attempt to be some- one, and underlying it is the fear that actually we are nothing much at all. It is the ego's effort to embellish our natural state. The ego inter- feres with our clear expression of power by trying to get us to add something to it. This is actually a ploy by which it thwarts our capac- ity to express who we really are and accept full recognition from others in return. Grandeur is our true spiritual power, the us that we dream we could be and that we only sometimes remember we are. It is the natural light of creation within us all. We really are that amaz- ing, but we usually forget this because of our years of conditioning, and because our society often doesn't acknowledge a living spiritual and sacred dimension to life. Our deepest need is not material at all. Providing for our material needs is part of the puzzle, but to know our own grandeur is what will fulfil us.

WE ARE AS WE WERE CREATED

We are created as love in essence; that is who we are. Our world is one of forgetting, a place where we have largely forgotten who we really are. We think we are fearful, but the true purpose of our life here is remembering. The purpose of our life – every life – is to awaken from the bad dream in order to begin to remember that we were created in loving wholeness, as a child of the creator, and that nothing has changed.

We have tended to worship the great spiritual teachers, putting them on pedestals and being in awe of them. Many religious teachings have encouraged us to do just that. In truth, no authentic spiritual teacher has ever claimed anything for themselves that they have not also claimed for the whole of humanity. They are our brothers and sisters: no better, just more awake or fully awake. They have known themselves in their full divinity, their full essence of love. Buddha taught that the Buddha nature is within all of us. Jesus told us that everything he did we can do, and more too. A number of spiritual traditions describe the path of self-realization, which is remembering the essence of love that we are, on a daily basis, in the midst of our lives, whatever we are doing.

We may have been brought up with the idea that the creative force of the universe is something separate from us, even remote and distant. The loving essence that we are is forever *inside* us and the handle to the door is on the inside. Mystics and some poets have always known this, and when I first heard the poem below, by Kabir and translated by Robert Bly, it inspired and touched me deeply. We are the clay jug:

Clay Jug

Inside this clay jug there are canyons and pine mountains
and the maker of canyons and pine mountains
all seven oceans are inside
and hundreds of millions of stars
the acid that tests gold is here
also the one who judges jewels
also the music that comes from inside the human body
even though no fingers are touching those strings

also the source of all water
Kabir says
you want the truth, I'll tell you the truth
friend, listen
the God whom I love is inside.

When we begin to remember that all we want we already have, we know instinctively how to live more authentically and this is one of the greatest joys and triumphs of human existence. We feel we can move mountains, we feel we are at home within our own skin, we feel that we are doing the work we were born to do, spacious within ourselves.

UNCONDITIONAL SUCCESS IS BEING MOTIVATED BY LOVE

We are not sent into this world to do anything into which we cannot put our hearts.

JOHN RUSKIN,
1819–1900, writer and art critic

We think that success is about competing and winning in this world, and that what we want are power, money and material things. These things are valuable but the greatest gift and joy in this life is to be wholehearted and to work wholeheartedly, to express the love that is within all of us. Ultimately the things of life will not take us the full distance to true fulfilment, because our fulfilment comes from finding and sharing love, talent, gifts, creativity. These take us all the way. We are spiritual beings and we want not just to know that as an idea, but to experience it ourselves. We do that by following our heart, by being authentic. This is also known as being true to ourselves; by allowing ourselves to trust and be guided, by beginning to give and receive fully in our lives.

What if we changed the purpose of our work? Instead of going to work to get money, to get appreciation and a sense of meaning, we could go to work to spread love, to value, appreciate and enjoy people, to help create some joy. As we begin to do that, the material success and the money come automatically as a by-product; when we are willing to receive, they will follow.

Working wholeheartedly is not about *what* we do, it is about the energy, love and intention with which we work. With love, any work we do can be a joy to experience.

Wholeheartedness is about regaining our sense of value in who we are and not just what we do, our sense of sacredness and preciousness. In the West, we have been encouraged to separate our head from our heart, separate the way we make our living from our personal lives. Part of the work we must undertake on this journey is to reintegrate them. We are on the path towards finding our light, our true goodness, and having the courage to let that light shine in a world that values cynicism and greed. It is about stepping through our sense of 'Who am I?', 'Who do I think I am?' and being bold enough to find and share our own true value with others, giving value to them. It is about joining with others; it is about partnerships, vision and true win/win. Ultimately it comes down to one simple but not simplistic idea – replacing fear with love.

Our heart is our capacity to love, to live fully and freely, to receive, to feel, to enjoy, to be courageous, to value and embrace life. If we can find it in ourselves to love profoundly, all else that is truly important will follow. Very few of us make it through to adulthood with a whole heart; mostly we reach maturity with some degree of broken-heartedness, which leads to cynicism, defensive-ness, fear, bitterness, anger or dissociation, or to a life of roles and appearances, with little zest or passion. This leads to tiredness and burnout. We lose heart – and our true connection to the flow, love and abundance of life. Without love we may have all that should make us happy, but because we can't really feel it, we still feel empty and we wonder what is wrong. Without a full and joyful heart, we can make buckets full of money and have all the possessions we want, but still won't feel happy.

YOUR NEXT LEVEL OF SUCCESS

Often we know the general direction we want to take, but lack clarity about detail. The questions below are designed to help you get more specific data on what your next steps to success look like, and what you are being called to. Use your journal to help you to record your responses.

DATA-GATHERING QUESTIONS

* What do you like best about life?
* What is the first thing you'd grab if your house was on fire?
* What can you truly speak with authority on?
* What are you ripe for?
* What stands between you and your personal greatness?
* What are you most resistant to?
* What part of you that you've kept in the dark most wants to see the light of day?
* What do you need to let go of?
* What is your voice of No saying?
* What is your voice of Yes saying?
* Which mentors would you most like to connect with?
* If you were granted an hour of uninterrupted TV time, what would you talk about?
* If you knew you couldn't fail, what would you start now?
* What is the most important thing missing from your life right now?
* If you could predict – intuitively – the next big decision in your life, what would it be?

* What would you introduce into your life, right now, to shake it up positively?
* What are the greatest forces shaping your life?
* What has been your most memorable break with tradition, or with a taboo?
* Whose life do you envy and why?
* What would those who know you best say your next step in your calling is?
* What would be your biggest regret if you were to die next week?
* What is your most important guiding principle in life?
* What is the most consistent message you have been hearing within yourself about your calling?
* What lifestyle changes are waiting to happen in your life?

SUCCESS AMPLIFIES OUR FEELINGS AND BELIEFS

To find happiness, we must begin an inner journey to recover and remember who we really are. By looking inside ourselves, we will discover that the joy, love, power and peace we are looking for is already there. Those qualities are who we already are.

JOHN GRAY,
author of *Men are from Mars, Women are from Venus*

One mistake we make is to believe success will make us happy or take away the pain. It won't, because it can only really amplify what we were already feeling and thinking. New levels of success can trigger old and unresolved feelings. We aren't as happy as we'd like to be, so we think 'If only . . .' then we'd be happier, fulfilled, content and at peace. This is the biggest trap our conditional self creates for us around success – telling us it is outside and in the future, rather than inside us, now. I have a friend who has just achieved great success in his career, but when he chatted to me, he confided, 'Nothing made me feel such a failure as my success. I felt a fraud, that I didn't deserve it. I am so scared of being found out.' 'Have you ever felt like that before?' I asked. 'I suppose I have, I just hoped success would make me feel different somehow,' he replied. Our concept of success must start as a consciousness within our mind first, then take an outer form in our life as a result. First within, then without.

I remembering hearing J.K. Rowling, author of the *Harry Potter* books, talking on the BBC Radio 4 programme *Desert Island Discs*. One of her selections was the song 'Guilt' by Marianne Faithfull. When she began to get very successful, she said, she hit an enormous layer of guilt. Some of us think, why me? when things go wrong, but she felt like that with her success. Why her? Why not all the other good children's writers? Did she really deserve it? Surely other people deserved it more.

Sometimes life offers us a level of success too great for the limits we've created within our minds. At these times we face a choice: either go into meltdown and probably sabotage ourselves, or transform our inner landscape, say 'Thank you' and open wider. J.K. Rowling said she struggled for a while, but in time began to allow herself to feel the gift of her success, what a blessing it could be to her, her child, family and friends, and the world at large. She discovered she could help, support, encourage and inspire many people. This is recognition of success as a shared process. Success is about learning to *receive* and *give*.

The important thing is that unconditional success is both an inside and an outside job. Most of us want to skip the inner work, or deny we need to do it. We need to look at our thoughts, beliefs and feelings to increase our receptivity to having success, or to allow ourselves to truly enjoy it when we have it. Success without inner readiness may bring unnecessary baggage – the feelings of guilt and inferiority that J.K. Rowling expressed.

Being successful – having a great marriage, relationship or family, having money, getting what you want, a great career, recognition, fame or any form of outer success – can be like a magnifying glass turned inwards. Whatever you feel, believe and think, your success will magnify and amplify. If you feel happy and loving, you'll feel greater love and happiness; if you feel confident, your confidence will rise; if you feel grateful, your gratitude will be multiplied; if you feel worthy, your worthiness will increase; if you felt connected, you'll feel even more blessed.

On the other hand, if at first you felt empty, you may well feel even emptier; if you felt a fraud, you may feel even more of one; if you felt you weren't good enough, you may feel even worse; and if you felt lonely, you could feel even lonelier. This is one of the things that most shocks people about success – it doesn't feel like they expected it to. It can actually be very disappointing, but not because success is essentially disappointing, it's just that we have misunderstood what it really is. We are overtaken by our ego's version of success. It doesn't necessarily give us the joy we sought. We want success to help us remember our grandeur. Our un-conditional self has a plan that does and will work: it knows our joy and how to experience it.

I was very touched by Geri Halliwell's autobiography *If Only*, in which she very honestly describes her deep desire as a child to be famous and wealthy, and how she achieved that through the Spice Girls and then through her own solo career. Growing up, she was often desperately unhappy as well as lonely and bulimic. She fantasized that success would change all that, and would be her escape. Geri describes the day the Spice Girls fulfilled their ambition, and signed their contract with Virgin Records. The deal was huge, and at last she was achieving the success that she'd dreamed of for so many years. The Spice Girls went out and partied, got drunk. This is how she described the next day:

'*A strange thing happened the next morning: I woke up and didn't feel any different. Somehow I'd imagined that I would. We had a record contract that was huge for an unknown band. And people were falling over themselves to work with us. I was going to be famous; there was no doubt anymore. Yet it felt almost like an anti-climax. I guess I'd expected that once I'd had a day like yesterday, every day would be like that. Why didn't the high last?*'

The Buddhists have a lovely expression: 'Wherever you go, there you are!' Geri had taken her feelings and thoughts – her consciousness – with her, as we all do. Her new outer success would provide lots of new opportunities, but not the expected escape from all that she didn't like about herself. We may have a temporary high, but lasting happiness can only come from within. Having more will not take away our inner pain. Sometimes disappointment can kick in immediately; other times it creeps in gradually, leading to boredom, lack of energy, or even sabotage and self-destructive behaviour like addiction. One of the best descriptions of addiction I have heard is never being able to get enough of something that you never really needed. This is the illusion part – our ego says this will make you happy, but it doesn't, so it whispers you haven't had enough yet, more will make you happy, or a different way or person will. But unconditional success is not a high that comes and goes; it is the happiness, joy and peace that abide within us, right now, and we take this gift with us wherever we go. We are not unhappy because we haven't got what we want or need, we are unhappy because we haven't found what we are looking for and we are looking in the wrong place.

Once we've realized that outer success alone will no longer do it for us, it is time to start putting down and building on our personal foundations, doing the inner work of restoring our connection to our unconditional self and clearing away what stands in the way.

We need to build our inner self-belief and confidence, and sense of peace and well-being. True success is an inside job: it is concerned with accepting all aspects of our self, and feeling good about our self, our past, our present and our future. This is our goal. What is the point of:

- *achieving a goal and feeling it wasn't enough or good enough?*
- *getting what you wanted and then being disappointed?*
- *having a fortune in the bank, but no love and sparkle in your heart?*
- *entertaining others but being bored yourself?*
- *being loved by many but disliking yourself?*

To be happy, we have to make a crucial and significant shift in our thinking – to make our inner success the focus and priority. Seek the kingdom within, and all else is added.

WE CAN BE TRULY OURSELVES AND BE SUCCESSFUL

The greatest joy is to be successful at being ourselves, yet I think many of us have grown up with one or both of the following beliefs: we can either sell ourselves or our soul in order to do something we don't want to and we'll be compensated with financial and material success, or we can retain our integrity, be ourselves, do what's really us and be happy, but we'll have to forgo a high level of material success. Can you relate to either of both of these? The message underneath is: you can't have it all, you have to choose between inner and outer success, choose one and sacrifice the other. We are going to explore this later in this chapter when we look at how we can work for love and money, but in the meantime be aware of any dilemmas this choice has created in your life. Happy but poor, rich but soulless are conflicting choices. Unconditional success means being able to have both.

In my life I have followed through on both beliefs. As I said in the Introduction, for the first ten years of my working life I focused on external success and sacrificed my happiness, my inner desires and inspiration. I even prided myself on how good I was at not listening to my inner voice. By my late twenties I was burnt out – successful on the outside, pretty dead on the inside. I was beginning to realize that I had neglected my inner world, so I began to address this. I soon began to experience more happiness and fulfilment, and decided to leave the corporate world, believing that I couldn't experience joy there. I'd rather be happy and poor than wealthy and unhappy, I thought. At that time I didn't believe I could have both.

I began another successful career in the world of spirituality and personal development, and didn't worry so much about the money. I was happy for a number of years, and then it began to dawn on me that I was still not living my truth. I also loved having money, enjoyed material things, and wanted them to support me in my new-found happiness and sense of purpose, yet I didn't have as much money as I wanted. I began to understand that this was not an either/or dilemma, but an and/and possibility. I saw that I was dogged by a lot of old conditioning on the subject: money was bad, spiritual things were good, and the two didn't combine. I realized that the spiritual path does not demand sacrifice. Happiness does not demand sacrifice; we don't have to give up anything in order to be happy. Money won't make us happy, but it can support and encourage our happiness. Later, in Chapter 2, we'll look at the mistaken belief that money is bad and spirituality means sackcloth and ashes, poverty and sacrifice.

Mostly we have sold out on our unconditional self because we think we have to be different from how we are in order to be successful. When you were a child, were you told every day, 'You are fine just as you are. You are and have everything inside you to be happy, creative and successful in your life'? I doubt it. On the whole we are told that to be happy and successful we need to be different, try harder, mould and distort ourselves, force ourselves to jump through hoops and repress and deny big parts of ourselves. Then we follow the path of playing roles and these roles lead us to become disconnected from our natural state, less able to experience the richness of life. Yet true happiness can only come from being ourselves, and being connected to our self. This is the greatest paradox: success and happiness are actually very easy and natural – many of our difficulties in life arise from us trying to be someone or something other than what we actually are.

As we become aware of and connect with our unconditional success, outer success must follow, it cannot fail, but the funny thing is that it won't matter so much! The journey is one of transforming old beliefs, ideas, emotions and perceptions into more positive and helpful ones. This is a lifelong journey, enabling us, a step at a time, to grow into greater abundance, creativity, trust, happiness and success. It will probably involve some stumbling, but also learning how to get up again. That is one of the major differences between those who succeed in achieving what they want and those who don't – the willingness and ability to get back up. We may fail to achieve all we set out to, but we must always believe that we will succeed eventually.

The secret of unconditional success is first learning how to be happy, loving, more confident, more trusting, creative and inspired, regardless of our outer conditioning.

WE ARE NOT OUR WORK

Many of us think that work is a cornerstone of our identity: one of the first questions we ask and are asked when we meet someone new is 'What do you do for a living?' One of the greatest lies the ego tells us is that to a great extent we are our work, our achievements and our material success. It tells us we are the labels by which we identify ourselves, and that these are the best measures of how we are doing in life. That is why work and the success it brings is so important to us – it is the major foundation on which many of us build our sense of who we are. We work so hard, struggle to achieve so much, because we fear that without it we might be nothing, or might be found to be somehow lacking.

We need to begin to recognize that we are much more than our work, and that 99 per cent of what makes us unique and powerful beings isn't visible at all to the outside world. We are our thoughts, our imagination, our love, our motivation, our aspirations, our memories. None of these vital aspects are visible, but they are part of our spirit, and this is beyond measure; *we* are beyond measure.

UNCONDITIONAL SUCCESS IS THE EXPANSION OF WHO YOU ARE, NOT AT YOUR EXPENSE

Being a success in the world is no substitute for being a success as a human being.

K. BRADFORD BROWN, co-founder of the Life Training Programme

A lot of what we regard as success is about achievement and the more tangible things in life – having the right car or clothes, keeping up with the Jones'es, being seen to be doing well, and even conspicuous consumption. We've become accustomed to viewing these as major parts of success. Material wealth and symbols of success are two ways of measuring how far we have climbed up the invisible ladder. Yet it is not just *having* and *achieving* that makes us successful. Unconditional success is *knowing* your own value, *knowing* you are precious, having an abundance of love in your life, being able to be yourself naturally and being creative. It is a journey of discovering the gifts and treasure that lie within you right now, and knowing the richness of your own spirit. Unconditional success is not a narrow target to aim for and one day to hit, but a way of travelling through life on an ever-broadening adventure of discovery.

Ambition is a double-edged sword. Much ambition is based on lack, on emptiness and unhappiness with how life is now. We are driven, so that one day life can be all different, and we'll be happy: the emphasis is all on the destination. A more positive form of ambition is analogous to an ever-opening flower. We see the great things in life, we appreciate more, we feel blessed and are inspired to create more and more of it.

SPIRITUALIZING MONEY

I propose a radical, yet ancient, notion: To build the life you want – complete with inner satisfaction, personal meaning and rewards – create the work you love. By this I mean invent a way to earn an income doing what you do the best, while serving others, becoming authentic, fulfilling the highest standards of your vocation. This is spiritual work. It's life assignment. And most of us are well equipped to do it.

MARSHA SINETAR,
author of *To Build the Life You Want, Create the Work You Love*

A deep desire that rests in many of our hearts is to be able to work at what we love, what we value and what inspires us, and to be able to receive money in return to support ourselves and our families. Not many of us truly believe and experience that we can make a good living doing what we love, and what gives us joy. Usually we're in a dilemma: we can only have one or the other.

The good news is that we can have both. My friend Dr Chuck Spezzano suggests that some of this can be traced back to the childhood belief that we have to choose between the love of our mother and of our father, and that we believe we can only be close to one of them, not both. He believes love, fulfilment and creativity represent the feminine, and work, money and career the masculine. It's an interesting idea. Another aspect of this is the belief that we need to sacrifice something. If something goes well in one area of our life, we feel (usually unconsciously) that we need to pay a price; we don't believe we deserve both. We think that success in one area will get in the way of success in another area, or divide our focus. Using your journal, look at the following questions:

> ### FOCUSING QUESTIONS
>
> * Do you think it is possible to have success in all areas – in career, love and intimacy?
> * Do you think you deserve success in them all?
> * If you had such success, would you feel good or guilty? Joy or meltdown?

MONEY – OUR SPIRITUAL EXCLUSION ZONE!

This is a split in many of our minds, corresponding to the belief that the material and the spiritual are separate. This is simply not true, and never has been. Paramahansa Yogananda, the first Indian Yogi to live in the West, described it this way: 'As cooling water and condensation become ice, so thought by condensation assumes physical form. Everything in the universe is thought in material form . . . Matter is not only frozen energy but also the frozen consciousness of God.' Money is the frozen consciousness of the creator. It is holy, not evil.

So the answer is not to have to choose but to integrate both within our minds. For many of us, money is a spiritual exclusion zone. It is the one area that our spirituality doesn't stretch to. Those who have chosen to set up a business supplying spiritual knowledge, spiritual healing or spiritual products are often criticized for charging money for them. But on this planet, money is the material form of power and exchange for most of the goods and services we need for survival, growth and pleasure. Everything is made available through this form of exchange, including spiritual knowledge. Everything is paid for one way or another.

Money isn't evil. Like anything else, it can be used for both good or ill purposes. But don't judge those who have more, or who are greedy. Seek in your own life to have a relationship with money that is based on love, abundance and trust, and the absence of judgement.

We may do with money what we do with sex: we love it and desire it but we judge or feel ashamed of that desire. But it is our judgement that distorts our healthy desire, turning it into an ugly expression. We are ashamed to be honest and admit that we want these things, so we have insidious ways of pretending we don't – such as condemning our desires even as we act them out. Money is not the source of greed. The mind is the source of greed, and money is one of the ways in which it finds expression. The challenge is to spiritualize our relationship to money.

HOW DO WE SPIRITUALIZE MONEY?

In truth, money has never been unspiritual, we have simply believed it to be so. All the beliefs we have been fed about money being unholy are untrue. It's never been holy to be poor; it's never been evil to be wealthy. So how do we spiritualize our relationship to money? Here are some ideas:

DEDICATE OUR RELATIONSHIP TO ABUNDANCE, NOT FEAR AND GUILT

You may not know it, but there are vast quantities of money in the world, enough for every person on the planet to have over a million pounds each, if it were equally shared out. Our consciousness of money and our relationship to it is the issue. When our relationship is based on awareness of lack and scarcity, and then on guilt and fear, it can become distorted. We need to recognize that money itself is neutral: it is the way we use it and the value we place on it that's important.

Because money is such a big symbol of success, and we need it for survival, we become very attached to it, and this attachment skews our thinking. We get very emotional about money. My friend William Bloom runs a course called the Money Game, which is designed to reveal some of these emotional issues. The exercises act as a microcosm of our whole life, and can be very challenging, but the awareness they offer also helps us begin to liberate ourselves from these issues.

Just imagine if, as children, we had been told every day: 'Don't worry about money, there is an unlimited amount of it in the world. You just focus on finding and developing your gifts, finding your inspiration and passion. When you grow up you'll discover that there are literally thousands of ways to generate money in your life.' How would we have grown up? Very differently, I suspect, and yet this belief is still true. We'll explore it more in the final chapter on being entrepreneurial. As we will discover, the greatest paradox in life is that the less we need and are desperate for something, including money, the more of it we can have!

MAKE MONEY THE BY-PRODUCT, NOT THE MAIN PURPOSE, OF YOUR WORLDLY ACTIVITIES

What would the purpose of your life be if you didn't need to go to work to make money? How would you then organize your life to inspire you and give it meaning and purpose? So many of us work mainly for money: we work to survive financially and materially. We wonder why we are stressed, unhappy and unfulfilled. We need to shift our thinking to be clear about the true purpose of our life. Then we must build our life around what is important to us, and develop ways of creating money from that.

RELEASE YOUR JUDGEMENTS ON MONEY AND THOSE WHO HAVE IT

Most of us have a lot of views about money and about those who have a lot of money. At one end of the spectrum, we give it too much value, and at the other end we deny its value and try to have as little to do with it as we can. Many of us received strong messages about money during our childhood: that the pursuit of money fosters greed, or that you are nothing without money. We may be afraid that people won't like us if we don't make money, or that they won't like us if we do. We can be very confused. Both individually and collectively, we need to commit to a radical healing of our thoughts and habits. We need to remind ourselves that the only judgements on money are our own. Money is neutral.

We can apply the Buddhist idea of sympathetic joy to money. Buddhists encourage us to share in the joy and happiness of others, not just in their suffering and pain. We can celebrate the success of others, and know that their success is an affirmation and encouragement for us too. See money as a blessing, and be willing to receive and give it.

GO BEYOND DESERVING INTO THE REALM OF WILLINGNESS TO RECEIVE

You may have heard the story about a man who dies and goes to Heaven. As it's a quiet day in Heaven, God is waiting at the pearly gates. He welcomes the man and offers him a quick tour around Heaven. The man is thrilled at the prospect, and enjoys the tour until God says, 'But I don't want to show you that room because it's such a sad room.' The guy is obviously curious, and nags God until eventually God capitulates. God opens the door and the man is amazed: the room is full of material goodies – money, possessions, jewels – as well as intangible things like peace, forgiveness, creativity, love and joy. The man is confused. 'Why is this such a sad room?' he asks. 'Because these are all the things I am constantly trying to give people and they continuously refuse to accept!'

Life wants us to have everything. God is the principle of giving all to all, constantly, eternally. God withholds nothing from anybody. We stand in our own way through our belief that we are unworthy and undeserving. But it is a question not of deserving but of willingness to receive, to give up the unhelpful beliefs that we all have about ourselves, so that we are ready to receive the goodness of life.

SHOW ME THE MONEY!

In the film *Jerry Maguire* Tom Cruise plays a sports manager who gets fired from a big sports management company for proposing that they take a more ethical and caring approach to their work and clients. When he sets up on his own the only client who remains with him personally rather than with the agency is played by Cuba Gooding, who believes in Jerry and his philosophy, and also wants to be financially successful. Cuba regularly telephones Jerry, shouts at him and implores him to 'Show me the money!' This is a thought many of us have – principles of love, integrity and spirit are great, but what about the money?! Deeply ingrained in us is the belief that only the lucky few – but never us – can make money doing what they enjoy. We don't have much experience of, and belief in, our capacity to attract money to us when we are doing what makes us happy or joyful and when we are being creative.

STEP UP YOUR SELF-BELIEF

Karyn Ruth lives in Colorado, and came to one of my seminars in London. Fourteen years a stand-up comedienne, she now worked in the corporate world, teaching about the power of humour in the workplace and how to learn to laugh more in the face of stress. We got on like a house on fire. Karyn asked me if I'd be interested in going to Denver to work, and I was excited by that idea, so she took a couple of my books home to give to some of her contacts. A few weeks later I had an e-mail from someone in Colorado saying that Karyn had suggested me as a possible presenter at an event, and was I interested? I was, and decided to call Karyn and ask her advice.

When we chatted I thanked her for putting me forward, and asked what she thought I should ask for as a fee. Her response almost caused me to fall off my chair. 'Go in at $9,000 plus airfare and expenses,' she said. I had never earned, or even thought of earning, that much money in a day, but it got me thinking. Why had I never thought of asking that much? Because I didn't believe I was worth it, came the answer. I knew some people could earn that much money, but I thought they must have something amazing and magical that I didn't have! Yet Karyn had seen me in action, and she thought I was worth it. In the end, I didn't get that particular piece of work, but was told that the fee was not the issue. In the most positive way, it really shook up my sense of self, and became a turning point in my career.

FOCUSING THOUGHTS

* Think for a moment about the largest amount of money you would feel comfortable receiving for a day's work. Be honest. Notice where you start feeling guilty, thinking, 'Oh no, I couldn't', or start feeling scared.
* This is the edge of your comfort zone: the amount of money you believe you deserve. Does it correspond to the amount of money you

actually do earn or receive? It is not what you are actually worth.

✳ Remember that in life we tend to get what we expect or what we think we deserve. You will get more when you ask for more, and when you expect more, and raise your self-belief. This exercise shows some of your more limiting thoughts. You may be able to get more money for your skills and experience right now, if you develop self-belief and a new strategy.

WE ARE MORE THAN ENOUGH

All that you need you have within you, waiting to be recognised, developed and drawn forth. An acorn contains within it a mighty oak. You contain within you tremendous potential. Just as the acorn has to be planted and tended to enable it to grow and become that mighty oak, so that which is within you has to be recognised before it can be drawn forth and used to the full; otherwise it lies dormant in you.

EILEEN CADDY,
co-founder of the Findhorn Foundation and author of *Opening Doors Within*

To me, one aspect of spirituality is rediscovering and remembering that we already have all we need. It is how we perceive ourselves that is the real issue. Do we see ourselves as good enough or as incomplete? Do we feel creative or uninspired? Do we love or judge ourselves? Take a look at the jumble of letters below, and see what you think it says.

SUCCESSISNOWHERE

Depending on how you look at it, it says either success is now here or success is nowhere. What we see is our choice, is our perception based on our life experiences. We may only be able to see one way. We may not even be able to recognize that there is another way of looking at ourselves and the world and that we can change these patterns and see in a new way. Just as success is a perception, so is almost everything else – it can be love is nowhere or love is now here, hope is nowhere or hope is now here, happiness is nowhere or happiness is now here. This is the power of our perception. We need new eyes.

This is what this book positively challenges you to do – to see that success is now here, that you have within you, waiting to be drawn forth, all the resources you could ever need to create what looks – and, more importantly, feels – like a successful life.

AM I GOOD ENOUGH?

The real secret of success is love. We must love ourselves enough to know that we are worthy to succeed. We must believe that those around us want us to win at life, and that our winning can only support their winning. We must know God wants us to be happy in all the arenas of our life.

ALAN COHEN, author of *Lifestyles of the Rich in Spirit*

When we don't feel we are good enough, we tend to focus on many unhelpful things.

How many of the following do you spend time focusing on?

- *what you aren't rather than what you are*
- *what you don't have rather than what you have*
- *where you fail rather than where you succeed*
- *what you don't know rather than what you do know*

We beat ourselves up, rather than believing that *we can learn, grow, heal, and develop new skills and attitudes if we need to.* We constantly compare ourselves unfavourably with others, are very sensitive to criticism and dwell on how life doesn't seem to work for us.

When we feel good enough we focus on:

- *where we have succeeded and are succeeding*
- *our inner wholeness and completeness*
- *feeling good enough*
- *the excitement of learning and experiencing more*
- *how blessed we are and how much we have to be grateful for*
- *how we love and support ourselves and others*
- *what inspires and fascinates us*
- *how many people like, encourage and support us*
- *how life does work out for us*

We will be exploring the power of focus more in Chapter 5.

INTUITION – OUR INNER INTELLIGENCE AND GUIDANCE SYSTEM

Whether we call them hunches, gut feelings, senses, or dreams, they're all the same thing – intuition, speaking to us, giving us insight and knowledge to help us make sound decisions about any actions we take. Intuition occurs when we directly perceive facts outside the range of the usual five senses and independently of any reasoning process.

MONA LISA SCHULZ, author of *Awakening Intuition*

Our soul contains the natural intelligence with which we were created; it knows the big picture of our life and reveals it to us through intuition. Many of us have been trained to believe that the way to get through life successfully is to focus on what we want, to set goals, make a plan, take massive action, force things to go the way we want and not to give up until we get there, wherever there is. We have valued logic and pushing over evolution and unfolding. We may actually have learned to pride ourselves on not listening to our inner calling, on being able to override it and not let things like that get in the way of our accomplishments. Yet misery is most often caused by not following our intuition. Indeed many organizations reward people well for doing precisely what they *don't* want to do and what goes *against* their grain. That is how much of the business and corporate world works, and for some of us it works well. But often this striving results in stress, imbalance, loneliness, a feeling of emptiness and even questioning what life is all about. When do we arrive? Where's the sense of purpose? Where's the joy? Where's the love? Without a sense that our work and success have a strong inner connection, and that they are an expression of our inner self, it can all seem a little meaningless.

We wonder where we can turn for help when everyone else around us is on the same rollercoaster and isn't questioning the ride. The answer is to turn to ourselves, our unconditional self: it has a plan for our happiness and success that won't fail, and this plan is revealed to us through intuition and inspiration. The solid ground of our inner knowing never goes away, and intuition is the way our unique path is revealed to us. In work and in all areas of our life, it has always taken courage to follow our unique path, exactly because making our own path takes us off in directions which can seem profoundly unsafe. This is the road less travelled, it is listening to the beat of our own drum. We've been told that life is precarious enough anyway, without leaving the well-trodden path that everyone follows. Adventure is a nice idea, but not when it comes to our work and our career – even though our soul longs for adventure and evolution.

Our unconditional self is driven by our inner guidance system, and unfolds through listening to and following our intuition, the natural intelligence that we were born with, but which, too often, gets lost in the maelstrom of contemporary life. So much of our motivation is guided and driven by outer forces – market forces, peers, economic downturns or booms, trends, future directions, what the competition is doing, regulation, keeping up, salary, rewards, keeping busy and doing what we think we must, should be and ought to be doing. These come and go. Of course we need to take all these things into account, but sometimes we forget to listen to our inner guidance system, which is consistent beyond time and outer changes.

The beauty of intuition is that it is equally available to all of us, regardless of our credentials, experience, age, sex or where we live on earth. You don't need years of experience to use it, just insight and awareness, now. Anyone can have insights at any time. If we reconnect with this vital life force, our intuition can lead to inspiration, which is the energy that carries us forward and motivates us into action. Intuition is our natural compass in life. It can guide us to our purpose in life, to success, to opportunity and to happiness. A recent report in *Time* magazine showed that over 70 per cent of business leaders said they made their major business decisions using intuition, gut feelings and hunches.

As it is, under years of conditioning, programming and neglect, we may have learned not to listen to it fully, or to listen but not to trust it completely. Generally we override our intuition, and overvalue our logical, rational and thinking mind. We may not even realize it is another wonderful intelligence we have at our disposal. Yet our intuition is both intensely personal and at the same time connects us to everything and everyone else. Intuition is a demonstration that we are not alone. The challenge is that to listen to and follow our intuition more fully we need to clear away any resistance, and the cobwebs of old conditioning, beliefs and attitudes.

Intuition isn't just about having one idea and then following it through until everything works out and you sail off into the sunset.

While some people may have that sort of experience, for most of us, using intuition is about how we create our lives on a daily or even a moment-by-moment basis. We can be guided literally in every moment by our intuition, when we ask and are willing to listen.

WE ARE ALREADY WISE

Many years ago there was a *Candid Camera* television programme in which Federal Express delivery drivers were set up to have a joke played on them. They were sent to make a delivery, and when they arrived at the delivery address, they walked in to find a temple decked out with flowers and photographs, and full of devotees. They then discovered that the photographs were of themselves, and that the assembled people were their followers. The drivers were greeted as gurus, and asked to sit on a temple throne and dispense words of wisdom. Initially, the FedEx men and women were shocked, but many did get on to the throne and start to dispense deep and pro-found wisdom: they talked about the power of love, kindness and integrity as well as many spiritual teachers I have met.

It struck me deeply that we all do this; we often relegate our own innate wisdom, and defer to the wisdom of others. We all have access to a very profound wisdom, but we are asleep to it. Deep down, we know who we are, who we are supposed to become, but we resist, and don't trust ourselves.

LEARNING TO TRUST OURSELVES

You know that if you get in the water and have nothing to hold on to, but try to behave as you would on dry land, you will drown. But if, on the other hand, you trust yourself to the water, you will float. And this is exactly the situation of faith.

ALAN WATTS, author and Buddhist teacher

One of the most powerful ways I have heard intuition described is by Nancy Rosanoff, author and workshop leader. She suggests, 'Intuition is knowing the *what* to do before the *why* to do it.' Isn't that the way it works? We get an intuition to call a friend, go to a talk, visit somewhere, read a particular book, share an idea or say something. We have no idea why, but we have a positive motivation pulling us forward. Intuition calls us to develop our trust, to be open and often unsure, and can stimulate us despite our doubts. Sometimes it's hard to explain to ourselves why we are taking a particular course of action, let alone explain to someone else why we are doing it.

This initial 'knowing what' can cause great conflict as our logical mind usually wants to know the why too before it will act. We want to know the destination and the direction of the steps on the path before we'll start walking. When I was still in the corporate world, it was my growing intuition that led me to believe that my future path would involve writing, training, inspiring, learning and teaching about love, spirituality, healing and creativity. Yet my mind raced with thoughts like, but how would you ever support yourself? But who'd ever be interested in you! Who do you think you are, don't be stupid!! I endured this conflict for three years. I knew what to do next, but not why or how. It was only when I began to get ill and my energy was sapping away that I decided to stop clinging to the familiar and began to be more willing to trust. Eventually, after much soul searching, I decided to do just that – trust – and decided to follow my heart and intuition.

That decision initiated the greatest adventure of my life. I have felt such fulfilment and have learned and developed in ways I could hardly imagine. I have also been called to face many fears in the last 12 years. When I look back as an observer, I can see how my intuition has always led me yet I didn't want to hear it. I thought *I* had a better plan, and my pain and suffering have largely been caused by my resistance to what I was being led to, not by what I was called to do. The path of intuition is not necessarily pain-free; it often requires us to challenge the boundaries we have created for ourselves. It may bring us up against our perceived limits but only in order to lead us beyond what we thought was possible, even into whole new worlds and perspectives. Intuition is our voice for freedom. Being on our knees is an invitation to change. Life is always calling us to be free of our untrue self-concepts and emotional wounds. Intuition will always lead us to shed what is untrue and embrace what is true. Our soul calls us to greater levels of authenticity and ultimately to wholeness.

WISDOM QUESTIONS

What is your relationship to your intuition?

❋ Is it your trusted partner?

❋ Is it a stranger?

❋ Do you regard it as your enemy?

❋ Is it like a naughty child that you like, but humour and don't give credence to?

What kind of relationship would you like to have? How could you improve it?

Intuition and inspiration are self-organizing. Just as iron filings arrange themselves around magnets, when we follow our intuition and fight our resistance, our life becomes easier. Instead of having to figure out all the details, life does much of that for us. We start to become a magnet for the people, insights, circumstances, ideas and energy we need to move us along. Once we've set our mind in a direction, life uses its creative ability to bring to us what we need. Being in the flow opens the door to synchronicities and meaningful coincidences.

WHAT IS OUR EXPERIENCE OF INTUITION?

The work will teach you how to do it.

Estonian proverb ·

Our intuition offers us inner tuition: it is our inner teacher, and even our inner coach. What is even more amazing is that our inner tuition is effortless, always on tap, instantaneous and best of all – free! It is our way of knowing what we already know but had forgotten. We may have learned to trust others more than we trust ourselves. How would it be to trust ourselves and our inner guidance?

Our problem is that we ignore and override intuition. There is evidence that much illness is caused by ignoring feelings of unease and disease until they escalate into illness. Much of our un-happiness in work is caused when we know deep down that we are not happy and are unfulfilled. Our unease calls us to change, but without inspiration, clarity or courage to take action, we may dis-miss our feelings. We hate the job, but need the money. We know we're fed up but don't know what we'd rather be doing. We have an idea, but don't know what to do about it.

INTUITION REVEALS OUR OWN WISDOM

The head asks the questions; the heart gives the answers.

BYRON KATIE, founder of *The Work*

In a world filled with so many conflicting messages about what we should think, feel and believe, finding our own inner guidance, listening to the small voice within, and hearing the rustlings of our own heart can be difficult at first. Yet it is our direct line to our authentic self. We are already wise. In fact we have all the answers we need within us now, and all the resources too. This doesn't mean that we don't need other people; friends and colleagues add love, richness and gifts to our life. We are often, in fact, encouraged to believe that others know better than us; we are taught to relinquish responsibility for ourselves and our actions and are trained to give away our power. We can, however, learn to re-own our power.

Intuition reveals our path and our calling one step at a time. As we trust and take each step, the next step becomes clear.

Here are some ideas on how to restore or strengthen your connection with your intuition:

- *Take quiet or meditative time and just observe your thoughts and feelings, without any judgement or attempt to change them.*
- *Notice how you really feel about particular situations in your life. You may well have overridden your feelings, so start by noticing how you truly feel.*
- *Notice how you try to rationalize away your intuition, deciding it can't possibly be true or make sense.*
- *Ask yourself great questions like 'What would I love to be doing?' 'Where is my heart?' 'What's inspiring me?' 'What is my calling now?'*

INSPIRATION

Perpetual inspiration is as necessary to the life of goodness, holiness and happiness as perpetual respiration is necessary to animal life.

WILLIAM LAW, 1686–1761, author and clergyman

What's inspiring you at the moment?

Mary, the human resources manager of a utility company, had invited me to meet her and discuss a management development programme she was creating and running for the top 50 managers in the organization. About 20 minutes into our discussion, I had one of those slightly uncomfortable feelings. I sensed her energy was low, and that she was struggling to work out what everybody else might want her to do, and how she could satisfy them. Mary wasn't excited about this programme, and neither were they! 'Can I ask you a couple of questions?' I boldly piped up. 'Of course,' Mary replied. 'How would you love to run this programme? What inspires and excites you about it? What would make you proud to be running this programme? How would *you* love the managers to be benefiting from this programme?' After a few seconds' hesitation she came up with a number of ideas, which we captured on a flip chart. Then we continued pouring out ideas for 30 minutes!

She had a very clear idea of what she'd love to be doing, but had discounted those ideas, because nobody had ever asked her about her inspiration, or valued it. As we discussed the way she'd love to be running the programme, her energy changed totally – she became more animated, and ideas tumbled out. It was as if she'd turned on a tap, and her energy was flowing freely.

By the end of our time together, not only had she marshalled her ideas, but she had decided to take responsibility and move forward with them, even though she had anxieties. She'd planned to talk to the MD, the directors, run some ideas past them, ask them for their views. She'd decided to go to a taster day on inspirational leadership at London's Globe Theatre, which took Shakespeare's story of Henry V as a basis for developing great leadership qualities. There would be a theme of creativity and innovation running through the entire management programme. She also had a number of other innovative ideas she wanted to incorporate. Most importantly, she would push to both give and receive guidance and direction. Where before there had been some apathy among her senior colleagues, now she inspired them to take more of a leading role in the new programme she had devised.

When we met again three weeks later, Mary admitted that she'd had to face a few challenges, but was still on track, purposeful and bringing it all together. She was growing in confidence as she tried new things, followed through on her inspiration; she was heartened by the feedback of other senior managers, and was learning from what wasn't working. Six months later she was halfway through the programme, and receiving great feedback and gratitude from the senior team for organizing a programme that inspired and stretched them.

This is the power of our inspiration. Each of us has a reservoir of innovative ideas that we can draw upon, and this reservoir will never run dry. We don't just have one inspired idea – we can have an unlimited number. Our inspiration is a direct line to the universal mind behind all creation. The whole history of human evolution is one of people having inspired ideas, and then the *courage* and *self-belief* to follow them through. Ordinary people can do amazing things when they are inspired, because inspiration goes to the heart of creativity itself. Inspiration allows us to see new horizons, to grow beyond the limits we have created within our mind and reimagine ourselves in the world. Inspiration is the force of unseen hands gently pushing us along to become what we truly are; it ignites the embers of forgotten promises of what we are here to do in this life. Inspiration overrides our blocks and dissolves our sense of limitation. And it occurs in *every* area of our lives – from deciding to paint a room in our house an unusual colour to inventing a game our children love to play.

WISDOM THOUGHTS

Spend some time answering the following questions:

* I am someone who is inspired by . . .
* I am someone who is inspired when . . .
* What blocks my inspiration is . . .
* What three things could you put in place that would support inspiration in your life now?

While inspiration is always available to us throughout our lives, what inspires us may change. Have a think for a minute:

- *What kind of things inspired you 15 years ago and would that spark, if reignited, be able to help you in your life now?*
- *What kinds of things inspired you 10 years ago?*
- *What or who once inspired you but no longer does?*

Inspiration activates the law of attraction. When we are inspired, our energy shifts, we are more aligned with the essence of ourselves. We are in tune with our love and our highest energy, and begin to resonate at a new level, and then we start bringing new situations, events and people into our life that resonate with our new energy. We discover a whole new world that was always there, but we hadn't seen it because of our limited perception: we were working at a lower energy level. Inspiration opens doors in our mind and transforms us. Inspiration leads us to new levels of self-belief and self-worth.

WHAT CAN WE DO WHEN WE DON'T FEEL INSPIRED?

Be kind to yourself! Trust in yourself. Inspiration cannot be forced; as much as possible, relax and accept that you are where you are and let go of negative thought patterns. I meet many people who beat themselves up for not being inspired, who are harsh on themselves for not having found their vocation yet. Age seems irrelevant; I have met teenagers who almost write themselves off, twenty-somethings who think they've left it too late, and thirty-somethings who think they've missed the boat. Yet by being harsh we diminish the very self-esteem and strength that would open up our inspiration.

Inspiration, guidance and new direction are there for us at every age. You may be trying too hard. Focus on a different area of your life; perhaps relax and play, and then come back to doing what you know cultivates and sustains your inspiration. To some extent, inspiration is a mystery; although it's always there, we can't control or manipulate it. But we can allow it and be willing to align with it and receive it, and we can be determined to discover it.

ARE YOU STIMULATING YOURSELF?

We can encourage our inspiration in many ways. Some of our personal inspiration is stimulated by stillness, contemplation, walks in nature, or prayer/meditation. It may also be stimulated by being with other people who are inspired, and putting ourselves in situations where we are exposed to new and often challenging ideas. I know that when I go to interesting conferences and listen to experts I can get incredibly inspired. Their great ideas and successes – and even sometimes their mediocrity and lack of inspiration – can bring me to life in new ways.

We need different perspectives on situations and new trains of thought to keep us inspired. We need to do things that shake up our existing ways of seeing the world. On my first trip to India, during the journey from the airport to the centre of the city I felt like I had arrived on a new planet. I knew it would be different, and I had travelled to other third world countries, but nothing had prepared me for this poverty, the cows on the streets, the beauty and the dirt. It shook me but expanded my sense of life. Many of these images and experiences will stay with me for ever.

SPEND TIME IN AWE AND WONDER

The world is not exhausted; let me see something tomorrow which I never saw before.

SAMUEL JOHNSON, lexicographer and author

If we are bored with the world, we are probably bored with ourselves (simply feeling uninspired, lacking in hope). We've lost our connection with our sense of awe and wonder, but we can find it again. We need new eyes with which to see the world. Do you remember how when you were a kid everything was fascinating? Remember when you loved learning new things? That desire may still be with you, but if not you can rekindle it. Here are some ideas:

- *How about discovering one new fact every day? Learn something new – a new word, something from the* Guinness Book of Records, *a poem, a quote.*
- *Be in awe of yourself! Discover some amazing fact about your body. For example, even as a simple mechanical pump, our heart is a miracle machine. The biggest muscle in the body, it weighs only 12–14 ounces and yet pumps between 40 and 80 million gallons of blood, beating 72 times a minute (that is over two and a half billion times in an average 70-year life). In one day alone, eight tons of blood pass through the heart. The heart produces enough energy to lift a ton weight three feet off the ground: a truly phenomenal little machine.*
- *Be in awe of this extraordinary universe we live in. Did you know that there are a million stars in the universe for every grain of sand on the planet? Did you know that there are estimated to be as many as half a million species of fish and crustaceans in the oceans of the world that are yet to be discovered because only 1 per cent of the ocean beds have been explored?*
- *Satisfy your curiosity. What would you love to know? What has always fascinated you but you've felt you'd leave it till later?*
- *Share inspiration – this is a great way to tune into our inspiration. The nineteenth-century American writer Edith Wharton put it beautifully when she said: 'There are two ways of spreading light: be the candle or the mirror that reflects it.' Bring your favourite quote to work, place it somewhere where you'll be able to read it and be inspired by it. Send it to your six best friends, and ask them to share their favourite quotes with you.*

We can be fascinated and curious our whole lives. A couple of years ago I was with my father Harold, who was then in his late seventies, and his friend Ted, who was in his eighties. They had both been keen gardeners all their lives, and I took them to a garden that was open to the public. I loved watching them ask each other, 'What's that one, I don't recognize it?' and talking excitedly about different flowers and plants. They were still curious, fascinated, appreciative and learning. We need never stop.

INSPIRATION CAN LEAD TO EASE

Trust generates confidence. Trust is not being naive, which ignores information or intuition. Trust takes all of the situation at hand, no matter how seemingly negative, and begins to turn it into advantage. For trust, like faith, uses all the power of your mind to unfold the situation in a positive manner.

DR CHUCK SPEZZANO, author of *If It Hurts, It Isn't Love*

Many of us have grown up with the belief that to have anything you want in life you need 1 per cent inspiration but 99 per cent perspiration – the good old work ethic that says everything needs to be worked hard and struggled for. We need to remember that inspiration is always available and we must align ourselves with it. Like any tool, we need to know how to use it. Questions are a great way to link in: ask yourself what would or could inspire you. Do this regularly and you will receive answers. Surround yourself with the inspiration of others as expressed in visual art, music, writing or spirituality. Simply being with people who are living authentic and creative lives is great too. All too often we see our limits as *the* limits, so we need to challenge ourselves positively by thinking bold, loving and courageous thoughts.

I had a powerful experience of this when I was writing my first book. As I was about to sign the contract with the publisher I had some anxiety. 'Can I actually do it? Does the world need another book? What if I am fooling myself and can't really write as well as I thought? What if it doesn't succeed?' were just some of the fears that flowed into my mind. But I'd known since I was a child that I wanted to write at least one book, so I went ahead and signed. Almost immediately after I signed and returned the contract I felt a peace washing over me, and although I had a date only two and a half months away in which to deliver the manuscript, I felt confident.

My commitment to saying *yes* to writing seemed to activate the flow of inspiration. Every day I would have so many thoughts and ideas that I felt almost overwhelmed. I felt like saying 'Enough already – I am only writing one book now!' and had to save many ideas for future books. I had an image of planes stacked up waiting to land at Heathrow airport – all the books in embryo waiting to be written. Far from being hard work, the first book was actually a joy much of the time. My partner, Helen, said she'd never seen me as happy. Inspiration flows as a result of our commitment to doing what is true for us. We don't do inspiration, it does us – we can welcome it, be willing and cultivate our minds to be ready to receive it. We can learn to trust the small voice that says, 'This might work, I'll try it.' Inspiration gives us direction and the energy to carry us forward. Inspiration is always available, even if it doesn't get through to us. I like to think of inspiration as a programme that is always being broadcast, 24 hours a day, 365 days a year. There are times, places and states of mind that allow us to tune into it better than others. But the variable is our reception – not the transmission.

INSPIRATION STUDY AND FOCUS PLAN

It is a universal law that whatever we focus on expands, so if we want more inspiration in our life, we need to focus on it more.

Imagine that you are a student of inspiration for one month. For just one month, what if you focused an hour or two of energy on inspiration every day, being curious about it, fascinated by it and immersing yourself in it? What if you read what had been said about inspiration across the globe, throughout history? What if you read something every day that inspired you? What if you spent more time in inspiring places and with inspiring people? What if you created an inspiration team for yourself? Do you think that would influence you? Of course it would. Will you? Here are some pointers:

- *Notice what percentage of your time you focus on inspiring and uplifting thoughts and ideas, and how much on depressing and soul-stealing ideas.*

- *Develop more awareness of what does or could inspire you – what people, poetry, other literature, music, places and situations uplift you?*

- *Who can you be around who will help you nurture your inspiration? Which friends and colleagues uplift you? How can you be with them more? Create a regular connection with key people and encourage each other to keep your focus.*

INSPIRATION IS ALCHEMICAL

As we choose to commit to inspiration, we are transformed by the experience, even if at first we take small and tentative steps. As we continue taking steps, we grow, learn, heal and develop. At first we may not feel worthy of the idea, we may have many limits to our thinking, we can't see how to follow through, or we get scared, but we can still take tiny steps. It is important to remember that sometimes the path reveals itself as we move along it, as each step prepares us for and reveals the next one. I once heard the poet Robert Bly say, 'Each step we take towards our soul, it takes two steps towards us.' We build up self-esteem as we go, we work out the strategy, the way becomes clear, we meet the right people, our confidence increases, our trust grows, our skills increase. It is an evolutionary process. By making the commitment and asking for inspiration at each step, we move on, we are refreshed and renewed. Dormant forces and talents can come alive in us, and we discover ourselves to be greater by far than we imagined. Audiences of all ages, in all countries I have visited, seem to resonate with this idea and recognize its relevance to their lives: the power and alchemy of inspiration is truly universal and eternal.

INSPIRATION IS TODAY'S COMMODITY

A few years ago John Naisbit, author of the Megatrends series, that identifies and predicts future trends of books taught us that we live in an age where information is power. There is a lot of truth in that. However, we can get overwhelmed with information, and inspiration can easily get pushed out. Bernie Siegel, author of *Love, Medicine and Miracles* and spiritual cancer surgeon, told me, 'We live in an age where inspiration is power, not just information. Someone can have all the information about how to help themselves get over a cancer, but unless they are inspired enough to want to change, grow and continue living, their chances are reduced. An inspired patient with so much to live for stands much more chance of recovering than one with all the information but no will.'

Most of us – whatever our age or social circumstances – want to be inspired about something. Create an inspiring place to work and you will have people queuing around the block wanting to work with you, because most work is so damn boring! I heard a British management guru speaking at a conference, who told a story about a colleague who was chairman of a major British plc. 'I had lunch with the chairman, and the chairman said, "I know we need some new talent and energy to work here. I know who I want to come and work with me here, but my one big problem is that, other than the money, I can't think of why they would want to come and work here! It's so boring! We are efficient but so dull!"'

Many organizations today are boring to work in. They don't nurture the human spirit, they don't encourage people to be creative and bring out their gifts. They can even be downright oppressive and insulting to human intelligence and spirit. They don't foster trust and co-operation. How many organizations do things beautifully, lovingly? How many really care about the emotional and even spiritual well-being of their workforce? Thankfully, more are beginning to realize the value of nurturing their staff.

INSPIRATIONAL PERSONAL COACHING PROJECT

In my coaching practice, a common theme is to help the people I meet become more creative and to excavate their authentic selves from beneath the roles they have been playing. One useful way of looking at this change point in their life is to see it as a project. This can help us define and encapsulate the purpose and outcome of the change they are being called to create. Here are some examples of their project titles:

- *Project Blue Skies – an adventure in exploring new territory*
- *Project Letting Go and Moving On. Time for rebirth and resurrection*
- *Project Breaking the Chains – expressing myself freely and letting my creativity emerge*
- *Project Regeneration – doing what I love and having a passion to live a fuller life*
- *Project Overflowing Love and Energy – embracing freedom*
- *Project Creating Flow in my everyday life, and living my destiny and calling*
- *Project Action Time – the courage to do it!*

WISDOM QUESTIONS

* What would be the title of the project for this point in your life?
* What are its key themes?
* What is new for you that you want to embrace?
* How would you describe the successful outcome of this project?
* What are some of your goals (goals for doing and goals for being)?
* How would other people know you'd changed and succeeded?
* What support are you likely to need to succeed? Who can you enrol to help you?
* What can you do to ensure your success?

Your unconditional self is the very essence of abundance, and unlimited resources reside within you, right now.

•

It knows nothing of shortages, lack or scarcity, as these are all of the ego.

•

As you move into putting your unconditional self at the centre of your work and success, you will become more abundant. Shortages are created by our unwillingness to receive, and we realize that there is enough room for us all to be successful, creative and gifted.

•

We discover that the more we give, the more we receive, and the more we are given to share.

2

UNCONDITIONAL ABUNDANCE

The ego's world is based on finite resources, but God's world is not. In God's world, which is the real world, the more we give, the more we have. Our having a piece of the world's pie doesn't mean there's less for anyone else, and someone else having a piece of the pie doesn't mean there's less for us. So we needn't compete, in business or anywhere else. Our generosity towards others is key to our positive experience of the world. There's enough room for everyone to be beautiful. There's enough room for everyone to be successful. There's enough room for everyone to be rich. It's only our thinking that blocks that possibility from happening.

MARIANNE WILLIAMSON, author of *A Return to Love*

Abundance is not about accumulation of money, clothes, cars, houses or gadgets: we can't buy rights to abundance, and indeed we can be incredibly abundant without owning a single thing.

Abundance is the richness of all the things that money *can't* buy. Abundance is how much happiness there is in our life, how much love, how much laughter. The support and encouragement we receive from others is crucial. Abundance is all about fun and friendship; it is about us and our relationship to our unconditional self.

As we've seen in Chapter 1, if we recognize our completeness, we recognize too that we already have all we need within us. The unconditional self can help us to reveal true abundance in our lives. It's simply a matter of choice. This is at the heart of unconditional success. All spiritual and material gifts flow from the boundless ocean of abundance that is within each of us. We may have come to think of abundance as having plenty of money or possessions, but it is so much richer than that; it is about seeing the many blessings in our life every day, and developing new eyes to see. Abundance is one of our greatest gifts, and because it is so precious, it is also where our conditional self, our ego, sets up the greatest number of traps for us. In this chapter I want to help you to gain a conceptual understanding of what abundance is, and then move into practical strategies that will help you to experience greater abundance in your life on a moment-by-moment basis. Remember that the power of abundance that lies within you can undo all the ideas of scarcity that your ego has created.

Most of us have had a thorough education in scarcity and lack, and deep in our subconscious minds, handed down from generation to generation, there are ancient beliefs that say life is hard, work is something we have to endure, it is natural to have to work hard to survive. With these beliefs so deeply ingrained at a subconscious level, many of us find ourselves in a frantic internal conflict. It is a conflict between what we would *love* to do and the way we *believe* life has to be in order for us to survive. The journey back to abundance is about confronting and reversing these scarcity beliefs.

Abundance is like a universal fund, the infinite bank account of the universe. It is the unlimited energy source available to everyone. We need to let go of our current belief that the only way to gain security on this planet is to have a large sum of money in a bank account. We must start recognizing and experiencing that security is the power within us, in every moment.

Abundance is primarily an experience and a state of mind, a state of awareness and consciousness. We create abundance and attract it to us by helpful attitudes and positive thinking. Abundance is both knowing and experiencing that there is a plentiful amount in life – of what? Of everything! We probably know people who seem to confidently let go of things that don't work, because they know that life is always full of opportunity. They commit to situations, and when it's appropriate, they let them go and move on. They know they will always have friends, make money, have opportunities, be inspired and be in demand. In essence, abundance reveals itself as a kind of generous and confident spirit.

Creation is abundant, and being the created, we are abundant too. But we may not be aware of this. You may have heard the story of the fish. 'Excuse me,' said one young ocean fish to another older fish, 'you are older and more experienced than I, and will probably be able to help me. Tell me: where can I find this thing they call the ocean? I've been searching for it everywhere to no avail.' 'The ocean,' said the older fish, 'is what you are swimming in now.' 'Oh, this? But this is only water. What I'm searching for is the ocean,' said the younger fish, feeling quite disappointed.

We are in the ocean of abundance, right now, we *are* abundance, right now, it is an ever-present reality. We may not feel this but if, like me, you take a few minutes of your day to stop and look around you, you will see that every flower, blade of grass or small stone offers endless beauty in a pure and unadulterated form. This spring I looked in awe at the daffodils, and wondered how many millions of years they had been on this planet. They looked as glorious as ever and I was fascinated by the thought that the abundance of all creation never tires. Every year daffodils come back as fresh as ever (as long as we don't get in the way!). Abundance is ceaselessly flowing, it is the essence of all things physical. It is the substance of all life. There has never been a time of greater abundance than this present moment. Only we, by our thinking and imagining, can and do separate ourselves from this supply of abundance.

WHAT WOULD GREATER ABUNDANCE LOOK LIKE FOR YOU, NOW?

So what's missing and what do you want more of? We are taught that we have to earn, deserve, suffer, sacrifice and struggle for anything good in this life, when the greater truth is that we merely need to define what we want, put a strategy together to have it, and most importantly be willing to receive it. If the situation we're in isn't working, we should be confident enough to take radical steps to change it, and if it's still not working, to move on. We can stand in the way of or deny abundance, but it is always there, waiting for us to claim what is ours by right. So what is missing in your life? You can use your journal to explore this further. Here are some ideas for questions:

- *Money – do you have enough, or are you in debt?*
- *Time – are you unable to spend enough time with people you love or do what you enjoy most?*
- *Inspiration – do you feel stuck and in need of direction?*
- *Creativity – do you feel you are just going through the motions and need to express yourself more freely?*
- *Stimulation – are you simply bored?*
- *Spirit – is there too little joy or excitement in your life?*
- *Health – how would you judge your well-being?*

- *Love – are you lacking love, support, intimacy or encouragement?*
- *Opportunity – can you see new and exciting avenues ahead or just more obstacles?*

Add any other areas of lack that you are experiencing. Getting specific really helps: you can then identify what you're missing and get moving forward with strategies to overcome the stumbling blocks.

Abundance is not something to get, or control, or even create – it is something to joyfully embrace and *be* because it's what you already are. Remember, true abundance is the experience of our unconditional self. Ponder this glorious thought for a moment – all the abundance that has ever existed in the universe is inside you at this moment, and is eternally yours. It is not just an idea, but an experience, something to be felt with the heart, not just understood by the head. The Persian poet Jalaluddin Rumi died over 700 years ago, but is one of the most popular poets in the West today. Often he would stay up all night praying, meditating and dancing with friends, and by dawn would have achieved a state he called majesty, which I think of as resting in abundance. He expressed that state this way:

This we have now
is not imagination.

This is not
grief or joy.

Not a judging state,
or an elation,
or sadness.

Those come and go.

This is the presence
that doesn't.

. This
that we are now
created the body, cell by cell
like bees building a honeycomb.

The human body and the universe
grew from this, not this
from the universe and the human body.

Translated by Coleman Barks

So relax into this thought. Abundance is who we are in essence, it is a quality of our unconditional self. We don't even need to think positive, we just need to stop thinking negative, and realign our mind with what is already true.

CONSCIOUSNESS FIRST

To run around trying to fix your world with the consciousness
that produced the problem in the first place will only aggravate
the situation even more. To change your world, you must change
your consciousness. You must draw forth from within a new
awareness, understanding and knowledge of the universe, the
power that sustains you, and the true nature of yourself. And
with each degree in the shift in your consciousness, more Reality
is revealed in your world.

JOHN RANDOLPH PRICE, author of The Abundance Book

Janice was successful, a lovely woman who ran her own business. She was financially secure, popular, had a loving husband, a beautiful house and her own horse. She seemed to have what most people only dream of. Yet, as we spoke, Janice expressed her unhappiness; she even hated at times her work and life. For all the money and trappings, there seemed real poverty somewhere in her life. She wasn't fulfilled and was forever running around taking care of others, feeling responsible for them and her business; she seemed to have left herself out of the equation. We discussed Janice's dream: to give up her business, to take time for herself, to discover what she loved and what she wanted from life. Her poverty was of time for herself, self-love, self-nurturing and support, as well as of love, connection and friendship. For all her success on one level, she realized that she lacked on other levels and began putting her strategy together to fill in the gaps in her life.

One of the most powerful lessons in life, and a hugely powerful universal principle, is that whatever we concentrate and focus on, what we give our energy and attention to, will grow and develop. What we continually look for and see, we become. So, without putting unnecessary pressure on ourselves, if we want to be more aware of the abundance inherent in life, and to experience it to a greater extent, we need to focus our attention on living an abundant life.

A CHANGE OF FOCUS

You give birth to that on which you fix your mind.

ANTOINE DE SAINT-EXUPÉRY, author of *The Little Prince*

I had just finished a presentation to 30 human resource directors on how to get people to shine and excel at their work, when one of the delegates said, 'I have just realized that more than 90 per cent of my energy and attention goes into dealing with difficult people and difficult situations in my organization. It has just dawned on me that my organization would look very different if I spent a fraction of that time focusing on developing my *good* people.'

Our focus of attention is one of the most influential factors in how we think and feel, and what we achieve in our life.

Another human resource manager I know has a scrapbook that she calls her happy book. In it she collects all the appreciation, positive feedback, gratitude and other good things she has achieved in her career. When she is having a challenging time or a down day, she gets her book out, reminds herself of her success and how well she has coped with challenges so far. Her happy book gives her a change of focus, which in turn changes the way she thinks and how she feels. You may like to compile your own happy book as a reminder of the achievements in your life, relationships and career.

HOW GOOD ARE YOU AT NOTICING WHERE YOU ALREADY *ARE* SUCCESSFUL, NOW?

Do you feel successful every day? Do you notice the things you've done well, the achievements you can be proud of? Do you congratulate and appreciate yourself each day? How much of the time do you feel a success? Or do you only notice the things you haven't done on your 'to do' list? Do you think about what you could have done better? Do you notice where you think you have failed? Do you tell yourself how far away the finishing line still is?

The best way to expand our sense of success is to choose to notice where we are already doing well and when we have already succeeded. Otherwise success is always just around the corner, coming soon, on its way, but never quite here. Today, start noticing what you can feel good about, now. Many of us have pretty good lives, but do we notice *how* good? Do we habitually focus on the bad parts? One of the saddest things would be to get to the end of our lives and look back and say, 'I had a pretty great life really, but I didn't notice it at the time!'

This is why keeping a daily journal can be so valuable. It helps us focus on what we want more of, helps us monitor our progress and change course when necessary. Our life may feel like a trudge through mud with just a few precious moments, but it's our choice whether we spend our energy focusing on the mud or on the precious moments.

One of the real skills of unconditional success is noticing the good things of your life, all the time. I love the idea that a successful life is a series of precious moments – of connection, of love, of beauty – each to be treasured.

ENOUGHNESS

A key element of abundance is the concept of knowing what is enough. Our ego flourishes on 'never enough' – we don't have enough time, enough money, enough love, enough security, enough self-esteem, we are not good enough, powerful enough, happy enough . . . the list is endless.

To recognize when enough really *is* enough we have to step off the treadmill of striving and prepare ourselves to arrive. To be content and fulfilled, to be happy with your lot, to be grateful and feel blessed may be regarded as soft and weak in some areas. In the world of business, to be successful we must be lean and hungry, ambitious, and always wanting more. Greed is good! In much of the business world *not* enoughness is seen as a great strength. I meet many people who play the role of being hungry, motivated and ambitious, while in truth they long for a quieter life, they don't want to push so hard, they want to slow down and enjoy life. They want more time with their family, to pursue hobbies and travel. They are frightened to admit this openly for fear of being isolated and seen to be out of step with the company ethos. So they play the game as best they can and carry on – miserably.

There is a distinction here: if we are starving, we need more food, if we are broke we need money. But there is a big difference between actually not having enough, and the fear of not having enough, and it isn't always easy to recognize this. To survive physically and emotionally, we need very little. In contrast, our psychological needs can seem endless.

I am not sure that many of us do know what enough is for us in many areas of our life. Think about the following list for a few minutes:

- *How much is enough money for you to earn a year?*
- *How much money would you need to feel safe and secure in your life?*
- *How much time is enough time at work?*
- *How much is enough time with your family?*
- *How much love is enough love for you?*

These can be hard questions to answer, often because we don't even think about them. We are so encouraged to keep striving, and going for more, better and best, keeping up, looking good, not falling behind that we don't even consider what is enough for us.

There is huge positive power in deciding for ourselves what is enough. When we aren't clear, we can be slaves to the treadmill, to the struggle. When we draw our boundaries and make some decisions about what is enough for us, we open the door to greater freedom and begin to take charge of our own lives.

FOCUS ON ABUNDANCE AND NOTICE IT!

Spirit just loves to prove to you that you live in an abundant universe . . . the fabric of life is one of infinite riches, and the material world is not separate from God's love; it is an expression of it.

ALAN COHEN, author of *Lifestyles of the Rich in Spirit*

In one of my workshops on 'Turning Passions into Profits', we were talking about abundance, and one participant, Brett, said that he found this concept very difficult to understand. His experience of life was much more about struggling along doing things he didn't enjoy. He was in the process of changing careers to do something he loved, but was finding it hard to believe that abundance would follow. I burst out laughing, and he looked quite upset. 'Why are you laughing?' he asked. 'How did you get to be on this workshop?' I asked him. 'I came to your talk two nights ago, you gave away a free place on this weekend by picking out a name from all the people at the talk, and I won it,' he explained. He still didn't get it. 'Do you not see? Here you are changing directions, needing help, support and new ways of thinking, and you won a free place on this workshop! Isn't that a sign that you are already being supported and moving into greater abundance?' Grudgingly he began to smile and saw the joke of how life *was* supporting him, but he wasn't seeing it. Often the problem is not that we aren't abundant, but that we miss the abundance happening around us and to us all the time.

Start noticing what you have rather than what you either think you don't have or actually don't have. To have more of what we want we must first want what we have. Remember that what we are seeking to do is change our consciousness to abundance.

So look at your life and see if you can view it a little differently:

- *If you have debt, notice how much capital or collateral you have – however much or apparently little.*
- *Instead of noticing your partner's faults or shortcomings, notice what positive things they bring into your life and others'.*
- *If you don't enjoy your work, notice what it does allow you to do – like pay the bills, have holidays, structure your time, allow you to learn and develop, provide a set of relationships and help you get clear about what you don't want, acting as a springboard to a new phase of your life.*

- *Think about how much money you have earned throughout your career so far.*
- *If you sent everyone you knew, even reasonably well, a postcard, how many would you need to send?*
- *Think of everyone who has ever been kind to you, loved or encouraged you in any way.*
- *How many countries have you visited and what did you gain – emotionally and physically – from your travels?*

Notice where abundance has already appeared in your life. Begin to resist any feeling you may have that it isn't enough. You may be surprised to find that you have more than you thought, that you know more people than you imagined. If you need or want more, try to examine why this is. What lies behind your need for more?

- *Is it a feeling of needing to compete and prove yourself?*
- *Is it out of joy and expansion?*
- *Do you feel that you are a failure unless you reach out for more?*

It is natural to be expansive and to long for more rewarding experiences. Our unconditional self, in fact, urges us to explore the possibility of more fun, love, happiness, inspiration and creativity. In contrast, our conditional self always starts from a place of emptiness, and its desire for more is usually an attempt to keep us struggling and striving, but never quite arriving. The ego's hidden mottos are 'Strive but never arrive', and 'Seek but don't find'! The only way through our need to strive is not by more striving, but by shifting our attention to our unconditional self.

John came to see me after a painful split from his partner, with whom he had co-founded a business 11 years earlier. He seemed to be in an enviable position. As part of his settlement he had negotiated a deal whereby he would be paid for another three years after leaving the business. He had already been able to pay off his mortgage, had a comfortable sum of money in the bank and his family were pretty well set up for a while. I had half expected to meet a man excited by new possibilities and blessed by his current freedom and good fortune. Instead I met a man burdened with worry. 'What if I never get to work again?' John asked. 'Is that likely? You are obviously very talented and skilled, so there must be lots of other places that would want you, and you can take time to explore the possibilities of starting a new business and see where you'd like to go next,' I suggested. But for every positive suggestion I made, John countered with a worry. He seemed to be an expert at seeing what he thought he didn't have, and overlooking what he did have, right now. John felt that he must work hard all the time, otherwise he was valueless; he didn't have permission to relax, enjoy the fruits of his labour and discover what was next. He was very hard on himself: although he had the circumstances of abundance, he had the mindset of lack and scarcity.

Like John, we must look at where we have erected barriers to the awareness of abundance. Only then can we begin to choose a new, more positive path.

AN HOUR OF GIVING THANKS

A grateful mind is a great mind which eventually attracts to itself great things.

PLATO, 428–347 BC, philosopher

As the maxim goes, we don't know what we've got, until it's gone. We are often grateful in retrospect, sometimes only when we've lost something. We can learn to be more grateful in the present moment, and even ahead of time. We can give thanks for what we have now, and what we will have. John's story reminds us to live here and now, to notice what we have. I read that one of the great Buddhist teachers, Sogyal Rinpoche, author of many books including *The Tibetan Book of Living and Dying*, taught people who lived in the streets in India, near starvation, the power of gratitude and thanksgiving. We can easily put off gratitude, thinking: when I have more or when I am more successful, I'll be more grateful. It is always a *when* thing, not a *now* thing. Obviously I don't know you, but I imagine you have a pretty reasonable life – food to eat, a roof over your head, friends, family, employment, clothes. But you may not see it that way. Sometimes we need some contrast, a different perspective, in order to see how fortunate we are. When I went to India in 1995, I came back with a profound sense of gratitude, realizing how blessed I was in comparison to the majority of the world's population. I vowed always to keep that sense of gratitude, but I often slipped up and needed to remind myself.

On a visit to the Findhorn Foundation, a spiritual community near Inverness in Scotland, I found myself free on a Saturday evening. I decided to go along to one of the meditation sanctuaries they have there. I sat quietly, on my own, and enjoyed the peace and tranquillity of the sanctuary. Slowly a few friends came to my mind, and I decided to send them love and gratitude for being in my life. I enjoyed the process so much I chose to bring more friends to mind and I sent them my gratitude and thanks. As I pictured my friends and family, I felt a deeper peace and calm, and before I knew it, three hours had gone by. I was feeling wonderful and didn't want to stop! What dawned on me later was how good it felt to be sending love and how wonderful to experience gratitude.

Gratitude can be used as a guilt trip – you should be grateful for food with half the world starving; you shouldn't want more when so many have so little. This is not the kind of gratitude I am talking about. I mean the willingness and ability to feel truly blessed, to accept with an open heart the goodness of what you have. True gratitude reminds us of our wholeness. True gratitude is remembering our unconditional self, which is already whole and full. To concentrate on abundance means not only looking at the material world, which is only the effect of abundance, but focusing on the source of abundance – the divine consciousness behind all things, the effulgent energy, the invisible force from which all things come. There are many ways to do this:

- *be in awe and wonder of nature*
- *pray and meditate*
- *read poetry, listen to or play music*
- *laugh and play*
- *be in love*
- *see a newborn child*
- *be with a loved pet*
- *stare up to the stars and heavens at night*

We can all become aware of this energy. It is not just an idea: it can be an actual and real experience. Remember it's hard to be grateful and depressed; it's hard to be grateful and unhappy; it's hard to be grateful and cynical; it's hard to be grateful and alone. Gratitude transforms so much negativity in our lives, by helping us receive.

ABUNDANCE IS THE ART OF RECEIVING

Be very honest. On a scale of 1–100 per cent, how good a receiver are you? How much do you allow yourself to receive love, support, inspiration, happiness, money, healing, guidance and appreciation? How much do you allow yourself to have, before you feel guilty, afraid or withdraw? The more we have grown up believing we need to be independent to be successful, the worse we are at receiving. Were you ever told, or have you come to believe, that it is holier to give than to receive? It is a popular religious teaching, and is the way I lived much of my life. I was a pretty good giver, and prided myself on how little I actually needed to receive. A few years ago I began to question this, and the thought ran through my head:

if we are all supposed to give but not receive, who is supposed to be doing all the receiving? I began to realize that not receiving is another guilt trap set up by our conditional self.

Yes, it is holy to give, but it is just as holy to receive. Without our ability to receive too, all giving can deteriorate into sacrifice, burnout and resentment. The act of receiving refreshes and renews us, it bonds us to people. Indeed, our unconditional self thrives on receiving because of the connections we make with others. It's worth spending a moment or two to reflect on how much we receive from others on a daily basis. Here are a few examples:

- *guidance and advice*
- *inspiration*
- *support*
- *practical skills*
- *fun and laughter*

TO RECEIVE IS ALSO TO GIVE

When someone truly accepts, appreciates and enjoys what you have to give, don't you just want to give them more? Consider where in your life you might be pushing things away because you don't feel worthy, you feel guilty, or believe others deserve them more than you. I am beginning to think more and more that the only true shortages are caused by a lack of willingness to receive. The first time I heard this idea I got quite angry – I believed I was pretty open to receiving things and the problem was that life just wasn't delivering the goods I wanted. But as I have delved into the deepest recesses of my mind, I have seen how many hidden noes I have harboured, and still do. I have discovered places of guilt and unworthiness, places of self-attack and self-loathing, that act as an enormous internal Keep Out! sign. My defences against truly receiving were like barricades. A great strategy for bringing greater abundance into our lives is to find and heal those places inside where we are putting ourselves down and generally just not loving ourselves; when we do so, abundance will naturally flow into our lives at new levels.

There is a big difference between taking and receiving. Taking is where our ego is at work; it loves collecting badges of honour, toys, certificates, qualifications and other proof that we're really OK, when deep down we feel we aren't. Sometimes we accept enormous amounts of love, money or success, but they don't really reach us because we don't receive the essence or heart of the gift. It's a craving that doesn't feed the soul. Our ego tells us that we need or want something, but we can still be left empty. It is then that we look around at our life and think, 'Is this it? I have all I thought would make me happy, but I am not.' My good friend Ben Renshaw wrote in his first book, *Successful, but Something Missing*, about this very phenomenon. To be happy, we need to be great receivers; to be truly successful, we may need to step up our willingness to receive, regardless of how much we actually have.

To be truly ready to receive we need to let some of our defences down, to begin to let people be important to us, to value others and ourselves. To truly receive we need our feelings, we need our heart, otherwise our life just becomes a collection of things that we neither want nor value.

OUR RESISTANCE TO RECEIVING

- *We fear being under an obligation – we don't want to feel beholden to anyone else and lose control.*
- *We don't want to bother people.*
- *We may feel guilty, thinking that someone else deserves more than we do.*

A RECEIVING PROJECT

Decide that every day for the next month you will spend 15 minutes in meditation, opening the doors within your heart and mind to receive what you seem to be lacking. Imagine how you would feel if you dropped your defences, opened your life up to new and exciting avenues, and generally allowed yourself to explore freely and without inhibition.

EXPAND YOUR GIVING

Abundance also hinges on our willingness to transcend our fear of giving. Remember our conditional self's belief system is based on scarcity, it tells us that when we give, we lose, we no longer have, and at the surface level this is true. But there is a deeper force at work within us, which knows that in our giving, we also receive. Paradoxically, we can't have abundance through simply trying to get, but only through giving as well. Have you noticed how when you truly love and share, you are transformed in the process?

But our ego is likely to have wired us up to believe that to give and to contribute will lead to burnout. We'd need to be some kind of saint to give more! We need to realize that the next step forward on this journey to unconditional success is about being willing to discover a new kind of giving.

In Buddhism, three kinds of giving are recognized:

- ***Beggarly giving***, in which we only give once we've received. We fight to get our needs met before we give anything back. Our giving is totally conditional.
- ***Friendly giving***, in which we are more generous, but only to those who are generous with us. Our giving is less conditional, but still has conditions. If we feel our giving is unlikely to be reciprocated, we withhold.
- ***Kingly giving***, which is both spontaneous and unconditional, beyond any demands or expectations. We truly ask for nothing in return, not even for

what we give to be received! We've learned that our giving will help us, and may help the receiver, but that is not our concern.

To live a successful and abundant life of purpose we need to remember and reconnect with our capacity for kingly giving, in order to stay fresh and open, not burned out, cynical and exhausted. In *A Course in Miracles* we are reminded that the only thing missing from any situation in our life is what we are withholding. That is the power of our giving. Being a leader in our life hinges crucially on our willingness to give our gifts: our love, humour, inspiration and ideas. The world awaits our kingly giving.

AN ABUNDANCE OF OPPORTUNITY

A big part of the consciousness of abundance is the realization that we are surrounded not only by beauty, but by opportunity too. It's the knowledge that there are many doors open to us, and many doors that we can open. The more we are conscious of our skills, the more willing we are to keep learning and growing, the more we discover that the world is awash with abundant opportunities.

GO TO THE HOLY PLACE INSIDE YOU

Abundance is inside you right now. It is the holy place within, an altar where all the treasures are laid out for you. It is a place of stillness, unshaken and unshakeable by all the appearances of the world. It is always there, even if we aren't in conscious contact with it. *Meditation* and *contemplation* are two ancient and proven ways to this place, and you don't need any particular religious or spiritual beliefs to be able to connect with it. All that is needed is a willingness to go to that place of tranquillity and peace, that in some ways can seem like *no-thing* but is the place of *every-thing*.

CONTINUE FOCUSING ON AND
NOTICING ABUNDANCE

Remember, whatever we look for we'll find, so ask yourself: what do I want to find? Be careful what you look for! If you want to prove or support your beliefs in scarcity, you don't have to look far. Every day the media is full of negative stories about lacks, shortages, battles, competition, lay-offs and fear and, most recently, the tragic attacks on the World Trade Center and the Pentagon. Yet behind all these are millions of stories of courage and kindness, love and generosity, abundance and inspiration.

Mark Victor Hansen and Jack Canfield saw this and thought: wouldn't it be wonderful to collect these true stories of love, courage and kindness? So they asked for stories and turned them into a book called *Chicken Soup for the Soul*. It sold hundreds of thousands of copies, so they compiled a second helping, and a third. They then began to specialize in stories for the workplace, for couples, for teenagers, for cancer survivors and war veterans. The list goes on. Their combined worldwide sales are now in excess of 33 million books, and growing daily!

We have an almost unlimited desire to be inspired and uplifted. Oprah Winfrey, apart from being one of the richest women on the planet, has also served to raise the spirit of hope in the world. People don't watch her TV show one day and say, thank you, that's enough inspiration for now! They can't wait for the next day's show, and then they go to her web site for more inspiration. Oprah recently began to publish her own magazine called O, which had the most successful launch in publishing history. As you can see, our need for inspiration and authentic living is healthily insatiable.

Every human need is an opportunity for us. If we want to bring inspiration and love to the world, we will find unlimited opportunities to do just that. As Martin Luther King Junior said, 'Everybody can be great, because anybody can serve. You don't have to have a college degree to serve. You don't have to make your subject and verb agree to serve. You don't have to know about Plato and Aristotle . . . Einstein's theory of relativity . . . [or] the second law of thermodynamics in physics to serve. You only need a heart full of grace. A soul generated by love.' When we focus on generating abundance through love and service, we will be amazed at how many opportunities there are.

TAKE ACTION TO BRING ABUNDANCE INTO YOUR LIFE

The doors to abundance fly wide open when we engage and utilize both our head and our heart. We need to be able to turn our inspired ideas into deliverable products and services, and into an income. The Dalai Lama said, 'Buddha always emphasized a balance of wisdom and compassion: a good brain and a good heart should work together.' When we can bring our business mind to support and be a servant to our inspired ideas, we become incredibly powerful. But we should not let logic alone be the master. I have often seen someone's inspired idea buck market forces, and transcend seeming limitations. At other times I have seen wonderful ideas stillborn, as people struggled to find the help to turn them into practical solutions.

I was recently invited to make a presentation in Cape Town, but the only time I could go would be at the beginning of December, the start of the holiday season there. When Helen, the promoter in Cape Town, talked to friends and colleagues they told her it would be totally inappropriate for me to visit at this time; everyone would be winding down for the summer holiday and Christmas, and consequently there would be little interest in talks and seminars. Helen and I talked about this, and we felt strongly that there were bigger issues at work here than simply market forces. We eventually decided I should make the trip as planned, and that we should trust our inner promptings.

How right we were to trust these feelings. When I arrived in Cape Town, I received a really warm response from everyone and in the six days I was there I had two sell-out talks, a sell-out workshop, two radio interviews, five press interviews and various other useful meetings – and all this at a time when nobody was supposed to be interested!

As you can see from this example, it's important to stay tuned to our inner voice. In order to achieve unconditional success, our business head needs the support of our spiritual heart. Quite simply, business needs spirit and spirit needs business. Without spirit, even amazing material achievements can turn to joyless, clinically efficient experiences. At the same time, without organizing, marketing and commercial skills, the most beautiful and inspired ideas may never come to fruition. True abundance calls to us to aim our heart at heaven while keeping our feet firmly on the ground.

When I asked my friend Barbara Winter, a self-employment advocate, what qualities were needed to be a successful entrepreneur, I expected her to talk about marketing or financial skills. Instead, she responded by saying, 'The most important things you need are joy and inspiration – to truly love what you do. When we have joy, everything expands, and becomes easier.'

Joy is a crucial ingredient of unconditional success. Perhaps it lies at the very heart of it. Wouldn't it be great if business and management courses taught a module on the subject of joy so that every student could be aware of the many opportunities that lie ahead when joy and skill come together.

WHAT CHANNEL FOR RECEIVING?

Many of us have grown up with the belief that the only way to have financial abundance in our life is to have a job, to work for someone else. We believe that earning a salary is the only way to security. Yet millions of people already know that a job is not the only way to earn money, and that their security comes from their own gifts and talents, and their ability to see and respond to opportunities to serve people's needs in a way that they enjoy. Being self-employed and running our own little businesses can offer us the greatest freedom to be abundant. Remember, though, that self-employment doesn't mean a limitless income, and balance in your life: those must be developed in your consciousness first, and then your business can be a vehicle for them. True abundance is the flow of giving and receiving, and our own business gives us the freedom to give what we enjoy doing and giving, and receive abundantly in return.

BE OPEN TO MIRACLES AND MONEY FROM UNEXPECTED SOURCES

Have you ever been given a book or something similar at some point in your life, smiled and said thank you very much, and then wondered to yourself, why did they give this to me? Why would they think I was interested in this? That happened to me with a book called *The Abundance Book*, by John Randolph Price. My friend Jai gave me a copy in 1990, and I looked at it, smiled and filed it away in a box somewhere. Many years later I came across it again, was curious, opened it and began to think, wow, what an amazing little book. It articulated beautifully some of the ideas and principles that I had been thinking about for a long while, and inspired me greatly. Its main message was that in order to create anything in your life, go back to the source of abundance within you. It also had a 40-day programme in it. I don't usually trust programmes like that, and I found my cynical side coming out, especially when I saw a series of endorsements from people saying how wonderful the programme was, and how it changed their lives and made them lots of money. They remind me of the infomercials you get on American television in the middle of the night. But a voice inside me said, give it a go. So I did.

Every day I read the daily lesson and meditated on it, and I could sense my thinking and feeling shifting in response to these thoughts. Secretly, I wanted one of those miracles that people said they'd had. It got to day 38 and I read my lesson, and then went off to meet my friend John, a coaching client, over breakfast. Secretly I thought: that miracle better hurry up and happen – only two days are left!

John and I had our coaching/breakfast session and at the end he gave me the cheque for my fee. Then he said, 'I have another cheque for you.' He reminded me that his mother had died the year before, and he and his brother had just sold the house that they grew up in. The brothers had received the money from the sale of the property and John told me, 'I tithe [give away] 10 per cent of all my income, and want you to have some of this income as a thank-you for helping and supporting me.' He handed me the cheque and I wondered if it might be for £100 or so. As I opened it I discovered it was for £5,000! I was flabbergasted! Lost for words, after a few seconds I came up with an inspired response, 'Thank you!' I was so grateful: I really needed that money right then, it was literally a godsend. We talked more, and I told him about the abundance programme I was doing, and he said, 'I bought that book three years ago, and have been following the programme ever since. It has helped me enormously.' Breakfast was on me.

I learned a couple of valuable lessons that day. Firstly, abundance is an inside job. By changing some of my inner attitudes, thinking and beliefs, I overcame my resistance to receiving. Until then, I had always believed that the only way I could really receive money was through hard work, effort and struggle. I had to earn and deserve it before I could justify it. Secondly, I learned that some people just love giving money away. It brings joy to their life, and at least one wanted to give some to me! I also learned not to limit the ways that abundance can come into my life. It wants to come in any way it can.

I saw more deeply that money will not make us happy, but that prosperity consciousness will bring forth happiness, love, joy, peace, contentment and fulfilment and a tangible supply of material things too. Money without consciousness is not our goal; a spiritual under-standing of our unconditional self is our goal, and money becomes a spiritual experience by working with this principle.

ASK!

Are you good at asking for what you want? Or do you hint, and hope people will know what you are asking for? Or do you see it as sign of weakness to have to ask? Or you don't want to be a nuisance? Many of us grew up with conflicting messages about asking for what we want. But don't forget that old adage, those that don't ask, don't get. Much of what we want in life comes from other people – love, encouragement, feedback, recognition, support, money, practical help, being listened to, learning. There is also incredible unseen help available to us from our inner worlds.

It is very hard to feel the joy of abundance when you are doing work that is not true to your heart. If you don't do what you love, or love what you do, you are blocking true abundance, however well you are paid. The money will be a compensation for your lack of joy, not a way of adding to your joy. One of the biggest blocks to abundance is the belief that we can't be well paid for doing something we love, and that we have to take any work that gives us the income we need.

Our lives so far will have been about the developing of blueprints etched into our consciousness through our conditioning, our beliefs and the attitudes that we have collected. That is the principle of life – we can only see what we believe. So to change our life, we need to change our core beliefs and attitudes, which will allow us to experience greater abundance.

What do you believe about abundance, lack and scarcity? Using your journal, write down some of your most apparent limiting thoughts; don't deny or hide them. For example:

- *Life's tough, that's just the way it is.*
- *There isn't enough to go around.*
- *I'm lucky to have any job, let alone one I love.*
- *If I thought about changing now, I'd just be throwing away everything I've achieved so far.*
- *Only lucky or special people get to be really happy and successful, and I am not one of them.*

ABUNDANCE IS OFTEN MOST SEEN IN THE LITTLE THINGS

We often find abundance in the simple things of life – the precious moments, the landscape, moments of laughter with a friend. On a recent business trip to the USA, one of my greatest joys was taking advantage of getting over jet lag in a very hot Denver. I woke at 6 a.m. for three days in a row, and my luxury was sunbathing at 7 a.m. and reading a couple of chapters of the latest John Grisham novel before I ran my seminar. It felt so delicious to be working, sunbathing and relaxing all at the same time.

Using your journal, make a note of the little things that make you feel abundant and lucky to be alive.

KEEPING IT FRESH

There is something within us that knows our wholeness. It's an innate wisdom which if used as a guide, will always lead to an experience of peace, harmony, and Love. There's nothing magical or special about it, it is in everyone. It may seem mystical, but that's only because it's little understood and seldom used.

BURT HOTCHKISS, author of *Have Miracles, Will Travel*

A big part of abundance is about taking a fresh, energized approach to what we do. My friend Barbara Winter, author of *Making a Living without a Job,* loves people who are passionate about their work. She told me the story of her visit to the Milky Way restaurant run by Leah Adler, the 81-year-old mother of Steven Spielberg, the film producer and director. The restaurant is not very big, so Leah meets everybody who goes there. She sits down and chats with the customers and asks them if they are enjoying their meal, how their day is going. Barbara asked Leah why she loved running the restaurant, and Leah explained, 'I am here at 8.30 a.m. every day, I get to help create the menu, get to chat to so many interesting people; I get to flirt with the men and have a party every day!' She was so enthusiastic that Barbara assumed that she must have opened the restaurant very recently. 'No,' she replied, 'I have been going for 25 years!'

Wouldn't it be wonderful to be able to still be that enthusiastic about our work and our life? We can be, but it's unlikely just to happen. It will need to be a conscious choice, a commitment to change. Here are some ideas about how to keep it fresh:

- *Don't tolerate your own boredom – if you are bored, ask what you would like to do that would get your energy flowing again. Life is too precious to be bored with it. Take a risk or two every day, and do things differently.*
- *Quit blaming – the problem is not out there even if it may seem to be. The way through is always by making a new decision, a new choice. Take responsibility for knowing and getting what you want.*
- *Stretch yourself – take risks, be bold and have the courage to do something different. Try to do something every day that creates butterflies in your stomach, gets your imagination flowing.*
- *Commit to self-discovery – there is so much you still don't know about your gifts, talents, skills and creativity. Commit to discovering more about what is inside you.*
- *Commit to love – work and life stay fresh when there is love, so if you don't*

have love in your life, think about how to create a more loving and nurturing environment.

- *Stay open to new possibilities – keep tuned to your intuition, inspiration and hunches: they will always be prompting you to stretch and grow, but you may not be listening.*
- *Stay curious and fascinated – there is so much to learn and discover about life and love and people, so keep being curious. Understand or learn something new every day.*
- *Stop waiting and take action – do something you know you want to do but have been putting off. Cure your wait problem.*

Our problem is not always with the work, it is with our attitude to work and our thinking about work. No work is intrinsically interesting or boring. Work – as with anything – can only be soulless if we refuse to bring our heart and soul to it. I have met toilet attendants who have loved their work because they met interesting people, took a pride in their job and loved being able to provide such an essential service. I meet people desperate to get into PR, and coach others desperate to get out of it. I used to run a career board on a well-known job web site, and everybody wanted to change their job – bankers wanting to become teachers, teachers wanting to become bankers! I felt like I should start a career dating agency! I have seen so clearly that no work is intrinsically interesting and no work will *make* us happy. It depends on self-knowledge: knowing our own shape, strengths and passions, and the part of us that we bring to our work.

KIND AND LOVING LANDLORDS

John has always inspired me. When we first met, he was on a career break from his sales career in the corporate world, and his partner Jackie was an accountant at a City bank. I loved John because he was a down-to-earth man, fascinated and immersed in spiritual and metaphysical principles, yet just as happy watching Chelsea play football. He'd started his spiritual journey six years before, after an illness, and was in recovery from alcohol addiction. He was fascinated by prosperity consciousness, and read all the books he could about people who had been successful and happy, so that he could apply these principles to his own life. He was a great student of wisdom, and a voracious learner.

He built his financial life on abundance and generosity: his belief that there was an unlimited supply, and the more he shared, the more he would have. He'd begun to tithe some of his income as an affirmation of abundance, and explained to me, 'I can trace my steady increase of income from the point at which I started to tithe 10 per cent of all money I ever received. It truly seems the more I give, the more I receive.'

He and Jackie had a plan to build up a small property business of houses and flats that they would buy and then rent out, which would give them a capital base and an income, although they had no previous experience in the area. 'My idea is that if we look after our tenants, give them great places to live, and make it a win/win situation for everyone concerned, we will be successful. I'd like them to be friends. I think we will have money flow to us as we focus on serving our tenants.'

One by one they bought properties and spent money refurbishing them. John spent a lot of his time organizing builders, decorating, and buying appliances. Before tenants moved in, he made the homes as beautiful as possible. He also researched the local neighbourhood and provided an information pack with details of the best places to shop and eat, emergency services, and other important contacts. John's intention was also to build good relationships with all his suppliers, including his lawyer, accountant, builders and appliance suppliers. 'My intention was to make their business a vehicle for service, generosity and love,' he explained.

Within 18 months of applying these principles of abundance,

John and Jackie had built up a portfolio of eight properties, worth over £1.3 million, and they had a substantial monthly income. He had put in a lot of effort and been on a steep learning curve. 'One of my biggest problems, though,' explained John, 'was understanding that what I was doing was still work. In my mind, going to an office every day from 9 to 5.30 was work, and this was somehow cheating! I am at last getting it that this is now my work, and that I don't have a boss breathing down my neck. I am the boss, and I am doing brilliantly!'

HOLDING ON BLOCKS THE FLOW OF ABUNDANCE

Every time we try to hold on too tightly – whether to people, things or situations – we are trying to control, and abundance can't come through where we've closed the door in this way. Control blocks flow, and abundance is about flow in our life, and not about grasping. Often we fear that if we don't hold tight we'll lose everything, but the looser we can hold, the more we can truly have.

FOR LOVE AND MONEY

We open another door to abundance when we believe we can have both spiritual and material abundance. It's not holy to be poor: the rich can still be spiritual.

I was having supper with Dina Glouberman, co-founder of the Skyros Institute, which consists of holistic holiday centres on the Greek island of Skyros, founded in the early 1980s. The two centres are generally very popular and successful, with hundreds of people visiting every year for rest, renewal, inspiration, learning, community and the stunning natural beauty of the island. We were at Atsitsa, one of the centres. Dina said, 'I remember clearly a visitor in our early days, who said to me, "This is such a beautiful place here, thanks for creating it. It helps so many people relax and find themselves. I do hope you are not making any money out of it!" '

It is a common idea that good, spiritual and life-affirming activities shouldn't make money. Our conditional self tells us that if it is spiritual, it should be free. This derives from the mistaken idea that money is bad, unspiritual and unholy, and that anything that makes money must also be tarnished.

The ego belief that poverty is holy, spiritual, and makes us good people, and the contrasting idea that wealth is unholy and un-spiritual are both untrue and unhelpful. It is not necessary to go without in order to reach God or get to Heaven. Worldly success does not necessarily lead us to live unspiritual lives. You can have outer success without selling your soul. What's crucial is discover-ing *why* we want more money or outer success.

YOU CAN GET PAID FOR DOING WHAT COMES NATURALLY

Many of us hold the belief that what is easy, natural, fun and enjoyable can't possibly be work! The feeling that it is only work if we'd rather not be doing it can go very deep. When I met Jo, she had spent years in the corporate world in the high-pressure area of newsgathering and had taken an early retirement package when it was offered. Financially she was pretty OK, but she wanted to create new work that she would enjoy and that would give her a sense of purpose and occupy her. She had trained as a therapist, and in the process of her work discovered a passion – spontaneous storytelling! She loved the way people could tell and create stories, almost out of thin air.

Although she loved creating these opportunities, as we talked she explained that she didn't do it very much. 'What happens when you start doing this work?' I asked. 'Well, I start off enjoying it, but then I lose momentum and don't enjoy it any more.' I asked her about her Scottish upbringing and her father's attitudes to work. She explained, 'My father told me work was tough, something to be endured, not enjoyed, and that's just how life was.' I suddenly made a link in my mind, and responded, 'Do you realize that you start off loving and enjoying the storytelling, but then you turn it into hard work!' Jo saw that she didn't allow herself to just enjoy the storytelling and charge for what it was her joy to do anyway.

I meet many people who are very talented, with gifts in many areas. Yet although people may love and appreciate them for their gifts, they can't conceive of charging money for them. Whilst some of their reluctance is based on a wonderful desire simply to give and share of themselves, a considerable amount is driven by the guilty feeling that they just can't have it that good! Because the work ethic, which values struggle and difficulty, goes so deep, we undervalue ease, grace and naturalness; we may even think it is cheating. Yet we are here to make things easier, not to struggle and suffer. Life does have pain and difficulty, that is inescapable, but we do ourselves a great disservice when we mistakenly believe that we are better people, more noble and valuable, for the amount of struggle we put ourselves through. It's a bit like the Monty Python sketch where the Yorkshiremen compete in telling stories about how tough their lives were when they were children. Our ego loves struggle, even thrives on it, while our spirit knows only ease. Our goal is to give less value to the struggle and value and celebrate ease more. We are here on this planet to undo the suffering ethic, not create more suffering.

We think that to have money, we have to deserve it. We create rules about what we must do to deserve it, and then when we have kept to these rules we feel able to have the money we want. But the vital question is, 'How willing are we to receive it, and receive it with ease and grace, in return for doing things we enjoy and value?'

One of my own big challenges is that I felt fine earning a lot of money when I didn't particularly enjoy what I did to earn it, when it was compensation. But when I started to do work that I valued, enjoyed and found relatively easy, I noticed that a part of me resisted receiving money, as if I hadn't really earned or deserved it.

FOCUSING QUESTIONS

＊ What rules do you have about what you must have done to deserve money?

＊ How do you feel about people who seem to earn money easily and joyfully? Do you celebrate or do you judge them and feel jealous?

THRILL 'EM AND BILL 'EM!

So much work and commercial activity is done with boredom and resentment. How many places have you shopped and been served by indifferent staff? How many restaurants have you eaten at with average food and poor service? How many businesses seem to be operating for their own benefit, not yours? Subconsciously we are drawn to return to sandwich bars or pubs where the service is kind, efficient and effective. Simply to shift into working with the attitude and energy of love could be enough for you to be successful.

With all that mediocrity about, you only have to do your work with love and enthusiasm and the door to succeed must begin to open. We accomplish this by switching from a sales to a service mentality. This creates an inner shift: from 'What's in it for me?' to 'How can I serve?' It's a move from the conditional to the unconditional self which desires to give all our gifts away as service to the world, and is willing to receive money as a reward for doing that. When we work for the upliftment of those we come into contact with, we have shifted gear into the spiritual fast lane.

To make money we have to deliver our energy in some way,

either through a product or a service. But if our overriding energy is boredom or resentment, people will know that we don't want to be doing our job, and so don't want to deal with us. They would rather deal with someone who lifts their spirits and makes them feel important while they spend their money.

Our ego will also tell us that we can only make money by focusing on meeting our own needs, and will scare us by trying to keep the attention solely on us. A key aspect of money mastery is to recognize that your success comes from serving someone else. If our starting point is how can I make a load of money or rip people off, we may succeed for a while, but eventually people will go elsewhere. So we need to have a new starting point – how can I help? how can I serve? how can I meet the needs of others? This doesn't mean becoming a charity worker or disempowering ourselves financially, but it does mean subjugating our egos for a while, subtly shifting our mindset while we focus on others. By asking how we can meet others' needs, help them to feel more fulfilled, we will make money in the process.

When we decide to work in this way, we are beginning to align ourselves with the unlimited supply of energy, the lavish abundance, that is within each of us, and that is what makes the difference. We can begin to move beyond the limits that most of us have been conditioned to accept and have grown up believing in. When our intention is loving and serving, then we work with the incredible inner power within that is ultimately greater than any outer power that seems to dominate or control us.

The world of work and business believes in supply and demand, that an over-supply brings prices down, and an under-supply raises prices, and that we are always in competition with other suppliers in a limited market. But when we move into the area of energy we can start to transcend these laws. With six billion people on the planet, each with hundreds of different and ever-changing needs and wants, we can see that there are limitless ways that we can help and serve others, and limitless ways of making money for ourselves. Instead of a mindset of fear and lack, we move into a mindset of abundance. We only need to know how to serve others, and ask for money in return for it. When you are involved in some activity that you enjoy and where there is love, your energy and enthusiasm will not be in short supply.

We serve others by finding out what it is they want and need, and then discovering the gifts that we uniquely have to meet their needs. We may not provide anything different from what hundreds of others offer, but we can offer it our own way, with our insights, our love, our caring. Our uniqueness can make the difference in a world hell bent on conformity.

God wants you to be rich

PAUL ZANE PILSER, author of *Unlimited Wealth*

To really understand money, we need to understand the source of money, which is the source of everything – our own consciousness, our own inner spirit. Both mystics and quantum physicists say that behind all physical appearances lies a non-physical reality, an 'invisible' field of energy. Depending on your persuasion, you might call this field the womb of creation, spirit, the field of pure potentiality, the unified field, God or the universal mind. It is also who we are in truth. The name is not really important: the idea is. There is a source of all that is, was and ever will be in this physical world, and we are all part of that source. We can – and do constantly – draw forth what we want into our physical realm from this invisible source of energy.

Rose explained to me at one of my abundance seminars, 'My husband is from India and I have lived there for quite a while. There, they have no problems with money being holy, and they even have a deity, Lakshmi, that they pray to for good fortune and wealth.' As we spoke, I was reminded how unhealthily many of us have learned to deal with money. Either we see it as a god, an idol to be worshipped and chased and cherished, or we see it as unholy and a hindrance to spiritual growth. We need to undo the belief that money is bad. The Church may have done a lot to spread the belief that money is bad, but it has also taught that if we give a lot of it to the Church then we can be forgiven and get to Heaven. What a great marketing strategy!

Ultimately we all want to live the life that is right for us; we want to experience happiness, security, love, fulfilment, and believe that they lie in some external circumstance or situation. They don't. (A recent survey by *Forbes Magazine* revealed that 37 per cent of America's 400 richest people were unhappy – and this was self-reported unhappiness.) Money can invite, encourage and support us to be happy but won't make us happy, because we already carry all that we want within us; we *are* what we are looking for. Whilst this is a reassuring idea, it can also seem frustrating. *How* can we get to these inner resources? The answer is that to get what we are truly looking for, we need to discover that the root of all experience is within us; that we can gradually become less dependent on the physical props, and go straight to the source.

HOW DO WE TRANSLATE THIS IDEA OF ABUNDANCE INTO EXPERIENCE IN OUR DAILY LIVES?

When we are in nature, in beauty, relaxed and at peace, it is much easier to be aware of abundance. When we are at work, with pressure on and a boss breathing down our neck, it may be less easy. We must take responsibility for bringing more abundance into our life; others can encourage, or criticize and put down, but it's our choice. A great key to abundance is self-belief and a deserving attitude, which means *freedom from guilt and fear*. Jerry

Gillies, author of *Moneylove*, says: 'The strongest single factor in prosperity consciousness is self-esteem: believing you can do it, believing you deserve it, believing you will get it.' For us to have, no one else has to go without. Abundance is for all.

30-DAY ABUNDANCE PROGRAMME

Ideas help to transform us and the purpose of this 30-day programme is to help you shift from an awareness of abundance as *things*, to an awareness of the presence within that is the source of all abundance. When we understand the abundance within we know that it is forever working in our life to bring into form what we want and need, including creative ideas, opportunities, money and inspiration.

Below are ten principles and ideas that will help to focus your awareness on the abundance within, and realize it within your life. It takes 30 days to build up an energy around an idea, so decide a day on which you'll start, and on that day sign and complete the following affirmation:

Today [*enter today's date*] I cease believing in money and material things as my support. I see the material world as the cause and effect that it truly is, and put my attention fully on the inner world of cause. Today I give up my belief in lack and scarcity, and I give up my belief in separation that may have caused seeming lack in my life. Today I restore to my mind my eternal awareness of the all-sufficiency of supply within me, and clear the way to receive incredible abundance in my life.

Then each day read one of the following affirmations and spend a few moments letting the idea sink deep into your mind, infusing your subconscious. Make a note of all your responses to it, including disbelief and resistance. Don't judge, or even try to change:

just notice. Once you have been through each principle once, go back and start again, until you have been through it three times.

The ten principles

1. *Creation is lavish abundance, I am lavish abundance. The abundance of the whole universe is individualized as me, the truth of me. Manifesting wealth alone would teach me nothing, but understanding that all things flow to me as an extension of my being is to understand everything.*

2. *Money is not my supply of security, no bank account or job is my security. My security is the abundance within me and my ability to manifest what I need in each moment of my life.*

3. *Today I choose to acknowledge the presence of abundance within me. It has always been there, and always will be, and today I give thanks that in truth I can never go without.*

4. *Abundance can't wait to happen in my life.*

5. *Today I surrender up all notions of struggle, sacrifice and difficulty, and allow abundance to flow naturally, easily and effortlessly in all areas of my life.*

6. *I am an inspired receiver, and an inspired giver, knowing that the more I share, the more I truly have. What I have is what I can give.*

7. *Today I choose to reveal the power of abundance that has always been within me. I remember that the divine presence that I am is the source and substance of my abundance. My awareness of the presence of God or creation within me is my supply of all things.*

8. *My unconditional self is forever expressing its true nature of abundance, and this is its responsibility, not mine. My responsibility is to be aware of this, and to be totally confident in letting go and letting God or creation appear as the supply of all I want in my life.*

9. *Today I let go of all thoughts of lack, scarcity, struggle and sacrifice, and*

restore the truth of abundance to my mind. Everything to fulfil my needs is present when I have no limitations on receiving it. Today, I will get out of my own way!

10. *I keep my mind and focus off this world, and place my entire focus on the god within as the cause of all my abundance and prosperity. I acknowledge this inner presence as the substance of all things visible in my life.*

Within my own life, and the lives of hundreds of others, I have seen amazing things happen when this philosophy of abundance is practised: offers of work, pay rises, opportunities, money out of the blue, problems resolved – all this can happen as people begin to change their consciousness.

We are all full of gifts, and the greatest joy of our unconditional self is to make its creative gifts visible in the world.

•

Within each of us are incredible contributions waiting to be released, and the more we find and share our gifts, the more we are helping others to find theirs. Life is a big jigsaw, and we all have pieces for each other.

•

Our gifts need to find a home by being brought to the light of day and being shared with the world, and our work can be the way in which we bring our gifts to the world, and make our soul visible.

3

UNCONDITIONAL CREATIVITY

What we have to confront in the present workplace is the reluctance to engage in conversations that really invite the creative qualities hidden deep inside each human being.

DAVID WHYTE, author of *Crossing the Unknown Sea*

I met Hazel at the Skyros centre in Greece where I was teaching. 'When I was a teenager, I loved being creative, I felt a real call. I enjoyed writing, painting, making jewellery and singing. I longed to do something creative as a living, but my family discouraged me and pushed me into more sensible things, to make money. So reluctantly I let my creative dreams go, overrode my intuition, and trained as a lawyer. Now here I am, at 33, successful on the outside, doing well materially, but dying inside. I have managed to ignore and discount my creative longing for 15 years, but it's killing me to do that. Rather than fight it and regard it as my enemy, I think it might be time to turn my attitude around and start listening to that creative calling again.'

Hazel's story is very familiar. Most of us have creative callings when we are younger, but we are encouraged to abandon our creativity in favour of seemingly more sensible and logical pursuits. I remember having to decide at 16 whether I was an arts or science person. I was torn: I loved both but wasn't able to do both. I chose science and it wasn't until my late twenties that I began nurturing and reintegrating my creative side again.

True creativity is our unconditional self expressing itself, it is accessing that spiritual electricity that resides in all of us. Creativity is about moving forward into the unknown, into wonderful surprises, into the magic that can happen in each moment as it is revealed and brought into the light of day. We can't be truly creative if we know what the outcome will be because it's not about endless planning, it is not about being the best in the world at anything, it's certainly not about being perfect. It is simple, and ultimately it is easy, but to be creative we also have to deal with all the anxieties, doubts, conditioning and fears that are within us. In developing our creative self we add a new dimension to the journey of discovering unconditional success.

IT ALL STARTS WITH AN IDEA

So, let's start at the beginning. We all long to be creative, to express ourselves, and put our unique stamp on our life and work. Creativity starts with an idea, and an inner longing to create or express something. This may manifest as inspiration, an inner calling or, as in Hazel's case, boredom and frustration, or even a sense of dislocation. The old ways of being are no longer working.

Creativity can also start with initiative. Initiative is the creative spark of inspiration and doesn't need to be told to do something by some external force. The spark begins with that little voice inside that asks you to bring something into being, or accomplish an act, dealing with all obstacles as you go. Initiative creates something – an idea, a thought, a vision. Creativity enables us to be powerful, and is a major attribute of success.

During my career I have heard thousands of people's ideas about what they would love to do with their work and businesses, and most people have very creative ideas. However, a lack of self-belief, direction, motivation, information or encouragement to follow these ideas through usually prevents us from voicing, sharing or implementing them. We may have tried something before that didn't turn out the way we wanted, so we associate creativity with a sense of failure. We try to save ourselves from repeating that old pain. Alternatively we allow our ideas to be undermined by the well-meaning opinions of others, and the cherished buds of inspiration never come to full bloom.

Creativity can also represent a new and different response to a situation. One man had enjoyed a wonderful holiday with his young daughter, and had taken lots of beautiful pictures. When at the end of the holiday she discovered that she couldn't see the pictures immediately, she was distraught and burst into tears. He could have yelled at her, taught her that life is full of disappointments and that patience was a virtue. Instead, he asked himself: How would it be possible to have instant pictures? and this one question led him to develop the Polaroid film.

It is easy to undervalue ideas, but it's important to remember that everything starts as an idea. Look around you for a moment – everything, literally everything, starts off as an idea in someone's mind. Whether it's a computer, TV, car, home, book, song or even a person, they were once just an idea in someone's mind. So the question is either:

- *Do we need to generate more ideas? or*
- *Do we need to do more with the ideas we already have?*

The stronger and deeper our roots are, the taller we can grow and I am often amazed at how far a single idea can go. In the film *Field of Dreams* the character played by Kevin Costner is continually prompted by an inner voice to build a baseball field in the middle of nowhere: 'Build the field, and they will come.' Eventually he heeded the voice, built the field, and in time they did come. He listened to his inner voice and his calling.

When I look back over the last 10 years of my life since I started my own business I can see how my life has evolved as I have followed my inner creative promptings. In 1996 an idea came to me – 'The Work We Were Born to Do'. The words simply came into my mind, and they really resonated. I felt that for much of my life I'd been doing the work I was expected to do, not the work I felt I was born to do. So I began by undertaking a small speaking engagement on that subject. People came and it went so well that I thought I would create a workshop, and made an audiocassette of the ideas. Both were well received. I had always wanted to write a book, and wondered whether I could turn the ideas and experiences into a good book. So I started writing, began to show it to publishers and found they were keen. I chose one, finished the book, and it came out in 1999. The ideas have resonated with thousands of people all over the world, and have allowed me to travel to many parts of the globe to teach, have fun and meet lovely people. And it was all down to one single idea! Ideas have their own life – they evolve at their own pace and sometimes in ways we cannot imagine. The Roman philosopher Epictetus expressed this in the first century AD when he wrote, 'No thing great is created suddenly, any more than a bunch of grapes or a fig. If you desire a fig, I answer you that there must be time. Let it first blossom, then bear fruit and then ripen.'

Our loves and beautiful ideas cannot and should not be held in some kind of limbo inside us where they can do no harm. They are too powerful to be held in. They have set off on a voyage from far inside us to find a home in the clear light of day and demand to be expressed in the world, particularly in the work we do. Through our work we can make ourselves visible in the world, and as the poet David Whyte describes it, 'This is the soul's individual journey, and the soul would much rather fail at its own journey than succeed at someone else's.' (We'll discover more about David's work as a poet in the corporate world in Chapter 6.)

My description of the evolution of the idea is merely factual – the experience is even richer. During this creative journey, at times I have experienced great joy, fulfilment and pleasure as I have become more creative and have learned and received feedback from around the world, feeling deep connections with people, some of whom I have never even met. The journey has been a challenge – but an enriching challenge. It has led me to face and heal some of my greatest fears and doubts, I have felt insecure at times, I have been called to believe in myself more than ever, and I've had to be willing to receive more, and give more than I'd previously dreamed possible. At times I haven't known where I was going with these ideas. I simply had to step forward in faith and let the path reveal itself. The ideas themselves led the way and I merely followed – but not as a victim, more a powerful co-creator.

Ultimately the creative process is a mystery. As we've heard, we can't control or manipulate this process. However, it can be encouraged and welcomed, and we can become willing and clearer channels. Creativity is like electricity: few of us truly understand it, but we all know how to use it. We can use it to light a cathedral, keep a person on a life-support system, or electrocute them. Creativity is like that. It makes no judgement; we can do with it what we will. None of us can say we truly understand a simple question like 'Where was an idea before we had it?' We simply don't know, but what we can know is what to do with ideas when we get them.

Our creativity can have different motivations. In such a rapidly changing world we are told we must be creative in order to survive, in order to be successful, in order to be employable. Creativity can be a means to an end but one of the greatest joys in life is being creative for its own sake. It is natural for us to create, and it is our joy to be self-expressive. Birds sing because it is natural for them, flowers bloom, stars shine because it is in their essential nature. It is our essential nature to be creative and to express ourselves. Let's take a look at some of the barriers we create to block our creativity.

- *We don't believe in a constancy of supply. We may have a few good ideas, but to have to rely on them daily would create too much uncertainty for us. Creative endeavours are fickle, we believe. John Cleese, the comic actor and writer, said in an interview with the UK chat show host Michael Parkinson, 'The toughest thing about being an artist and a creative person is waking up each day and not knowing if you can still do it!'*
- *Creativity doesn't pay the bills. We have been educated and encouraged to believe that only sensible jobs pay the bills, not creative work that we truly enjoy; or that our creativity will only be rewarded when we are dead or too old to enjoy it any more.*
- *Our creativity or authentic self-expression are somehow not good enough. We've been teased or ridiculed in the past, so we want to save ourselves the pain of repeating that process. We'd rather play safe and conform even if this leads to boredom.*

BUT WILL THE WORLD WANT OUR CREATIVITY?

Maria had the idea of creating a training and development programme offering inspiring talks and workshops to the public and businesses. We talked and it became clear it was her purpose, the one thing she felt called to do at this point in her life. 'But no-one else is doing it,' she said. 'That's because you are being called to lead the way, and create what doesn't now exist,' I told her. 'But what if no-one wants what I'll offer?' she asked. 'You want nothing more than to give what you think people need. Have faith in yourself and your creativity and don't be frightened to try,' I suggested.

Creative expression can be very fulfilling but to get to this place of joy we need to be courageous and determined. There may not be interest in our offering, but we can create interest. There may not be a market for our work, but we can create a market. Remember: we need to give our ideas nourishment. We need to dedicate them to the benefit of others. By adding our love to them and giving them the purpose of love and healing, our ideas will fly miraculously. Using your journal, try to respond to the following questions. Take the time to really focus on them and to jot down any creative ideas you may have previously dismissed.

WISDOM QUESTIONS

✳ What do you do with your ideas?

✳ Do you collect and cherish them?

✳ Do you ponder on them, get curious about where they came from and how they could possibly come to fruition?

✳ Do you dismiss them if you can't see any way of making them happen?

What is your style? Your spirit and subconscious mind are pregnant with an abundance of ideas. You can be having great ideas for the rest of your life; there is no shortage on the supply side, only on our receptivity to the ideas. We criticize them to death, or lack the self-confidence to follow them through.

WHAT'S YOUR CURRENT CREATIVE CALLING?

So what idea is calling you right now? Have you had an idea that has never gone away, and keeps reminding you of its presence? What's nagging you? Has something always fascinated you? Did you have a passion in the past that you never pursued, or that you long to take up again? Has something always appealed to you?

Here are some suggestions to nurture your creativity and ideas:

GIVE IT ROOTS

- *Begin to take your ideas seriously. Think of why you should do something with them, and the joy that they could create.*
- *Keep focusing on an idea in a positive way.*
- *Remind yourself that you are a creative being. You wouldn't have been given the idea without the resources to follow it through.*
- *Spend time with other creative people who will nurture and support your ideas.*
- *Initially resist the temptation to share your ideas with those who are less likely to understand or support them, or may actively criticize.*
- *Build your personal foundations – your own self-love and your own self-belief.*

GIVE IT WINGS

- *Research the idea – collect more ideas and information, and start working on how to make it happen.*
- *Listen to inner guidance, hunches and intuitions about where to go next.*
- *Watch for synchronicities and signs that you are on track once you start to take action.*
- *Start to follow through and take small actions to make the idea real.*
- *Recognize your resistance – your fears or doubts – and see it as a sign that you are on track. Our greatest gifts are sometimes buried under our greatest fears and doubts.*
- *Have the courage to continue through any resistance.*
- *Begin connecting with supportive and encouraging people.*
- *Invest time, energy and, if necessary, money in the project.*

Generally we won't follow our creative callings until the pain of doing so is finally exceeded by the pain of not doing so, and it's appalling how high a threshold we have for this pain.

But at some point, the idea becomes more important than our fear and defences.

THE CHALLENGE OF CREATIVE DIALOGUE WITHIN ORGANIZATIONS

Historically, fear has been used to great effect to motivate us in our work. You know the kind of thing – if you don't perform, you're punished, rewards are withheld, or you're out – and because work, money and survival are so interconnected, our compliance is bought. We scare people into working hard, performing, jumping through hoops and seemingly giving their all and more. And to some extent it works. Fear can get jobs done, fear can produce results and increased profits.

Many organizations have inbuilt guilt mechanisms, and we carry psychic guilt around with us. When the two meet, we have compliance. We are so used to them that many go unspoken, but we know the messages: you will be in on time, you will work as long as is necessary, you will sacrifice balance in your life, you will not argue, you will do as requested, you will take on the workload we give you. The guilt and the accompanying compliance are already programmed into us, often before we ever reach the work-place. Like animals who have been on the receiving end of shocks from an electric fence once too often, we have learned not to go too close to the fence, even if the current has been turned off. Not a conducive and supporting environment for creativity.

But on the whole, fear is only a short-term solution; we are all worth more than mere compliance. Fear can't allow our creativity to flourish; it can't create trust or inspire people to consistently give their best. Only valuing can do that; only appreciation and recognition can do that, and only love and care can do that. We need a change of intention and purpose for our work, from material survival to nourishment of the soul, from stagnation to growth and creative fulfilment.

Every organization should seek to encourage adaptability, vitality, imagination, and the enthusiastic willingness to go the extra mile – ancient qualities which human beings have wanted for themselves since the beginning of recorded history. We are not automatons who can perform at the press of a button. Nurturing qualities cannot be legislated for or coerced, and no handbook or regulatory body can make them happen.

There is no lever to pull inside a person that will activate their creativity, and no specific slogan that will bring about a passionate response. Programmes are programmes, and creative people are creative people, and the two do not meet happily. If there were a specific lever, we would have pulled it for ourselves a long time ago. But it is just as difficult for individuals to find their own creative powers as it is for any organization. When it comes to the moment of truth, both the organization and the individual are called upon to commit to creativity.

In the workplace today we need to encourage conversations that really invite the creative qualities hidden deep inside each human being to come forth. Our reluctance is born of the knowledge that by inviting creativity and passion, the organization must allow for fear and failure. It must acknowledge shadows previously not spoken of. It is a high-stake game for the company, and it also involves high stakes for the individuals playing out their life's destiny within the company.

GIVING UP OUR EXCUSES FOR NOT BEING CREATIVE

We are ourselves, creations. And we, in turn, are meant to continue creativity by being creative.

JULIA CAMERON, author of *The Artist's Way*

One of the most profound and inspirational lessons I ever learned about our ability to be creative came about during a visit to a former concentration camp. My partner Helen and I were on holiday in Poland, staying in the beautiful city of Krakow. I hadn't realized that we'd be only 90 minutes from Auschwitz and Birkenau, the concentration camps of the second world war. We saw bus trips to Auschwitz advertised in our hotel, and although we felt it was a strange thing to want to do, we felt called to go there, as Helen is Jewish.

It was mid-November, and there was already six inches of snow covering the ground when we arrived at Auschwitz. The snow continued to fall heavily, adding an eerie feeling to our visit. The sign above the entrance to Auschwitz cynically reads ARBEIT MACHT FREI – work makes free. Auschwitz was a shockingly huge place, and we were even more shocked when we were told that we were later to visit Auschwitz 2, at Birkenau, which was only two miles away and was 10 times the size.

We were shown the gas chambers, the mountains of possessions and the furnaces, told stories and given information by a guide in a caring and factual manner. It was a harrowing and humbling experience. It is one thing to hear about these places, another to be there, see the photographs, and be told just some of the stories by the guides. It's another thing to literally stand in a gas chamber, on the spot where such atrocities were perpetrated only a few decades earlier.

Then we were shown the huts where the prisoners were kept,

and the conditions and sense of isolation truly appalled me. We were led to a tiny room where a priest had been kept in solitary confinement for months on end, often with no clothes and hardly any food. Our guide drew our attention to the walls and the back of the door and showed us little etchings of the crucifixion, the cross and other images. They were beautiful and moving. She then told us that the priest had carved these with his fingernails. I was stunned, and moved that in the midst of all that horror someone could still be creative, extend and express beauty, and share of himself. In the midst of death, he had a spirit for life. Of course, I am sure it was a way for him to try to keep his faith and stay sane in the midst of such madness, but I can't imagine how many thousands, perhaps millions, of people have been touched, moved and inspired by this one man's gifts. His was a small light of creativity in the middle of total darkness.

I left the camp wondering how many excuses I make in my life for not being as creative as I could be. If only I had more time, more courage, more money, more encouragement, more support; the list goes on for me – what about you? Excuses are usually rationalized fears; we look for reasons to justify why we can't, but our can'ts are usually won'ts – our hidden noes. In truth, we may be scared to express ourselves, to show ourselves, be authentic or take a risk and look stupid. You may have heard the expression that it is better to light a candle than to curse the darkness for eternity. Some of us are good at cursing the darkness, and others are good at trying to snuff out our candle.

Here are some ideas that might help you to bring the gift of creativity into your work and your life:

- Give of yourself – *Emerson wrote, 'The greatest gift we can give is a portion of ourselves.' When we express our creative selves we connect with other people, in ways that we will not always know. Whatever we experience, millions of other people will have gone through too.*

- Be authentic – *in a world obsessed with appearances and image, expressing your true self is a unique gift. When the world is dark, it needs us to shine a light.*
- Trust your creative spirit – *if the human spirit can prevail in the midst of the horrors of the concentration camps, it can also prevail in our work and life if we are willing to step courageously past all our excuses and resistance.*
- Bring something into being – *the Latin root of the word create is creare, meaning to bring into being. Bring some beautiful idea or vision, whether small or enormous, into the world as a gift from your heart to the hearts of others.*
- Be unattached – *you will never know the impact that you and your creativity will have, even in years to come, beyond your own life and beyond your own awareness. Think of your creativity as an anonymous gift to the world and to the future.*
- Know your inner power – *there is a power within us that is greater than any circumstance and any power outside us. Our creative spirit has the power to overcome anything.*
- Follow through on intuitions – *notice when you have ideas that you generally dismiss out of fear or doubt. Go ahead with them. Capture ideas and follow through before you censor and rationalize them to death.*
- Don't get bogged down in minutiae – *try to keep the 'big picture' in mind – particularly during the early stages of your vision. Details are important, but they can dishearten and distract you from your ultimate goal.*

FROM PARALLEL TRACKS TO ON TRACK

Many of us have chosen, often unconsciously, paths that run parallel to our true creative spirit, but not the path itself. We may work as an art critic, but deep down we'd like to paint or sculpt ourselves; we dream of film-making, and work as a production assistant; we long to write, and work in a bookseller's. This way of living means that we are in the vicinity of our creative calling, but keep it at a distance. We allow ourselves the luxury of wondering, what if? Promise ourselves *one day*! For me, my parallel track was to spend nine years promoting other people's creativity and spirituality, when deep down I wanted to shine my own light. But I was scared. In her wonderful book *The Artist's Way*, Julia Cameron calls this the path of the shadow artist: we keep our creativity in the shadows, and never quite put ourselves in the spotlight.

This is safe, but unfulfilling; we'll never experience the joy of letting our own light shine fully, discovering just what we are capable of, what our calling truly is. By devoting ourselves to our creativity we set up an energy field that draws others to us. This energy field creates interest and opportunities that manifest as incredible synchronicities.

WISDOM QUESTIONS

* Can you identify the parallel track in your life right now?
* What would you love to put more at the centre of your life, but are resisting?
* How could you put yourself 'on track'?

CREATE YOUR IDEAL WORK

Did you know that at the age of four, 96 per cent of children think they can be anything they want to be, but that by the age of 18 only 4 per cent of them still believe it? Generally, as we grow up and get sensible, we tend to close down our sense of possibility. We begin to draw a veil over our imagination, trading our dreams for a salary, and excitement and adventure for security. We need to thaw our frozen imaginations and envisage a future that isn't dictated by the past.

In my workshops I get people to do the following imaginary exercise:

Imagine that you have a meeting with the CEO of a large and successful company who says to you, 'Hi. I have heard about you – I have heard that you are very talented, gifted and resourceful, but you haven't yet found your niche or fulfilled your potential. I'd love you to come and work for me, but I only want you to do work that you really want to do, work that will utilize and inspire the best of you. I want you to come in every day and be excited and motivated. Don't worry about the money, that's not a problem. All I need to know is what you'd like to be doing. Please send me a job description of your ideal work, and we'll create it for you.'

What is your reaction to this? 'Great! Just what I have always dreamed of'? or 'Oh, what do I really want? I'm not sure.' Is a lot of your energy going into moaning and complaining, or are you clear about your vision and welcome every opportunity to create it? Whilst we may be frustrated about our current working situation, the real problem might lie in our scarcity of imagination and vision, and our difficulty in seeing a future that is different from the past. All too often we go round in loops of frustration, not realizing that the way out is through our imagination and creativity, which come from our unconditional self. We need to light a fire under our frozen imaginations: the future is not there waiting for us, but is in embryo in our hearts and wanting to be brought to fruition.

Imagination is more powerful than memory. How much do we base our work decisions on the past, on our memory or the memory of others? Most of the memories we review regularly are of things that didn't work out, that went wrong, and how disappointed or how silly we felt. We then decide along the lines of 'never again' and, as we've discussed, we retreat to that seemingly safe place. Safe, perhaps; bored, more likely.

Problems arise when we let other people imagine and determine our futures. The debt we owe to the play of the imagination is incalculable, because the imagination is where all invention is born.

IMAGINATION

Imagination is a place of abundant possibility and unlimited ideas. Imagination is God's gift, and our passport to a new future. When we don't live in a life of vision, we live a life dictated by the past; it's just a life dictated by old programmes, old patterns, with unfinished business dogging our every step. Remember, imagination is not fantasy. Fantasy is in the mind, and usually stays there. Deep down we may use fantasies to avoid engaging fully with life. Imagination, on the other hand, is the forge of our soul, where our most cherished dreams are fashioned. When Martin Luther King made his speech 'I have a dream' he spoke from his heart to the hearts of millions. He had a vision of a future that has yet to be realized. He acknowledged the present, and inspired others to work together to create a new future. We can do that for ourselves too.

Susan was 52, and had been a personal assistant (PA) for 30 years. She'd never been out of work except through choice, yet had very little self-belief. She felt that every day was a test that she might fail. She explained, 'My uncle was the eccentric one in our family. He was creative, drew, painted, played music, he was happy but not very well off, and was looked down upon by the rest of the family. His brother, my father, was also very creative, but dropped all creative ambitions to get a sensible job and career. My grandparents were very poor, and there was always a terror in our family of being poor. So I guess I have followed my family's script and done the sensible thing all my life – sensible job with money and pension – and have marginalized my creativity, and passion. I feel dead, yet I can't imagine myself doing anything different.'

Susan felt she must now try to find and follow what inspired her. 'I feel like I don't have a choice; if I don't change I will die, emotionally if not physically. On my tombstone it would read "Died at 52, buried at 80!" But I am terrified. I don't really believe I can change, and don't believe I can earn money doing things I love, and enjoy. I guess I don't really believe in myself so I am going to need a lot of support.'

What was it that was calling Susan to change? What force was at work? There is a force, an energy in us, that calls us to lead authentic lives, to drop the roles and façades and bring out the true us. In Greek there is a word *physis* which means *life force*. However off track we may feel, and for however long we have been off track, there is always an inner pull back to our true centre – our home. Creativity doesn't cause pain: only our resistance to it will do this. It doesn't matter what name we give this inner compass or knowing, only its existence and purpose are important.

I asked Susan to imagine that she *did* believe in herself, and that she could earn money doing things she enjoyed. I asked her to let me know what came to mind and quite suddenly ideas began to tumble freely from her: taking up a course in massage, singing, learning languages, writing, teaching and coaching. Within twenty minutes she had given birth to a new set of possibilities. It was beautiful to observe. Susan had the courage to thaw her frozen imagination, to have a future that was qualitatively different from her present and her past. We then started to look at how she could start building bridges from the imagined future to today, tomorrow and next week. It took time but she went away with a new sense of hope; having planted some seeds in the future, she could start nurturing these seeds to create a new beginning for herself. One of the roles we can play for each other is to be a midwife to each other's dreams.

Think about some of the following ideas and jot down your responses in your journal.

- *What qualities would you most like to experience in your work?*
- *Who would you like to work with and why?*

- *How would you be growing, learning and stretching yourself?*
- *What would be your motivations?*
- *What varieties of rewards would you be experiencing?*
- *What contribution would you be making?*
- *How would you like to be appreciated?*

GETTING OUT OF OUR WAY

The ego never created anything. It just comes along for the ride and offers a constant commentary.

K. BRADFORD BROWN, co-founder of the Life Training Programme

I was thrilled to be invited to run a seminar and take some time out in Cadaques in northern Spain. It is a beautiful town on the Mediterranean, is relatively unspoilt and has a long artistic history. Both Pablo Picasso and Salvador Dali lived and worked there for many years, and I found it a very inspiring town, rich in art and creativity. One of the attractions is Dali's old home, now a museum. It has been restored to its original state, with the artist's studio and work in progress left as it was when he died.

The whole house is filled with evidence of Dali's creative expression. Apart from the many drawings and paintings there are pieces of art made from bits of tinfoil and cans, rubbish and car parts transformed into garden furniture. As I walked around I had a strong sense that here was a man who had what I perceived as complete creative freedom. If he had an idea or felt inspired, he simply tried it out. He didn't stop to wonder whether people would like him or not, approve of him or not, or whether the work was any good. He didn't censor his urge to create, he simply followed through out of curiosity.

One of the greatest gifts that goes hand in hand with creativity is the sense of freedom and spontaneity we experience. Creative skill may be the smaller part; giving ourselves creative permission and freedom can be the greater part. All of us have a rich vein of creativity, so many gifts that never see the light of day because of our self-judgement.

WISDOM QUESTIONS

✳ When was the last time you followed through on a bold new idea?

✳ How good are you at being spontaneous? Do you welcome spontaneity or do you prefer to stay on tried and tested paths?

✳ How can you improve your willingness to try things out and take a few risks?

✳ Can you identify the greatest negative self-belief that prevents you from experiencing your creativity?

WE DON'T DO CREATIVITY, IT DOES US!

The artist . . . knowing that he can never create anything on his own account, out of the top layers of his personal consciousness, . . . submits obediently to the workings of inspiration; and knowing that the medium in which he works has its own self-nature, which must not be ignored or overridden, he makes himself its patient servant and, in this way, achieves freedom of expression.

ALDOUS HUXLEY, author of *The Perennial Philosophy*

As we've seen, creativity is beyond our conscious control, and indeed trying to control it can actually be counterproductive. But we can work in partnership with it. It is essential, however, to understand that our innate creativity can take centre stage in our lives if we have faith and trust in our creative spirit. All we have to do is recognize our own preferred way or ways of being creative. I heard the late Douglas Adams, author of many books including

The Hitch-Hiker's Guide to the Galaxy, describe how the creative process worked for him. When he sat down to write, he wouldn't know what he was going to write or how the story would evolve. He said that, for him, writing a book could be like looking at an almost empty canvas, with the full picture taking up perhaps a square inch of one corner and the rest blank. He described how, within his mind, the characters would show him the plot and story on a step-by-step basis. On the other hand, J.K. Rowling, author of the *Harry Potter* books, described how she always knew there would be seven books in the series in total, even before the first one was published. She has already written the last chapter of the last book, which is safely in a bank vault so that no-one else can read it! Paul McCartney describes how 'Yesterday', the most often recorded song of all time, came to him complete in a dream. Giacomo Puccini said that, 'The music of this opera [*Madam Butterfly*] was dictated to me by God; I was merely instrumental in putting it on paper and communicating it to the public.' The artist Jackson Pollock described the creative process this way: 'The painting has a life of its own. I try to let it come through.'

We need to understand there is no right way to be creative. We just need to find *our* way.

CLARIFYING WHAT IT MEANS FOR YOU TO BE YOUR CREATIVE SELF

- *How would you know that you were being as creative as you'd like?*
- *What would there be more of? And less of?*
- *What would you do differently?*
- *How might you be different?*
- *How would others recognize your creative self?*
- *What would they see that would be different about you?*
- *What achievements would they see?*

SET CREATIVE GOALS

Decide on the things that you would like to do, or like to do differently. In coaching hundreds of individual clients, it is evident to me that we want to be more creative but we do not recognize that this can take time and conscious effort, daily practice and daily choices. Our creative dreams and goals rarely, if ever, come out fully formed. They form first in the melting pot of our soul and imagination, and then move into physicality step by step, little by little.

GET CREATIVE SUPPORT

Creativity blossoms amongst friends and withers amongst enemies.

JULIE MACNAMARA, author and creative writing teacher

It is hard to be creative and grow creatively *on your own*. It's wonderful to share the journey with others who are committed to creativity too and we need to ensure that those who we engage with will be willing and able to support us. We should cultivate relationships with people who are prepared to be challenged, to grow, to struggle and keep going, celebrating and commiserating with us in equal measure on this journey.

Creative partnerships do, of course, exist in the corporate world but there is a dilemma here too. Most working environments are built on command and control, yet command and control generally stifle creativity. Control blocks the flow of creativity, and creativity needs to flow. To have more creativity means swapping control for trust, encouragement and accountability. Accountability means being responsible, but not being blamed. In most work environments people are terrified of making the wrong decisions, so they tend to avoid decision-making completely or make safe, less inspired decisions, rather than creative and bold ones.

Our happiness comes from developing and sharing our creative gifts in their fullness.

Your talents can hardly wait to be expressed. They are itching to get out and about. To go through life without releasing your strongest talents leads to feelings of frustration, resentment and even depression. You feel bottled up, envious and discouraged. You may even question whether you should exist at all.

LAURENCE G. BOLDT, author of *How to Find the Work You Love*

WE WANT TO GIVE OUR GIFTS

The real secret to successful management is discovering what people do naturally and then figuring out how to adapt the organization to take advantage of these natural gifts. Unfortunately, too many organizations deal with creativity in reverse: so many of their systems are of the 'one fit for everyone' variety, and we try to squeeze people into systems. What really makes us happy is finding, developing and sharing the gifts that we have been blessed with. Each of us has unique creative gifts to bring to this world and if we can tap into this we have no need to seek motivation from others. Naturally and effortlessly we evolve into self-motivators, passionate and excited by the un-conditional success that is within our reach.

A most powerful expression of the human desire to share our giftedness occurred recently at the Atsitsa holistic holiday centre on the Greek island of Skyros. As part of the community evening activities, it was announced that there was to be a pea fair. Hardly any of us knew what it was, although we'd heard this event had been organized on previous occasions. After supper, participants and staff would set up stalls around the centre where they would offer some gift or service to others – a bit like a big car boot sale, but without money changing hands. Everybody would be given 15 chickpeas as currency with which to purchase talents and services. It sounded strange but interesting. I was curious to see how things would turn out as the participants started planning what their contribution would be.

The evening arrived, and I was stunned and touched when I saw just how much people were prepared to give when their only reward was raw chickpeas – and, of course, the opportunity to give! There were people offering relaxation techniques, offering to sing if you paid them (and then offering not to sing if you paid them more!), crystal healing, Tarot readings, massage, cartooning or a five-minute art lesson. One man offered to create an on-the-spot haiku, a 17-syllable poem or phrase popular in Japan, on a subject of your choice. Another woman offered to play Cupid, writing and delivering love letters. There was such a buzz as people gave generously, offering things that were beautiful, outrageous, naughty or just plain fun.

My partner Helen and I had set up a stall too. We put up a sign saying COMPLIMENTARY THERAPY, FIRST ONE FREE, AND THEN TWO CHICKPEAS EACH. Many people were intrigued and some asked for their first one free, even though they didn't know what they were getting. Helen or I would then look at them and find something that we could honestly, sincerely and uniquely appreciate about them. We'd then tell them something like 'Your hair is really beautiful tonight' or 'That colour really suits you' or 'You have a beautiful smile' or 'I've enjoyed being with you on this holiday.' Generally the customer would break into a huge smile. Our therapy consisted of nothing more complicated than noticing and complimenting people on their appearance or personality. Once people had their first compliment, they were eager to give us their two chickpeas for another. It was a joy both to be able to give people genuine compliments and receive their gratitude in smiles (and chickpeas) in return.

The next day there was enormous gratitude for the evening. All 100 people on the site remarked on how amazing it was that people had so much to offer and how much they had enjoyed both giving and receiving. It seemed that for a couple of hours people's hearts and souls had opened wide and they had let the best of them pour forth. It struck me that this was a wonderful example of a community in action, with people giving, receiving, sharing, shining and appreciating. It was a precious evening. It reminded me how Patch Adams, clown, doctor, author and the subject of a film, created a hospital based on love, community and laughter. The treatment he offered was free, and he told me that every week he gets hundreds of letters from doctors, nurses and other medical professionals offering to come to work at his hospital for free. People want to give their gifts in a spirit of love, service and appreciation.

BUT WHAT IF WE DON'T BELIEVE WE HAVE GIFTS?

Anything that is **truly** *given is a gift.*

HELEN BEE, dancer and coach

It is impossible for anyone *not* to be gifted, because it's how we've been created. Sometimes, though, these gifts may be hard to spot.

Sheron worked in a work rehabilitation unit, helping people with brain damage and mental health problems get back into some kind of meaningful work. She'd had many people she found challenging to work with, like Michael who was deaf, blind and unable to speak. He spent nearly all his time in a home and needed round-the-clock care. Everyone racked their brains to find useful work for him. One day, Sheron took Michael to visit the manager of the unit's bakery with a view to finding a suitable job. During the visit Michael was given a bowl of flour and some ingredients and as he dipped his hands into the flour a huge smile came to his face. His sense of touch was very acute and it was obvious that he loved the texture. Quite soon, with some guidance, it also became clear that Michael could make pastry, and very soon he demonstrated a gift for making cakes and sponges. He loved the kneading and delighted in the smells of the bakery. Everyone was delighted that Michael had discovered a gift that was not only useful but one that he could truly enjoy.

Michael was only able to work on Tuesdays, and on that one day he was always up early, washed and ready to go. On other days of the week he would often stay in bed late. If Michael, with no sight, hearing or speech, had a gift that lit his heart and enabled him to contribute to others, how many more do we have?

Our conditional self often makes us feel that we are arrogant to think we are gifted, yet it's arrogant to think we are not. We are all precious and have the ability to touch the hearts and lives of others in a unique way. Think for a minute about all the people that bring gifts into your life. Think of the writers, artists, musicians, speakers, athletes, colleagues, family and friends who have somehow enhanced your life.

What if Shakespeare had sat down and thought, 'No, I'm just kidding myself, I can't write'? What if the Beatles did their first gigs in Hamburg and said, 'We're awful! We are never going to get anywhere'? What if Steven Spielberg had given up after making his first home movie? Just imagine for a moment how much poorer your life would be if people like this had succumbed to their self-doubt or self-criticism.

RECOGNIZING OUR GIFTS

Here are some ideas to help you discover your unique gifts. Remember, a gift isn't something that you alone can do. It is something that captures your imagination and makes you happy, present and engaged.

- *What activities, talents or skills have you been most appreciated for doing or contributing?*
- *What qualities have you been told you bring to people and situations?*
- *What do you most enjoy giving/receiving?*
- *Ask your unconditional self – intuitively – what you have come here to give in this life.*
- *If you could spend your days giving or sharing one particular thing with people, what would that be?*
- *What do you love about yourself?*
- *What do you think others love about you?*

GIFTS OF PRESENCE AND BEING

It is our fear of giftedness that complicates life. All problems have at their root the fear of taking the next step in life and the fear of acknowledging our gifts and talents. These so-called problems are resolved with ease and simplicity by simply acknowledging our life-enhancing gifts and unwrapping our Presence.

CHUCK SPEZZANO, author and workshop leader

In these days of hard work, busyness and achievement, when people are regularly regarded as simple resources to be used as efficiently as possible, it is easy to forget that it is we and our presence that are the most precious. Instead of being ourselves, we can come to believe that we aren't good enough, and that we have to take on roles in order to become acceptable.

Our gifts are not always gifts of doing: they can be gifts of being. One of the people who has most touched my heart was Marie de Hennezel, a French Jungian analyst who had been influential in setting up the hospice and palliative care movement in France. She explained that many of the people in their care would die within a very short period of time, and often doctors, nurses, family and friends would fuss around trying to help when there wasn't always a lot that could be done. More often than not, the patients said they wanted someone simply to sit and be with them, perhaps holding their hand or listening to them. They didn't need anything more than the presence of a loved one, or a loving presence, and to feel connected to them, which was difficult when people were busy rushing around all the time. Marie explained that even in the death of the body, there could still be great opportunity for emotional healing – the kind of healing that connects us to another, re-establishes relationships and sustains us with love during difficult days and dark nights.

Some of our gifts are in our very being, so remember that it is not just what you do that is precious and important, but also who you are, your presence. We can learn to bring our being into our doing. We bring our presence into our work by slowing down, connecting to our inner unconditional self, and by choosing to trust ourselves and know that we are good enough. It is an activity of heart, mind and will, not just of hands. It is letting our divinity shine through us. It is choosing to be the presence of love. Just being there for other people, in times of pain and grieving, can make a great difference.

DISCOVERING AND VALUING OUR GIFTS

All true gifts can be expressions of love, and because we are all love in essence, we are all gifted. I like the idea that in our soul we are rich with gifts, and that one particular quality more than others resonates in us.

The quality that most resonates with my soul is inspiration – I love it, need it and feel refreshed by it. In my early life I didn't pay much attention to it, but in my later twenties I noticed its absence. I wanted more of it, loved reading inspiring books that uplifted me, going to talks and meeting people that I found inspiring. I dreamed that I could build my life around inspiration, immersing myself in it as much as I could. Gradually, I did just that.

Ask yourself what *quality* you most enjoy and resonate with, for example, love, fun, humour, peacefulness, friendship. What quality would you most like to be experiencing every day of your life?

Whatever quality came to mind, I would suggest that you have come to embody and to *be* it. So whatever work you do, and however you live your life, part of your purpose is the giving and receiving of this special quality.

OUR PRESENCE RADIATES OUT

Did you know that people who pray and meditate have a huge impact on people and situations around them, even in parts of the world where they are not physically present? That is the power of our presence and again we don't have to *do* anything in the conventional sense, for it is the essence of the unconditional self that lies within us. The Buddha and other spiritual masters are said to have had incredible presence, and in the Bible it is said that when Jesus entered a village, people could feel his presence whether they were with him or not. In just the same way, our presence is a gift; our very being radiates and helps others. As Ralph Waldo Emerson said, 'Who you are speaks so loudly I cannot hear what you are saying.' In a world obsessed with only what we can achieve, measure, control and evaluate, our spirit and being are true gifts. They cannot be measured but they can be valued, experienced and appreciated and can serve to draw us to like-minded, supportive people.

HOW CAN WE DEVELOP OUR PRESENCE?

For thousands of years meditation has been known to be a wonderful way of centring us and connecting us with our unconditional self. Whilst meditation can be magical and mysterious, it is also simply practical. People who meditate generally are shown to be happier, more peaceful, more creative and, interestingly, don't show up quite so frequently in doctors' waiting rooms. In some countries, those who have trained in and regularly practise certain forms of meditation are given discounts on their medical insurance because they are likely to stay healthier.

Generally meditation works gradually to dissolve the belief and behavioural patterns buried deep in the conditional self so that we have more access to our unconditional self. As we become more grounded, integrating our inner and outer worlds, we become less thrown by change and any turbulence of life we experience.

BRINGING MORE BEING INTO OUR DOING – EXCAVATING OUR AUTHENTIC SELF

Jane, a gifted personal development teacher, realized that she was getting burnt out. Although she was respected, admired and appreciated by students and fellow teachers, she somehow felt she was missing from her work; she was merely playing a role, albeit a very good role, and not really contributing in a truly creative way. She'd been caught on that familiar treadmill that required her to get the work done, see the programme through to the end.

I asked Jane whom she most admired as a teacher. She described her friend Robert: 'He seems to have so much fun with his teaching, and seems so open and quite defenceless. I seem so concerned with giving people all the information in a well-structured way, and he does too. But he seems to give so much of himself in what he does. He gives from his heart and spirit; he laughs more, has more fun, and seems to get so much back in return.'

I asked how she thought she might be able to be more like Robert, and she responded, 'By having more fun, worrying less what people think of me, and taking creative risks. Also by noticing when I have ideas that I censor out of fear. I could try to go ahead with them, despite the fear. Also I would like to practise what I teach, not just talk about personal development but demonstrate it.' This reminded me of a response by Gandhi; when asked what his teaching was, he replied, 'My life.' There is no need to dedicate your life to your work, but it's important to recognize that we are the gift and we should share our true presence with others.

Jane decided to be a little less focused on the content of what she taught, to relax more and to let some of her defences down. She found it hard to start with, but as she began 'putting more of "me" into my work, my fear diminished. I feel more confident. I realize I know all I need to, and whatever I may need to learn, I can learn. I've also discovered that the more inspired I am, so too are the students. I am feeling more creative and getting more ideas all the time.'

Jane's example illustrates that beneath the role she was playing, there was another dimension of her authentic self waiting to be utilized. As we commit to remembering our unconditional self, we discover that we are like a never-ending box of chocolates. Each time we find a new aspect of our self and step into our creativity, we find that there is another delicious layer of gifts waiting underneath. We discover how multi-faceted we are, and as we do so we grow in stature, confidence and self-belief.

BUT WHAT IF WE DON'T THINK THE WORLD WANTS OUR GIFTS?

I have had a series of livelihoods – all connected to my greater purpose which is to play some small part in the transformation of business into a place where work is once again honoured and all people can find meaning, purpose, dignity and nobility in their work.

James A. Autry, author of *Love and Profit*

James is a lawyer in a successful city law firm. He had built up the commercial property department from scratch, and had reached a point where he was questioning a lot of it. He loved earning the money to support his family, but was beginning to feel as if all his certificates and diplomas didn't amount to much. James had completed the introduction and foundation year of a psychotherapy training course but as he began to develop a greater emotional awareness, and an interest in spiritual matters, he felt he needed to keep that side of him hidden from his corporate life. He didn't feel that these two worlds could successfully coexist.

Although several colleagues were supportive of his psychotherapy training, he was often teased badly by others. The aspects of himself he was beginning to value and treasure sometimes felt like curses in the business setting. His gifts of sensitivity, compassion and understanding weren't valued by his senior partner, who thought that nothing was more important than the financial success of the practice. James was supposed to be tough, competitive and business-focused. Gradually, as he began to gain inner strength, he found new ways to help both colleagues and clients through challenging and difficult times in their lives.

James experienced ridicule and rejection, and it would be naïve to think that everyone will appreciate us and the gifts we have to offer. Some people will reject and disagree with what we value and treasure so we need to decide that we want to give our gifts anyway – the joy for us is in our giving. We also need to develop a willingness to be a little more detached, but not distant; a little less in need of the approval or acceptance of others. We can choose to go through our life scattering seeds every day, and we'll never know how many will take root or what the harvest will be. That is true detachment – complete involvement but less attachment.

OUR CALL TO SHINE

What a Beethoven, Shakespeare or Picasso has done is not create *something, so much as they have accessed that place within themselves from which they could* express *that which has been created by God. Their genius, then, is actually expression and not creation. That is why great art strikes us with the shock of recognition, the wish* we *had said that. The soul thrills at the reminder of what we all already know.*

MARIANNE WILLIAMSON, author of *A Return to Love*

The film *Billy Elliot* is the story of a father and two brothers, during the miners' strike in Britain in 1984. They are dealing with the death of the mother and wife. It's a tough time and place where men refuse to show any 'soft' emotions. Young Billy hates the boxing lessons his dad insists he take, and instead is intrigued by and attracted to the ballet classes for the girls going on in the same hall. Slowly he begins to get involved in the lessons, and finds he loves ballet and is actually very good at it.

When his father learns that Billy has been missing the boxing and is taking ballet lessons, he is furious and strictly forbids him to carry on. Billy isn't conforming to the role his society has set out for him and it causes him and his family great distress.

In many ways, this child's dilemma mirrors the problems many of us face. Do we shine and show our true self, or do we defend and hide, for fear of ridicule and criticism? Do we dim our light, or do we shine it bright? Do we give in to the opinion of others or follow the guidance of our inner voice? To be truly successful, we must begin to become independent of the good opinion of others, which doesn't necessarily mean being defiant, conceited or rebellious. It simply means we should not give in to fear and doubt; we should try to keep trusting, giving and shining. As *A Course in*

Miracles reminds us, 'Every decision is a choice between love and fear.' This doesn't mean that there are right and wrong decisions, it simply means that we have a choice to align ourselves with the free and expansive unconditional self, or with the conditional self that sets limits on just how much we can achieve and be.

One of the things I enjoy most about my job is that it gives me the opportunity to support and encourage people to face what can sometimes feel like huge challenges. Very often the challenge is to reach through and trust in what we know to be the true path of our happiness. We may not always get it right, and may sometimes feel as if we've failed. It's so important to remember that the creative process involved in following our dreams is itself empowering and illuminating. Brick by brick we build our confidence and self-esteem, and the defences we have built in the belief that they will keep us safe begin to tumble. In truth, we can only shine when we have the courage to dismantle these carefully built defences, and let our hearts out. Defences don't help us achieve our goals: their only purpose is to try to save us from fear and pain. Paradoxically they often end up causing us more hurt and pain, as they block out creativity, stifle inspiration and shut off the supply of love in our lives.

To shine means to put our heart into what we do – to put love into our work, and life, and connect to our unconditional self. It's about bringing our spirit and uniqueness into our work. Most importantly, it's choosing *not* to defend ourselves. I don't think there are many of us who make it through to adulthood without pain, heartbreaks and disappointments – all of which give us adequate reasons to harden our hearts. The question is: do we have enough reasons for choosing to love, to shine and be true to our heart? It takes courage to keep going in the face of inner and outer resistance, to choose to give our love and gifts, for our sake and the world's.

ARE YOU A STAR WHO'S SCARED TO SHINE?

How could Leonardo da Vinci not have painted? How could Shakespeare not have written . . . we are to do what there is a deep psychological and emotional imperative for us to do. That's our point of power, the source of our brilliance. Our power is not rationally or wilfully called forth. It's divine dispensation, an act of grace.

MARIANNE WILLIAMSON, author of *A Return to Love*

We are perhaps the one and only part of creation that can refuse to be itself. Our bodies may be physically at our work, but our hearts, minds and imaginations can be placed firmly in neutral or engaged elsewhere. Some of us may have hidden so well and for so long that even we feel we can no longer find ourselves. But we all came here to live a purposeful life and within each of us is the light of abundance and love. Yet all too often we look around at the world and think to ourselves, 'Boy, it looks dark! I dare not shine – I'll be attacked or hurt in some way!' So we begin to learn to move off our centre, to hide, scared to show up fully in our lives, yet all the time we're aware that this isn't the *true* us. We take on guilt, we take on fear, and we take on roles or adopt personalities that we think will make people like us. We harbour a divine discontent, never really feeling fulfilled because we are not really being us. The answer to this dilemma is courage.

Have the courage to shine – give your best self to the world as a gift. People are hungry for inspiration, and a few good words or an act of kindness can bring nourishment to many. Notice when you are scared and want to pull back, and then go ahead and do it anyway! As Dr Susan Jeffers explained in her best-selling book *Feel the Fear and Do It Anyway*, behind nearly every fear is a gift waiting to be shared. So look beyond the fear and see the gift. You are a leader, so shine for people and with people. Show them how wonderful you are, but let your light remind them how wonderful they are. When we have the courage to shine we liberate ourselves from our fear, and in doing so we liberate others too.

HELPING OTHERS TO SHINE

My friend Karen became marketing director of a major company covering Africa. She inherited a team of people that she didn't choose, and had been advised to sack most of them. Being a rebellious spirit, and having a strong belief in people's innate ability to perform when encouraged and allowed to shine, she refused. She got them all together and told them, 'You are already winners. You have already achieved unconditional success, and you have nothing to prove. I simply want you to join with me and we'll achieve amazing things together. Will you do that?' It was like most organizations, quite political, with people covering themselves, and this positive and open stance went against the grain. But cautiously they all agreed to join Karen on this exciting journey of discovery.

In the three years that Karen was with the company, she and her team did achieve amazing results. They created a unified business for the 17 countries in which they operated in Africa for the first time ever. They increased sales by over 20 per cent, which had never been done before; they exceeded everybody's expectations, and their achievements became the stuff of legend within their industry. Karen had led her team with understanding and commitment, with a fundamental belief that her team's gifts and talents were merely waiting to be brought forth. Everyone had a contribution to make and all were equally valued.

POWER WITH INTEGRITY

When we shine we need also to learn how to use our new-found power with integrity. If we take advantage of people or use them in some way to meet our needs, we will fail to connect fully with our peers and will not reap the rich rewards that unconditional success can bring. When we shine with integrity our shining is a blessing on all. As we've seen, this world is an abundant and beautiful place and we have a responsibility to share all it has to offer.

Karen's story reminded me of a well-known speaker who started off his seminar by holding up a £50 note. In the room of 200, he asked, 'Who would like this £50 note?' Hands started going up. He said, 'I am going to give this £50 to one of you, but first let me do this.' He proceeded to crumple the note up. He then asked, 'Who still wants it?' Still the hands were up in the air. 'Well,' he replied, 'what if I do this?' And he dropped it on the ground and started to grind it into the floor with his shoe. He picked it up, now crumpled and dirty. 'Now who still wants it?' Still the hands went into the air. 'My friends, you have all learned a very valuable lesson. No matter what I did to the money, you still wanted it because it did not decrease in value. It is still worth £50.'

Many times in our lives, we are dropped, crumpled, and ground into the dirt by the decisions we make, and the decisions others make for us, and the circumstances that come our way. We feel as though we are worthless. But no matter what has happened to us in the past or what will happen to us in the future, intrinsically we will never lose our true value: dirty or clean, crumpled or finely creased, we are still priceless to those who love us. The worth of our lives comes not from what we do or whom we know, but from who we are.

Our spirits are always safe and protected; we are held in love eternally in the mind of the creator.

•

In essence, we can't lose anything that is truly valuable. Through learning to love and let go, and through forgiveness, we can remember that we are always standing on solid ground.

•

We can learn, little by little, to let go of our emotional attachments, and in doing so we become freer, less dependent on external circumstances, and know that love can transform everything, even our apparent failures, into successes that will foster our spiritual growth.

4

UNCONDITIONAL SAFETY

We turn to God for help when our foundations are shaking, only to learn that it is God who is shaking them.

CHARLES WEST

We can have things without being overly attached to them. I have always found Buddhist ideas very helpful, and many years ago I heard of the concept that all suffering is caused by the things of the world. So to be happy, I thought, we must renounce things of the world, because they only cause suffering. This is similar to the Christian idea of sacrificing worldly things in order to pursue spiritual growth. It wasn't until a couple of years later that I realized that I had misunderstood this concept, which was that suffering is caused by *attachment* to things of the world, not the things themselves. This is very liberating – have whatever you want, just don't get too attached to it.

Buddhism teaches that when we put too much faith and invest too much in the transient things of this world, we will experience suffering, because we have neglected to cultivate and nurture our inner nature, which is beyond time and space. The more we know our inner nature – our unconditional self – the more we can see through this world. Everything – success and failure, money and material things, ups and downs, suffering – is fleeting. Enjoy these things, play with them, but know they are not really *it*. That is what it means to be in this world but not of it. We know we are living in a material world, but who we are is far beyond anything material.

In order to embrace a new level of true, authentic success, we may well have to learn to let go of the attachments to some aspects of our life that we have clung on to through fear. We have to grow up and fully embrace the gifts within. By letting go we mature and grow into what we can be, what we were always meant to be.

I like the idea of cowboy logic which says, when your horse is dead, get off it! But many of us have been trained to keep going with what is no longer useful to us. Hilary, for example, was stuck and bored. She had co-founded a very successful public relations company, which promoted some of the top films in the UK, and was a publicist for several major actors. Her company had recently been taken over and she had lost all her energy for work. She was going through the motions, being paid a salary but knowing that she wasn't really contributing as she could or should. She discovered that because she had invested so much energy and time in money-making, and valued status above true enjoyment, she now felt empty and joyless.

As we began to talk, Hilary explained that her goal was to create something new, as well as to have more time to spend with her husband and two young boys, and to pursue new interests. 'So what would inspire you now?' I asked. 'That's the problem: I don't know,' she answered. She was unenthusiastic about everything. It seemed she had run out of steam and had been waiting for her energy to return. I suggested that she think about this as now was her chance to let go of the past and start something new that would excite her. This period of uncertainty could be turned into a time of action.

Although Hilary had spent many years successfully promoting other people's creativity, I also had a hunch she might be being called upon to put her own creativity more centre stage in her life. She had started work on a film script but had not followed through, as with a few other projects she'd dabbled in. Although bored and disillusioned she was terrified of new beginnings and had settled for that familiar comfort zone that had increasingly become very uncomfortable. She felt trapped: being seen as successful and competent, she was scared to take new, baby steps in other areas, in case she failed.

It soon became obvious to me that much of Hilary's identity was tied up in her position: her status within the industry, her reputation, how she was seen by others. These had once helped her build her self-confidence. Now, however, they were more like lead weights that served to hold her back. So much of her energy was going into holding on that she had none left for new inspiration and new projects. She was scared that if she couldn't be recognized for her past achievements and reputation, who was she? Where was her sense of identity? 'My deepest fear is that I would be alone and forgotten if I moved on,' she told me.

This is a big challenge for many of us. We tend to build our sense of identity on our external achievements, on our outer success, on money, on reputation, on respect and other tangible things. That's terrific, but what happens when they are threatened, when we lose them, or choose to let some of them go? These are important questions, and the answers, of course, depend on our sense of self – who we think we are. Hilary was scared that she might be nothing and nobody if she dared to make changes. The real question is: what sustains us, from the inside, when all else falls away? How strong is our sense of ourselves beyond anything tangible? The opportunity here for Hilary was to regain a sense of herself way beyond her job title and career history.

Hilary decided it was time to talk to the new owners of her company to see if she could negotiate a part-time position, which would free up some of her energy to start new projects of her own. On a previous sabbatical she had started a cooking venture, and would put some energy into that. She also came up with other ideas about how she could use and recycle her considerable experience and skills in ways that would serve her. Her future began to look exciting; the challenge she faced in this process of change was to shift her perspective from that of a victim to that of a strong, creative woman with choices and opportunities.

Once she realized she had nothing to fear and could actually embrace change she began to see how she could shape her future. It was time for her to take small, regular and consistent steps outside her comfort and familiarity zone, try some different things in order to put adventure back into her life, and possibly reach a whole new level, and definition, of success. What she hadn't yet realized was that these steps forward represented, paradoxically, a form of death and letting go. She was leaving behind a safe but disappointing world, and was looking forward to a rebirth, and a level of success that would be more stimulating and challenging.

Hilary's experience is common to many of us – we have what we think is success, only to discover that it hasn't brought everything it promised. It doesn't continue to bring us the happiness, fulfilment or the sense of joy that we longed for. We begin to wonder if we have success, or success has us. We must remember and rediscover that who we are is far beyond any material success or failure, far beyond any circumstance. Our safe ground is more than our success in the world; it is in the very ground of our being. We are already an unconditional success. The Buddhists call this our *ground of awareness*.

Change, growth and evolution are natural. New challenges bring neglected skills and interests to the fore as we start to explore unknown territories. It is only our resistance that causes us pain as we try to make ourselves fit into shoes that we outgrew years ago. We blame the shoes, or curse ourselves for growing! But our soul is always calling us to higher possibilities, to greater expression of our innate gifts. Sometimes we have to be dragged kicking and screaming to a new level of authentic success, because we are so attached to the familiar old ways of working and living.

On one South Sea island, natives have learned to trap monkeys by putting sweet fruit into a gourd. When the monkeys grab the familiar fruit, their hand makes a fist, and they can't get it out of the gourd. When the islanders come, the monkeys could escape by letting go of the fruit but they don't – they get caught and become supper. Grasping becomes their death. As you may know, only a few chromosomes separate us genetically from our monkey cousins so it's hardly surprising that we too often fail to realize the dangers of holding on when we should be letting go!

I don't know about you, but I think I could have been an Olympic gold medallist in *holding on*. How good are you at letting go? I think we ultimately change through either desperation or inspiration. Too many of us, it seems, have cultivated the ability to live with the unacceptable, sometimes for very long periods of time.

YOUR SUCCESS IDENTITY

How much is success a part of your identity? Using your journal, try these questions and see what answers come to you:

- *Identify 10 aspects of your life you consider to be successful. (These could be relationships, skills, talents or jobs. Your choice.)*
- *Write down at least 10 ways in which you feel satisfied (e.g. I feel successful when I am inspired/loving and kind . . .)*

- *Describe six of the greatest successes of your life.*
- *What would you like to be most successful at?*

Did you find that easy or difficult? Do you feel comfortable describing yourself as a success? Does this fit in with your story about yourself? Do you set the bar so high that you rarely achieve what you consider to be success?

LETTING GO OF OUR STORIES

The universe is made of stories, not atoms.

MURIEL RUKEYSER, 1913–80, writer and poet

I was in the middle of a tour promoting my first book when I received one of those telephone calls you dread. It was my mum telling me that my 79-year-old father had just had his second stroke. I raced to my parents' home and luckily Dad was still there and not in hospital. He was lying on the sofa, hardly able to talk and partially paralysed. I wanted to be strong, but I couldn't. I just took his hand and started crying. 'I am so scared of you dying,' I managed to choke out through my tears. I didn't know what to say to him, so just said whatever came to my mind. 'I've never felt I've been a good enough son to you, I feel like I've let you down.' 'Don't be silly,' he slurred, 'I've always been so proud of you. From the moment you were born and I held you in my arms I have always been proud of you, and I have never stopped. If anything I feel like I wasn't a good enough father.' We carried on talking, and I think I've hardly ever cried so much.

As my tears dried, lightness and relief began to wash over me. It dawned on me that most of my life I'd told myself that my dad didn't really love me. I believed that I wasn't worthy, and didn't deserve my dad's love. Somehow, as a child, I had decided that I wasn't really lovable, and I had made that into the story of my life. But as my dad and I talked, I realized that all my life I had told myself a story that had never been true. Sure, we had differences and had fought, but he had never stopped loving me. It really hit me that I had created much of my own pain. In those few moments of awareness, I rewrote one of the big stories of my life. The relief I felt was enormous. It was as if I had created a whole new beginning, a whole new relationship with someone I dearly loved. In essence I had forgiven myself.

When we achieve unconditional success we seriously challenge our personal stories and are able to take the opportunity to let go of old beliefs and move into greater happiness.

THAT'S MY STORY AND I AM STICKING TO IT!

Our ego – our conditional self – loves telling stories. Indeed, in many respects our ego *is* our collection of stories and many have negative or unhappy themes.

These stories form a core element in the foundation of our identity, and we want to stick to them! We do everything to prove that our story is right and that our meaning is the true meaning, even if it is full of pain and negativity. With my dad, I had been determined to be right that he hadn't loved me enough, but on that seemingly terrible day, I was given a huge gift. I saw that I'd made a mistake, I had simply misunderstood his behaviour.

We are the universe's great storytellers – we love to tell stories. Stories come from the infinite richness of the human imagination, but they are not necessarily cast in stone. We can change them, and in so doing can alter the course of our lives. Fiction is one of the largest categories of book sales; we love going to the cinema to see stories; as children we love being told stories. But we are not our stories, our stories cannot contain our immensity and cannot define us; our unconditional self is never altered in the slightest by the stories we tell and live out. Our trouble is that we forget they are just stories. In our forgetting, we become very attached to our stories, we invest our sense of identity in them and find it very hard to let them go.

Just look at how many stories we all play in our lives – victim stories, sadness, success and triumph stories, stories of revenge and tragedy, comedies, horrors, dramas, crucifixions and farces. We tell stories of betrayal, of redemption, of abandonment, and we tell stories of love. We are creative beings and are free to tell whatever stories we wish.

One woman's story moved me greatly because it demonstrated a willingness and ability to change the course her life was taking. Rhonda Britten had a horrific childhood. Aged nine, she witnessed her mother being murdered by her father, who then turned the gun on himself and committed suicide. From then on she didn't really want to live. But just when she hit a real low she suddenly saw she had a choice. She said, 'I realized that I could be fearful, be a victim, could stay angry and probably kill myself, or I could choose to make the most of my life.' She had what in Japanese they call a *sartori*, a moment of insight and clarity – a destiny-forming moment in which she turned her life around. Rhonda went on to teach people about the power of choice and she created seminars entitled 'Fearless Living'. She wrote a book about how our lives are created through choice, and how new choices are always available to us. She turned horrific experiences into an inspiring example because she chose to believe in herself and others despite what she'd been through. Rhonda's story demonstrates that problems, no matter how difficult, can be a source of pain or of empowerment, depending on the value and meaning we give them, and depending on our willingness to dare to change what seems like an unreconcilable disaster.

FOCUSING QUESTIONS

✳ What are the major stories you tell about you and your life (e.g. not being wanted, feeling unworthy or misunderstood, being wronged; is yours a victim or a disaster story)?

✳ Is your story a drama, an adventure, a tragedy?

✳ What are you trying to get through your story (sympathy, pity, love, revenge, etc.)?

✳ Are you enjoying your story of your life?

✳ If you were watching it as a film, would you be interested? Would you be thrilled, gripped, fall asleep, be touched or bored? Would you stay watching all the way through, or would you leave?

WHY DO WE CREATE STORIES?

As children, we unconsciously try to make sense of our experiences, both good and bad. Perhaps we experience emotional or physical pain and then create a story that seems to wrong us – otherwise why would these things happen to us? We usually end up thinking we are wrong, or they are wrong, or all of us are wrong. Transactional Analysis is a wonderfully easy to understand psychological model, and suggests that we grow up having decided on one of four *life positions* – stories about ourselves and the world – from an early age. They are:

1. I am OK, you are OK – I am basically a good human being, and so are others, although we may not always act in good ways.

2. I am OK, you are not OK – I am the only one I can trust; other people will hurt or let me down.

3. I am not OK, you are OK – everyone else is all right, but I am not.

4. I'm not OK, you are not OK – the world is a pretty lousy place, because none of us are any good.

All stories that aren't happy, abundant, loving and joyful have at their root the message '*I am not good enough, I am not worthy.*' The only way to change our story is to choose to give it up and accept that we are OK, now, and that our story is based on mistaken thinking and on attachment to the material things we think we must have in order to be happy and loved. Yes, material possessions and our status in the workplace can encourage and support happiness but ultimately they cannot make us happy, because our happiness is already within us. Those idols don't need to disappear from our lives altogether, we just need to put them in their place and value them a little less.

WISDOM QUESTIONS

Think about the story of your life, and what you have told yourself you must have in order to be happy. Also think about how you've spent the majority of your time and energy:

* What do you think or believe you must have in order to be a success?
* What do you believe that you couldn't survive or function without?
* What do you most fear losing?

Your answers to these questions will illuminate some of the idols that you are cherishing. It's not the thing itself that is the problem, but our over-attachment to it; our overvaluing of it creates the pain for us.

HOW DO WE CHANGE?

We are free to keep our story for as long as we want: no-one can make us give it up, but we can choose to give it up little by little. Our story is always about the past, and while we run our stories, we miss much of the present. Our story doesn't fulfil, it doesn't inspire us, it doesn't reward us deeply. Only being ourselves, living authentically, will do that.

Here are some ideas about how we can change our stories:

AWARENESS AND CHOICE

If we are not aware of our story, or not aware that it is a story, we have no choice other than to keep running it. But we have to be kind with ourselves as our stories are often based on mistakes and incorrect perceptions. Awareness of ourselves and others is essential. Without awareness, we don't even realize we have a choice. But we *can* choose to change our story, even rewrite our life in the light of a new perception.

FORGIVENESS

Forgiveness is the ultimate tool for letting go. Forgiveness restores what has always been true about us but we've hidden. It gives us a new beginning and allows us to be more connected to the people we interact with.

Our journey home to unconditional success is an adventure into our forgiving mind.

What could you want that forgiveness cannot give? Do you want peace? Forgiveness offers it. Do you want happiness, a quiet mind, a certainty of purpose, and a sense of worth and beauty that transcends the world? Do you want care and safety, and the warmth of sure protection always? Do you want a quietness that cannot be disturbed, a gentleness that never can be hurt, a deep, abiding comfort, and a rest so perfect it can never be upset?

A Course in Miracles

You may reasonably ask: what has forgiveness got to do with success? In the conventional view of success, very little. But the vision of success that we've been talking about places forgiveness at its centre. Our divine mind – our unconditional self – knows nothing of judgements and grievances, it looks upon all things with equal love. Whenever our life isn't flowing as we would like it to, we look for blame and turn to old grievances and criticisms, and this slows us down, or even stops us in our tracks. What we are being called to do is to forgive, to melt the icebergs within us and allow inspiration and creativity to flow again in our lives.

Real forgiveness, when seen from a metaphysical perspective, means we realize that only love is real. All the love we ever gave is real and never lost, all the love we received is real and never lost. All else is a hallucination, an imagining, of our mortal mind. This does not deny the physical reality of events, but it acknowledges that beyond the physical there is another greater world. Forgiveness is what enables us to remember and experience that world.

Forgiveness registers that all the mistakes of our personalities are errors to be corrected, not sins to be punished, and it is the divine correction of all our mistakes. It is the restoration of love. However many mistakes we have made (and we've all made many), forgiveness acknowledges that the innocent presence of love is still at the heart of every one of us and the possibility of transformation and renewal is within our reach.

In a world so built on guilt and on condemnation, forgiveness can seem crazy, even mad, but it's important to remember that negative judgements act like a brick wall, keeping our wholeness out of reach. Through forgiveness we start to remove the bricks from the wall. Our true purpose is not to search for love, joy and abundance, but simply to dismantle the barriers we have erected to their presence.

But why is forgiveness such a well-kept secret? If the description from *A Course in Miracles* quoted above is true, why isn't it being taught on every battleground, in every church, school, hospital and workplace across the planet? Firstly, it probably is; go anywhere and you will find someone who is practising and embodying the principles of forgiveness, but they are not usually the ones in positions of greatest power and influence. Secondly, our ego thinks forgiveness is its greatest enemy for it is through forgiveness that we dissolve every fear, every guilt, every pain, every grievance and every sense of separation – the very foundations upon which our ego is built.

Forgiveness builds the bridges back to the place we never left. Another way of understanding forgiveness is to see it as a relinquishing of our judgements, as resisting nothing, and accepting all that is.

Below are just a few of the characteristics and core perceptions of **the unforgiving mind**. They are so ingrained within us that we may need time to discover how deep they go.

- *Holding on to old grievances and judgements keeps me alert and aware of dangers.*
- *There are people in this world waiting to take from me what I value most.*
- *Others must change their attitudes and behaviour before I am willing to accept them in my life.*
- *I experience fear, guilt or separation because of an unhappy or difficult past.*

The unforgiving mind has a limitless capacity to perceive and create war and conflict, sometimes with other people, sometimes with different aspects of ourselves, sometimes even with whole nations and races. Most of what we perceive through our body's senses can justify our choice to view things with an unforgiving mind, but as we've seen from Rhonda's inspiring story, there is an alternative way of looking at the world and the future.

Below are some of the key characteristics and core perceptions of **the forgiving mind**:

- *We can make a conscious choice to forgive ourselves and others.*

- *We acknowledge our calling to give and to receive love.*
- *We experience compassion and a desire to support others.*
- *Our perceptions are based on the present, not on the past.*

Just as our unforgiving mind has a limitless capacity to perceive conflict, our forgiving mind has a limitless capacity to welcome unity and healing; as we abandon the limitations of the past, the future offers us endless possibilities. Giving up our story leads to transformation and as the Zen saying reminds us, 'What a caterpillar calls the end of the world, the master calls a butterfly.'

CULTIVATING OUR SENSE OF IDENTITY BEYOND THE OUTER WORLD

The ultimate work, then, is an engagement with soul, responding to the demands of fate and tending the details of life as it presents itself. We may get to a point when our external labours and the opus of the soul are one and the same, inseparable. Then the satisfactions of our work will be deep and long lasting, undone neither by failures nor by flashes of success.

THOMAS MOORE, author of *Care of the Soul*

True happiness and liberation come when we gradually develop our sense of identity beyond the outer world. We are all someone's son or daughter, a friend, perhaps a parent, a boss or employee, an enemy, a threat, an ally. But these aren't who we really are. They are who we have come to believe we really are. Who we really are is the silent witness to all the roles we play. The real you is the unchanging presence in the ever-changing landscape of your life. The Buddhists call this our ground of awareness. The ground we stand on is unshakeable, a place where fear is unknown and where we are not defined by the circumstances of our life. Here we dwell within ourselves and our happiness and contentment no longer depend upon the flow of continual change. It is here that our essential nature resides.

As the world speeds up, there is a real need to find an inner sanctuary that is constant, still and secure.

Stillness is an eternal state that we must find a place for in our busy lives. But it is an essential force for it allows our ideas to be born and gives us the opportunity to refresh our spirits. Many say it is the language of God. St James's Church in Piccadilly, where I have worked for many years with Alternatives, is literally in the heart of the West End of London. Yet this is truly a place of peace and tranquillity that nourishes hundreds of people every day. They come to sit, rest, pray, observe and drink in the beauty of the carvings and decorations. It is a sanctuary where people go to restore their spiritual batteries and to reconnect to themselves and others.

IMPRESSION MANAGEMENT

All right is not all right . . . We are what is greatest within us.

MARSILIO FICINO, 1437–99, Italian philosopher

How much energy and time do we put into impression management – getting people to believe that we are OK, in control, on top of things, intelligent, bright and aware? Too much, I would guess. We think we need to get it just right – whatever *it* is and whatever *right* is. We are trying to measure up to an imaginary idea of how we think we should be, and how we think they think we should be. No wonder we end up exhausted! We are terrified that someone will find us out, see through our façade and realize that there is nobody really there! All too often, we feel that if we lose this façade, any success will crumble and we'll be exposed or abandoned. Yet the management of our façade is probably what causes our problems: we can't be authentic, creative or build true relationships if all we are building is an impression. Unconditional success is not about appearing to win all the time. It is about remembering our unconditional value and recognizing that *everything*, including our most difficult times, seeming failures and uncertainty, can move us closer to home.

Julie worked as strategy manager for a major household name telecommunications company and we met while she took a break to re-evaluate her work, life and career. She told me her fascinating story. She'd been hired to work with all the directors in a very high-profile position, drawing together their ideas into a unified business strategy. She'd arrived in a blaze of internal publicity, and had meetings with all of the major players individually over a period of weeks. Then she went away to formulate policy.

After two weeks of synthesizing all she'd discussed with the directors, a sickening awareness began to dawn on her – she hadn't a clue what the strategy should be! Julie felt horrified: she'd been hired to formulate the strategy – she *must* know! She just sat with the problem for a while until the directors began to chase her for her results and she knew she needed to do something. She began to pray for inspiration! What came to her was to 'be honest'. She wished that there was another answer to her request, but decided that she would feel her fear and do it anyway.

She went back to the first director and confided, 'I feel very bad about saying this, but I can't see a clear strategy and I'm a bit lost.' Amazingly, the response she received was, 'I am so relieved to hear you say that because that's just how I have been feeling. I thought I was the only one.' Then, one by one, she went on to have similar conversations with the other directors. Once she'd had their feedback, she decided to call a meeting where they could all voice their concerns. Out of this meeting came, most importantly, a new honesty, a new trust and a new quality of relationship with the directors. A stronger foundation for developing a successful strategy also emerged. Julie had been willing to take a risk and let go of her apparent safety, and in doing this she found solid ground that supported honesty and authenticity.

In the corporate world of work there is often – from within our own minds and from outside – enormous pressure to know all the answers, look good, be strong, have no doubt or weakness. As the jungle law tells us, only the fittest will survive. We fear our weakness will mean that we are eaten or abandoned by the pack. That may well be true in nature, but in the corporate world now, only the wisest survive in the long term. In the short term it may be clever and productive to be competitive, defensive and guarded, but it won't work for us. In the long term, we all lose.

Denial is one of the most corrosive patterns we can play out in our life. If we deny we have a problem, we can't begin to solve it; until we acknowledge we don't know something, we can't begin to learn; until we acknowledge we are lost, we can't begin to find our way home.

STRENGTH AND VULNERABILITY – IT'S OK NOT TO KNOW ALREADY

How can we discover anything new, wonderful and exciting about ourselves and life if we think we know it already? Anita Roddick, founder of the Body Shop, once said that the difference between conventional management style and the style she encouraged was that conventional managers were trained to avoid saying that they didn't know, because they would appear weak or vulnerable. She wanted honesty. She wanted people to realize how much they didn't know and to be honest about it so that they could learn and discover.

Using intuition as our compass offers us the paradox of enormous strength and sometimes great vulnerability. It is our strength because it is our most true personal compass in life, and will lead us to live our most authentic and successful life. To embrace our intuition we are regularly called to acknowledge, 'I don't know', and that is an uncomfortable place for many of us. Only then can we listen, only then can we be taught, only then will we discover.

As we grow up, we don't necessarily look good, feel good about ourselves or have the answer to every question. I remember sitting down with my manager, when I was looking to leave my last company. 'What can I offer you?' I was asked. 'More money, a bigger portfolio of customers? What do you want?' I couldn't say that I wanted my heart and soul back, wanted to be creative, wanted to be in charge of my own ideas and thinking, and be the captain of my own life. 'I just want to be happy' was the best I could manage, 'and I don't think my happiness lies here'. I could feel the pain, knew something inside was calling me, but at that stage I couldn't articulate it very well.

But it's important at this stage of our journey that we understand the nature of our pain. Growing into our authentic self often generates the pain of growth, as we experience the healing of childhood wounds. This kind of pain challenges us and calls us to a new perception, a new way of seeing. Part of success is learning how to handle this pain and discomfort. Excess pain can be a sign that something isn't right, but it can also be a natural part of the growth process. Recently I was reading about the new phenomenon of the quarter-life crisis, where 25-year-olds are questioning the success that they've created. It seems that they often hit a crisis after just two months in a job, get bored and start looking around for a new one. It can be tricky to understand if boredom is true and someone is being under-utilized, or in the wrong situation, or if they have hit a temporary plateau, and will rise to a new level of success. It could be that by jumping from job to job we are actually *avoiding* true inner change, even though it looks as if we are changing. The change we need might simply be to delve deeper into ourselves, rather than radically changing our circumstances.

DISCOMFORT IS OFTEN A HEALTHY SIGN

Creating love from the ashes of negativity may be the most creative act.

K. Bradford Brown, co-founder of the Life Training Programme

It is little wonder that so many people are choosing to leave organizations and start their own small businesses where they can be creative and in charge of their destiny. Shirley Jamieson is co-founder of the Cambridge Entrepreneur Centre in the UK, whose purpose is both to help people become entrepreneurs and to help larger organizations develop a more entrepreneurial spirit. She told me, 'Hardly a day goes by without me getting a telephone call from a director of a major UK company saying, "I am bored! Do you know of a start-up company I can work with? I want some excitement and inspiration. Oh, and by the way I have a whole team of people who want to come with me!"'

All of these people are very gifted, with lots to offer, but they're bored because they feel uncreative and undervalued. They want a bigger challenge. They want their talents to be fully utilized, and want to be positively stretched, but it is the meaning that we give to our discomfort and how we perceive it that is crucial to our success.

If we believe that all work is necessary evil, our pain is just the affirmation of a cruel life. From a spiritual perspective our discomfort is an inner push, a wake-up call to the first stage of a new birth for our soul. The human heart seeks the freedom of authentic self-expression and cannot stay chained for ever. Although many people believe this freedom can probably only be found outside the corporate hierarchy, it can be found within when we change our mindset from one of command and control to genuine empowerment, appreciation and valuing of our own contribution.

Brian was nearly 40 and a senior manager with a major

broadcasting company. His second child had just been born. Although successful and an inspiration to many colleagues and friends, Brian explained to me, 'I feel like something I've been trying to run away from is catching up with me.' 'What's that?' I asked. 'I feel like I am actually a failure, and that all that others see about me is untrue. I feel I am a fraud, and that I could sabotage my life right now.'

Brian's is not an unusual experience. Many people report feeling like a fraud, that their success isn't really theirs, but is a show, a façade that they fear will be seen through. When we feel we are actually a failure we take on the role of success, which to most people looks like success, but to us doesn't *feel* like success. We can feel stress at the incongruence of our inner and outer worlds, and we don't experience success because all the rewards and recognition go to our role, not to us. Yet there is a force within us that is positively pushing for us to get these mistaken beliefs about ourselves out and healed, so we can be freer and more available to life. It's tough, though, dealing with issues like this when we are supposed to be strong professionally and not show any signs of weakness.

Brian and I continued talking, and I suggested that maybe this was a time for him to attend to his inner world and to ease up on the effort he put into his career. He sought therapeutic help, which helped him trace back his extremely painful feelings of failure and guilt to his troubled childhood amidst a warring family. This was the place inside him he had been running away from, trying to deny, cover up and compensate for. But now his life was calling him to change, to go back and undo some of his faulty thinking, and move to a new level of true success and confidence.

As he realized that it never was his job to fix his family's problems, Brian was able to free himself and move up a gear in his career. He also reconnected with his wife, his kids and his work colleagues. There was no longer a huge barrier of pain and resentment between him and those he cared for.

In *A Course in Miracles*, we are taught that, 'our weakness is Heaven's strength, and our strength Heaven's weakness'. Sometimes it's not until we are on our knees that we become open to the help and guidance that leads the way to our unconditional self.

BREAKTHROUGHS ARE ABOUT LETTING GO AND EMBRACING

When an old way of working isn't working any more, our ego will cry, 'Give up, I might as well die now' while our spirit will whisper, 'Hooray, time to let go of a mask and an illusion. Time to be more real. Time to quit hiding and start shining, time to stop playing roles and be truly yourself.' This hidden, secret voice is longing for a life *more full of love, abundance, success and flow*! It is also longing to shed the familiar but unsuccessful skin we have adopted. As we take that first crucial step through our fear, our confidence appears, but we have to take that step first, otherwise we end up waiting and wasting the success that awaits us.

In the Jewish Cabbala we are taught that we often need to take a fall before a rise – to gain energy. Don't misunderstand this as a call to suffering, but sometimes we need to heal broken, hurt and wounded places in our hearts in order to free ourselves. Our long dark nights of soul-searching are often trips into our own underworld, after which we come out stronger and more integrated, a little more whole.

But what has brought us this far may not take us to the next level of success. Many coaching clients I have worked with have spent their lives being tough, independent and self-interested, and are stuck in their careers, either blocked in success or not experiencing their current success. They have reached a place where they need to learn about partnership and co-operation. They are realizing that we are in this game of life together, and that the juice of life comes from being in partnership, being in supportive relationships, and that being king or queen of your own empire may give you a lot of control but it blocks happiness and joy, and can be very lonely.

Natalie was an actress who'd had some success in advertisements. But her success had been erratic, so she trained as a reflexologist to give herself another string to her bow and to keep herself active. After a particularly difficult period of resting, she wondered whether acting was still for her and so decided to take a holiday to visit friends in Australia, where she'd also consider her future. 'I said to myself that I would give myself six months. If my career didn't take off, I would let acting go. That felt good and so I went off feeling at peace, knowing that my career would either take off, or I would change direction completely. I had no idea what would happen but felt OK anyway.'

Natalie had a great time in Australia, and came back curious about what would happen next. She didn't have to wait long for the answer. 'Within days of returning, my agent called to say that I was up for some auditions. Within weeks, I had a couple of great advertisements, followed by a great part in a BBC drama. Then to top it off, within a month, I had auditions for a major part in a series, and after several meetings, got a part on ITV's *The Bill* that involved some really juicy storylines.' When I asked her what she thought created her reversal of fortunes, she responded, 'I truly let it go. I was willing to have success, and willing to let go of my need for it, all at the same time. This was the result!'

As we've seen, attachment takes so much energy: we hold on not just to future outcomes and expectations, but to the past and how we perceived it. It creates fear and worry. It robs us of the vital resources we need to be creative and initiate exciting new projects. Our focus becomes lost in 'What if it all turns sour? What if I am rejected? What if . . . what if . . . what if . . .' The joy of simply taking action is soon lost.

We also need to differentiate between letting go of something and letting go of our emotional attachment to it. Attachment can hide a level of fear of loss. So, the more we can let go emotionally, the more we are able to enjoy and appreciate all we have.

When we learn from every experience, we build up capital of experience in our emotional bank account. We have learned to be happy regardless of apparent successes or failures, as we find solid ground. We can be more confident, more at ease, less needy and more attractive, and that creates its own magic, because we get out of our own way.

LETTING GO INTO PARTNERSHIP

One of the greatest emotional patterns we need to break relates to our fear of being dependent. It's the fear of letting other people be *that* important to us, be that valuable and precious to us. The bottom line is our fear of love and of being loved, of being truly equal to and intimate with other human beings.

We fear that if we let people get too close, too intimate, we might then be abused: they'll hurt us, we'll lose them and then we'll feel devastated by that loss. Yet, paradoxically, what we thought would save us pain actually causes us pain – loneliness, a sense of isolation and a lack of true connection with and appreciation of other people. In reality, the worst has already happened, and is in the past. The future is waiting for us and to fully appreciate it and enjoy it, it is essential that we share our experiences.

We can learn to rely on others, and others can rely on us, creating a rich and valuable connection that is family and community.

Another key to unconditional success relates to our ability to value those around us more fully. Instead of trying to minimize the value of others for fear of being exploited, we can learn to appreciate the many gifts people bring to their work and life, and how closely our lives are intertwined. We move from seeing the world as a desperate competition to seeing it as a place where we coexist in harmony and for the benefit of all.

APPRECIATION – WHAT FEEDS OUR SOUL

I now perceive one immense omission in my psychology – the deepest principle in human nature is the craving to be appreciated.

WILLIAM JAMES, 1842–1910, psychologist

I was invited to speak at a career management conference, and one of the keynote speakers was Chris Bonington, a member of the highly successful Everest expedition of 1985. He gave us a fascinating presentation, describing how Arne Ness, the leader of the expedition, had the gift of valuing and appreciating everybody in the team.

At base camp, before they set off up the mountain, they had a number of meetings. Arne Ness wanted to transform them from a group of people into a true team. He explained to them that they were all equally important to the success of the expedition. The Sherpas were not paid servants but equal members, and if they wanted to reach the summit too and the conditions were right, they could. They played both a support and a leadership role. Arne knew that you need to acknowledge and value people to earn their commitment.

Eighteen of the team – nine Europeans and nine Sherpas – reached the top, the largest group of people ever to do so. Although the factors that created success were many – including of course physical prowess – appreciation, inclusion and a unique bond of mutual respect, Chris explained, were without doubt the most crucial.

In organizations we often forget the difference between evaluating and appreciating, and I think we are much better at evaluating.

Evaluation implies distance and objectivity, as with a specimen under a microscope. When we evaluate, it is like putting ticks in boxes, deciding whether someone has jumped through the right hoop and performed the way they should. Appreciation, in contrast, implies a greater closeness, and a greater respect for the individual.

I knew an MD of a company who always took the time to speak to the cleaner, the post-room workers, the man who cleaned his car and all the others in the organization. 'You are important, this company couldn't work without you,' he would tell each of them, overtly or covertly, and mean it. When he left, there was uproar and everyone wanted to go with him! People appreciated *him* because he genuinely appreciated *them*. He knew they were *all* partners in success, and that every one of them played their part in the overall success of the company.

APPRECIATION ENCOURAGES PEOPLE TO SUCCEED

Appreciation can make life more worth living; we can live without it, but our life is poorer. For those of us with low self-esteem, appreciation helps us remember that we are better than we think we are. We want peak performance from ourselves and others. But we don't beat virtuoso performances out of people with a stick, or threaten it out of them, or get it by ignoring them. We get it by encouraging them, helping, supporting, trusting and inspiring them to find, develop and give their best. Appreciation and encouragement is the sun that calls us to blossom. As we appreciate the gifts of others we awaken the gifts in ourselves, and we create more flow in ourselves.

In most working environments there seem to be hundreds of manuals, rules and regulations outlining punishments, grievances, things you mustn't do and what you must do when things go wrong. We tend to have a lot fewer, if any, manuals about how to encourage, value, appreciate and recognize people. I once sent out a partly tongue-in-cheek press release that said 'Heart at Work suggests that every organization in the UK should have a director of appreciation and inspiration.' The press release went on to explain that feeling unappreciated was a major reason stated by many people for leaving their jobs, and that this one thing alone could be costing British industry millions of pounds a year in lost productivity and recruitment costs. I didn't get much positive feedback from the British media!

WAYS TO IMPLEMENT THIS IDEA

- *Whenever you feel called to judge or criticize someone, find at least two things you can genuinely appreciate about them first.*
- *Appreciate something about yourself every day. Keep a record of this in your journal.*
- *Use your intuition to pick someone to appreciate today – find a creative way to express that appreciation.*

WE ALL NEED APPRECIATION

A friend of mine is a partner in a City of London law firm, and he gave me a copy of an article from the legal magazine *Commercial Lawyer*. It described a mini-revolt within another top law firm that was renowned for being thrusting, aggressive, competitive and successful, but was beginning to lose many of its good lawyers. Morale was deteriorating, and this culminated in senior assistants in the corporate department writing a letter to the senior partner. In it, the lawyers laid out their grievances, and one of the key ones was, 'A general feeling of not being appreciated, not valued as an individual, of almost being like cannon fodder, and not being thanked when they had worked all night.'

Although a critical letter, it was courageous and its intention constructive: it was aimed at creating positive change, suggesting solutions, and building greater success in the firm. The result was that it opened a whole new dialogue within the firm. It demonstrated that, however well you may be doing materially, or however wonderful an image you have created, we all need to be valued and appreciated, including lawyers! Behind the pinstriped suits beat radical hearts that want recognition for their expertise, effort and commitment.

GENUINE APPRECIATION

Look around your life and notice a couple of things that you love and enjoy, like your CD player, computer, cooker, music or videos. Think for a moment of who you have to thank for them, even if they are dead or living on the other side of the world. Appreciate the inventors of printing, the semiconductor and the microchip; the people that made your computer, those working to produce electricity . . . you can go on and on. Send them a silent thank-you and express your gratitude for the impact they've had on your life.

Apply these principles of appreciation:

ALWAYS BE SINCERE

Have you ever had a boss who came back from a course where he'd been told that he had to appreciate people more? His clumsy attempts didn't sound in the slightest bit sincere. This is counterproductive; better to keep quiet than try to appreciate in a way that is not genuine, which can be more of an insult than a motivator.

GIVE TO OTHERS AS THEY LOVE TO GIVE

You know the best way to thrill someone? Give to them what they give to everyone else! Have you noticed that you often give to people what *you*'d love to have yourself? It's natural and most of us do it, so if you want to make someone's day, notice what and how they give, and find a way of returning this. They will be very grateful.

Just imagine going ten-pin bowling for an evening, and every time you bowled, just before the ball hit the pins, a sheet came down and you didn't see how many you hit, you just got a final score at the end of the evening. How long would you bowl for? Probably less than a minute. We love instant feedback, it feeds our excitement, our motivation and, especially at work, it helps us to learn quickly. If you think you have been bowling strikes and spares, and your boss tells you that actually you have been bowling balls down the gutter for the last six months, how helpful is that? We need genuine, positive feedback fast in order to rectify problems before they take hold and become irretrievable disasters.

DON'T LET EMBARRASSMENT STOP YOU GIVING

If we have not been used to giving positive feedback, we may feel a bit clumsy and awkward to start with, and that is OK. Like any new skill, we need to learn as we go. Keep learning, keep practising and ask for feedback, so that you can become competent at it. As you learn to give and receive this valuable information, the quality of your life, as well as the lives of those around you, will improve greatly.

PRACTISE LEARNING TO RECEIVE

We often have three ways of dealing with appreciation that is given to us: we either change the subject, minimize, or justify the appreciation! 'You do look lovely in that dress' – 'What, this? It's nothing, I've had it for years.' 'Thanks so much for your help, I really appreciated it' – 'Don't be silly, it's what I am paid to do.' Recognize the traits? Here's the magical golden rule for how to receive appreciation. Smile, and say 'Thank you!' Nothing else, just let it in. Let yourself feel whatever you feel. Remember that the amount of recognition we are willing to receive from others directly relates to how much we love and appreciate ourselves. If we don't value ourselves, we won't see what's coming towards us, or will be uncomfortable with it.

The power of creation is within us now, a power that can transform our lives and those around us.

•

Our success relies less on skills, qualifications and experience than on our ability to access the spiritual power that lies inside us and to infuse our work and life with this power.

•

Belief in our self underpins all success in our life, and our power is manifested through our passion and our love, and having these motivate our action in the world.

•

Our greatest power lies in being ourselves, and being authentic.

5

UNCONDITIONAL POWER

There is in this world no such force as the force of a person determined to rise. The human soul cannot be permanently chained.

DR WILLIAM DUBOIS,
1868–1963, civil rights activist and writer

Our power lies in our ability to respond to and follow through on our intuitions, creative callings, inspirations and passions. This power comes from our unconditional self, right now. But many of our personality structures, beliefs and attitudes can get in the way of this power, and our purpose here is to undertake the inner work that allows our personality to be a vehicle for this power. When we can add love and self-belief to our deepest longings, we turn this power into accomplishments and achievements.

YOU ARE NOT BROKEN AND DO NOT NEED FIXING

As we've seen, so much of the world of personal development is founded upon the idea that we are broken in some way, and that we need fixing. Because we see ourselves as broken, we have problems in our lives, so our focus is always on trying to find ways of fixing those broken bits. I spent many years being a personal development junkie, going to many different teachers and healers, always hoping that the next one might be able to alleviate the pain I felt.

I am suggesting a new starting point – a recognition that we are already whole.

No amount of studying, learning, qualifications or self-improvement can fill the hole created by the belief that we are not good enough, whatever line of work we are engaged in. We can get caught in the trap of always studying, trying to earn, learn, achieve and deserve our way to being good enough. We are forever trying to get to an imaginary finishing line where someone will give us the medal that says 'You are now good enough'. The secret is we have already been given the medal – we've already won, but we've forgotten! The test is over, and in fact there never was a test at all. It is good to learn, to develop and to grow in knowledge and understanding, but do it from interest, from curiosity and fascination, not from a feeling of inadequacy.

THE POWER OF BEING OURSELVES

Fiona came from a tough, working-class background and had worked her way up to becoming a successful manager in a very successful telecommunications company. But she wasn't particularly happy. 'I feel like I've moulded myself to try to be what they wanted. I have given my power away. For years I have forced myself to do things that I didn't particularly want to do, and wasn't motivated to do, and I have grown to dislike myself for doing that. I have succeeded, but I've lost myself in the process. I can no longer push myself to do what I don't value. I am scared of them realizing my heart isn't in it any more. I am burnt out.' Fiona felt she'd been racing for years, but the finishing line seemed further away than ever. She talked about how she longed to be creative, to be in charge of her own work and life, and to do something that was really *her*. She wanted her life to unfold with some adventure, some surprises and inspiration.

Fiona's experience echoes what many of us have come to think about success. She'd climbed the ladder only to discover that it was leaning up against the wrong building! To be successful we often believe we must mould and distort ourselves and we don't believe that we can simply be ourselves. We believe we need to sacrifice either what we love, our creativity, our family, our authenticity, or our balance in life. But as we know, unconditional success is about discovering the unique shape of our own soul and letting it fashion our lives so that we can be truly happy and fulfilled.

SUCCESS IS 80 PER CENT ATTITUDE, 20 PER CENT SKILLS

Many of us today are re-evaluating what it really means to us to live a successful life. Some of us are realizing that our concept of success has had too high a price tag attached to it. Yet there is a plan for true success and happiness inside us now, and it is about being whole, not torn.

There was a fascinating article in the *Harvard Business Review* following up on a long-term research study looking into causal factors of success. This study discovered that what contributed most to success, surprisingly, was not skills, education and qualifications, but attitude, motivation and self-belief. Indeed it showed that only 20 per cent of success was based on knowledge and how much we'd learned, and 80 per cent was based on how we felt about ourselves, how motivated we were and what our major attitudes were.

Obviously we need a base level of ability and skill, but once we have that, it is how we develop our mind and spirit that makes the difference to our sense of success. Again, it's not the letters after our name, the certificates on our walls or the credentials on our CV but the love and courage in our hearts, the inspiration in our spirit and the attitude to serve and help our fellow humans that determine how far we go and how much we enjoy the journey.

ALTITUDE TRAINING

Sally was organizing a conference for 700 independent financial advisers. 'Every year we have keynote speakers at our conference, and usually they talk about the technicalities of the financial products, the ins and outs of them. This year we'd like something different. Can you help?' she asked me. We went on to talk about how important attitude, motivation and self-belief were for her members, and yet the attitudinal aspects of work are so often overlooked. We created a presentation called 'Your attitude determines your altitude' which was brilliantly received by the audience, and helped the financial advisers identify and move past some of their limiting ideas and beliefs and realize that their success was only partly determined by what they knew. We tend to hire for skills and then train for attitude. Perhaps we should consider hiring more for attitude and training for skills. One of my hopes is that more and more organizations will come to realize the power of attitudinal training, helping employees believe in themselves, building up their sense of self-worth.

This concept works in reverse too. Jane was amazing. At 48 she had been a successful dancer, trained as a psychotherapist and as an actress, knew a lot about astrology, had a degree in fine art, had learned how to teach aerobics and Reiki, and was loved by many. But she was broke, and felt as if her life was over because she could no longer dance. She is a wonderful example of the opposite – she is 80 per cent skills and 20 per cent self-belief! We all have a deep reservoir of talents and abilities. Noel Coward put it forcefully when he said, 'Thousands of people have talent. The one and only thing that counts is: Do you have staying power?'

The crucial factor in realizing our potential is self-belief. Self-belief is the magic key that opens up new perceptions, dissolves doubt and helps us take ideas and bring them into the physical world. Self-belief is not a guarantee that we will succeed in the way we expect, but it increases the chances that we'll put ourselves in the position to be successful.

WISDOM QUESTIONS

Think for a minute about the education, training and development you have had over the years.

* How much of it has been learning facts, hard skills, knowledge and techniques?
* How much of it has been about using your mind, developing your attitude, spirit and motivation?
* What have you most enjoyed?
* What kind of training and development could you benefit from?

Of course you can't learn to use a computer by having a positive mindset alone. Without skills you simply have a motivated idiot – and they can be dangerous! But our attitude towards what we are learning is crucial. Today, many athletes spend more time on developing their attitude than they do on technical skills. They make their mind receptive to success, they imagine themselves winning races, medals and titles. And the key word in this attitude training is self-belief.

GET YOURSELF AN ELECTRIC MONK!

In *Dirk Gently's Holistic Detective Agency* by Douglas Adams is a glorious character called the Electric Monk. The purpose of the Electric Monk was to believe, on its owner's behalf, what the owner couldn't yet believe! In a world full of strange concepts, the Electric Monk would build a bridge between our incredulity and what was true. What a wonderful idea. If our biggest problem in life is lack of self-belief, we can really do with someone who believes in us until we can believe in ourselves.

In my workshops, I often invite people to think of something they'd love to believe about themselves that they don't yet believe. It could be a belief like, *I can make money doing something I really love*, or *I can develop my creative passions into a career*, or *the world wants what I'd love to do*, or *I can make big changes in my life*. They share these beliefs with the group, and then I invite all participants to go to several people that they sincerely believe in and be their Electric Monk! They tell them that they believe what the person doesn't currently believe about themselves. It is a very powerful experience for many people and the key reason is that we all need someone to believe in us. To believe in someone means to get them to understand and appreciate their own gifts.

SOMEONE TO BELIEVE IN US

When my friend Niki made the transition from being employed to starting his own business, he told me, 'I consider encouragement from friends and family to be the single biggest factor in my success to date.' Being encouraged by supportive people – family, friends, teachers, bosses, mentor, coach or colleagues – is one of the greatest gifts. I will remember for the rest of my life the words of Mrs Jamieson, my O-level English teacher, who introduced us to Franco Zeffirelli's *Romeo and Juliet*. The film touched me deeply, and we all had to write essays on what we thought about the play, and the film version of it. When she returned my essay, I discovered she'd written, 'This is a joy for an English teacher to read. I am so glad you enjoyed the film, that you understood it so well, and that it had such an impact on you.' I felt she'd seen that deeper teenage part of me, both enjoying and struggling with love, sexuality and relationships, and it really helped me to better understand myself. So, although words can hurt, words can also inspire us for a lifetime, can heal, bless, create self-belief.

Charles Handy, author and co-founder of the London Business School, wrote a book called *The New Alchemists*, in which he studied a number of the most successful British entrepreneurs and a number of people who had created successful not-for-profit organizations. One common strand he found was that most of them had had someone who believed in them, someone who had seen their gifts and had identified in them what Sigmund Freud named a *golden seed*. It didn't mean that they were greater than anyone else, merely that their innate talents had been recognized. Like desert rain, this kind of recognition can help us to break off our sense of doubt or isolation and nurture us towards unconditional success.

WISDOM QUESTIONS

Whose words have had the most positive impact on you?

* Who from your past or present has most believed in you? Who have been the most affirming and encouraging people in your life?
* What did they tell you about yourself?
* What impact did they have on you?

In the Jewish Cabbala tradition there is a belief: that every blade of grass has an angel standing over it encouraging it and whispering to it, 'Grow, grow, grow.' If a blade of grass can inspire this kind of sacred belief, we probably have a lot more help and encouragement than we realize. The whole of life might well be on our side, supporting us, and whispering in our ear, or to our soul, to grow, grow, grow! It may only be us that is saying 'no!'

WHO DO *YOU* SEE AND BELIEVE IN?

The people around us need our affirmation and our belief too. Whether they are our partners, children, colleagues, bosses or friends, we can help them with our belief. A few words from us could make a great difference to them.

- *Close your eyes and ask yourself: Who most needs my support, belief and encouragement right now? See who comes to your mind. You don't need to understand logically.*
- *What do you think they need to hear?*

How will you tell them? Let them know you believe in them, either with a telephone call, a card, an e-mail or some other gesture.

HOW DO WE BUILD UP OUR SELF-BELIEF IF IT IS LOW?

Self-belief is natural, we are born with it. We learn to fear, we learn to doubt ourselves. We come to believe that we are inferior to others. One of the best ways to develop our sense of self-belief is to start doing or being what we would do if we had never lost it. This may sound a little tautological, but it works. If we wait for our self-belief to suddenly arrive, we may die waiting. We need to choose it. We need to start taking small but significant actions that demonstrate and build it.

So what would you do if you really believed in yourself?

Just imagine for a moment that you didn't have any doubts about yourself and your worthiness, and begin to answer some of these questions:

- *What would you start that you haven't started yet?*
- *What would you ask for that you are not asking for now?*
- *What would you give that you are holding back on now?*
- *How else would you be different?*

PRIMAL BELIEFS

Each of us has our own personal philosophy on life, and one of the biggest factors in creating this philosophy is our beliefs. Right now we are running our life according to our personal beliefs about love, money, work, success, relationships, business and happiness. We have had many good teachers from whom we have learned these beliefs, and we have had some teachers who were less helpful. Our inner beliefs and awareness are the causal levels of life; our outer conditions merely reflect this inner state. The world is a canvas on which we paint our beliefs, attitudes and thoughts. But our beliefs are only the operating software of our life. As we identify the bugs and glitches in this software, we can install new programming so that our life works more successfully, unfolding beautifully whether we realize it or not. We often don't see that the way we live our lives is the result of thousands of decisions we've made, often under the influence of other people, and sometimes in painful and difficult circumstances.

Do you want to start identifying and liberating yourself from some of your beliefs? Just look at some of the major achievements in the world and ask yourself, what would I have needed to believe to create that? Do you want to know how to change your life to be much better? Change your beliefs. This sounds very easy, and sometimes it is; once we are aware of a belief we can change it in the twinkling of an eye. Other times, the task is more challenging, because some of our beliefs reside deep in our unconscious mind and have been handed down through many generations. They can seem to be the very foundations of our identity until we remember that the power to change rests with us.

I like the way my friend Robert Holden describes how we develop our beliefs. He likens the process to Mary Shelley's *Frankenstein*, one of the best-known horror stories of all time. Dr Frankenstein is a young scientist who, with his creative ability, makes a person out of the parts of other people. His creation then becomes a monster that turns against its creator and the whole world. This parallels how our beliefs work. We make up beliefs about the world and how it works, let them loose in our mind, and then they come back as shadows to haunt and attack us. The one difference between the Frankenstein story and our own is that the doctor knew it was his own creation attacking him. We tend to forget that we adopted our beliefs, and now blame them on life, or other people; we say that's just how things are, and end up as a victim of our own creation, rather than the powerful architect of our life. You were the architect, but you hid the plans! Now it could be time to examine and restore the foundations of your life, and make them stronger. It's not about beating ourselves up for stupid and painful beliefs that we've adopted, but about recognizing the mistakes we've made, and choosing new possibilities.

We need to begin to truly comprehend that the world out there is like a projector screen on to which we project the story of our lives and our beliefs. If you don't like what you see on the screen you can easily make changes that will reflect your vision of a happy life. You wrote the script, remember.

Pick a new belief and simply imagine it to be true. See yourself in your own imagination as if it were true: choose it to be true. Identify a list of new core beliefs that you would love to see yourself living. Write them down and then repeat them to yourself. For example:

I see myself as a confident and valuable person, setting goals and achieving them.

I see myself being creative and inspired.

I see myself being fulfilled and authentic.

I see myself growing in confidence, self-belief and inner power every day.

I see myself making major changes and creating new ways of working.

Too often our beliefs don't seem to be beliefs, but seem to be 'reality', how life is. We need to create a compelling future vision of ourselves, and know that on the level of spiritual reality this vision already exists. It represents the truth of who you are. Your conditioning simply blocks your awareness of this. The key is to see in your mind what is happening now, let it be true in your inner world now and trust that the outer manifestation will follow.

LEAVE THE IBIWISI TRIBE AND JOIN THE ISIWIBI TRIBE

Every man's world is and always remains a construct of his mind, and cannot be proved to have any other existence.

ERDWIN SCHRÖDINGER,
1887–1961, Austrian physicist

Many of us were born into a tribe called the IBIWISI, a tribe who wait for their lives to change, are sometimes cynical about the possibility of change, and live with the belief, 'That's just how life is, there is not much we can do about it.' They believe that the world is pretty fixed and immutable. IBIWISI stands for I'll believe it when I see it. Recognize the traits?

Some of us were born into the ISIWIBI tribe, where we were told that the world is not about how it is but is more to do with how we are. We were told we are creative and powerful, and that the world is a mirror of our thinking. How we think is how the world is likely to be. We see the world as a playground of infinite opportunities, limited only by our thinking and vision. ISIWIBI stands for the I'll see it when I believe it tribe. Recognize the traits?

We may be less familiar with the latter than the former, but the good news is that it is never too late to change tribes! Membership is free, new members are always welcome, and application for membership is by changing your mind!

We don't necessarily need a lot of self-belief to get us going – that's a lie we tell ourselves in order to postpone taking our first steps. We can start with 99 per cent doubt, uncertainty and fear, but the remaining 1 per cent that represents our willingness to change will get us going wonderfully.

WHICH SELF ARE WE BELIEVING IN?

Self-belief is not about conceit or arrogance, it is not about thinking that you are the best or about trying to beat others. That is all ego. True *self*-belief is simply knowing that there is an incredible power within you, as there is within everyone, and that that power and want will manifest positively in your life. It will be for your good, and the good of those around you.

Are you believing in your ego or your unconditional self, your being? That is the question that determines the level and experience of success in your life. If you are believing in your ego you have every reason to fear and to be anxious, but if you are trusting in the power of the unconditional self you are on safe and solid ground. You are trusting in the power of the whole of creation within you, the power of the whole of life that is within you. That is worth believing in. The trouble is that at every turn our ego will try and stay in control and block awareness of the spirit within.

YOUR PASSION QUALIFIES YOU!

The ego says, 'Your value is based on your credentials. You need a Ph.D or its equivalent before you can get a good job.' But some of the best and brightest of our generation were educated more by life than by school. There's a mass of talent in our society, but few have credentials to show for it. Our achievements may have been mainly internal.

MARIANNE WILLIAMSON, author of *A Return to Love*

One of the most popular expressions I hear from people who are considering following their heart and calling in life is 'yes, but who am I to succeed?' Yes, but who are you not to? Jennifer came to a seminar, having had a successful career in computers. She was getting bored with it, her heart wasn't in it any more. I asked her what her real passion was, and she responded as quick as a flash, 'Cooking and entertaining!' She explained that she was never happier than when creating new recipes, feeding family and friends, with a group of people around a table. She had a number of ideas about how to make money out of her passion. When I asked her why she hadn't put any into practice, she replied, 'I am qualified in computing with exams passed and certificates on my wall, but I have no qualifications in cookery at all.' I wished I had a certificate in my pocket that I could have given to her that said 'You, Jennifer, are hereby qualified to cook and entertain, and be happy and joyful, because you are very gifted at it, people love it when you do it, and you love doing it. You can learn all you need to as you go. Your passion qualifies you, and your ability will see you through!'

This is a very familiar theme: we are qualified in one career but have a passion for something new. We don't feel competent to try new and exciting experiences because we don't have a piece of paper that says we can. We may want to strengthen our passion by learning new skills to implement these changes, but the passion itself is the gold, our revealing of the love within us. The word 'qualify' derives from two Latin words and means to endow with a quality: *qualis* means of what sort and *facere* means to make. To be qualified means to make something with a quality, so when we make things with love and with passion, we are making them with the highest quality of all.

Our passion, and the wisdom we have gleaned from our own life experiences, may have more power than a Ph.D, our love more power than a stack of A levels. Of course, competence is also crucial, but generally people who are passionate are also curious, lifelong learners, forever wanting to expand their knowledge through a sheer desire to understand life and how it can be improved.

Today, it is as if we have become obsessed with measuring our achievements by the number of certificates we have managed to gather. But did Beethoven write music in order to get a grade? Did Picasso paint to get a certificate? Did Callas sing because it was down as a goal on her appraisal form? Of course not. They did what they did because they loved what they were doing. Most of the greatest creative acts in life stem from this same passion. Creative passion is what we are most deeply curious about, most hungry for, will most hate to lose in life. It is whatever we pursue for its own sake, what we study when there are no tests to take, what we create though no one may ever see it.

When we find the power of our passion we begin to move from powerlessness to fuller participation in life. When love fuels us, everyone is empowered. This seems to be a big challenge for many of us – to own the power of our passion. We want someone else to tell us that it's OK. From childhood onwards we are taught to defer to others who have greater power – parents, siblings, teachers, bosses, church or political leaders. We may wait passively for some outside force to champion our cause and permit us to follow our calling, but that permission can only come from within, from our own soul. Friends, bosses and colleagues can support and encourage us, but the inner desire and choice must be our own. We must take responsibility.

When we work with love and passion we are calling on the power that is behind the whole of creation. We don't need pieces of paper to affirm our brilliance because brilliance lies within each of us. It is how we were created. Our personal power is not something that is going to reveal itself at some later date, but is revealed as a result of our decision to reveal it. We are powerful in whatever moment we choose to be, by choosing the unconditional self within us. The choice to be used as an instrument of love, right here, right now, and in each moment, is a choice for personal empowerment.

Once we've tasted the experience of that authenticity, personal power, passion and integrity, we can't go back. Our soul won't let us. Even though it may lead us to trials and tribulations, we must go forward. I love the expression 'heartbreakthrough' to describe this. We may be led to difficulties, and as we are, each one will allow us a breakthrough to new levels of creative power.

We are generally taught to give our power away, to let others have power over us, and to trust their judgement rather than our own. *Power over* is an idol for many people in this world – the ability to control and influence, to tell people what to do and how to be. Yet the greatest power of all is *power with* people – the ability to inspire, excite, support, educate, believe in, inform, develop and love people is the greatest power of all, and that power is within all of us now, through our unconditional self.

GOAL SETTING TO EMPOWER YOURSELF AND GET INSPIRED

Knowing and getting what you truly want in life is so powerful. That is why one of the best self-esteem builders is goal setting and goal achievement. By setting our heart and mind on what we want, we set ourselves on a lifetime journey of discovery with a growing daily awareness of our personal power. Positive goal setting is one of the most efficient ways we can use our minds, and it reveals to us the power that until now may have been lying dormant within us.

Although goal setting is so powerful, I have discovered that hardly any of us were taught how to do it earlier in our lives. Did your parents teach you about goal setting? Did they tell you at school? When did you learn? Most of us come to goal setting later in life, often through work or business training. I would love to see the power of goal setting taught to every child as they grow up.

We may be bored and uninspired because we haven't set ourselves goals that interest and uplift us, and that enrich our lives and enliven us. We haven't created a future for ourselves so compelling that we want to focus our energies to create it. People whose lives are successful, adventurous, exciting and powerful did not create their lives by accident. They planned them. They had a vision, designed and made a blueprint for their lives. Step by step they did what was necessary to bring the plan to fruition. They made conscious positive choices about what they wanted their life here on earth to be like, and then lived on a daily basis in such a way as to create the lives they wanted. They accessed their inner spiritual power and bought it forth into their lives.

Beginning with the end in mind helps us awaken forces within us, draws support to us and unleashes a mysterious magic residing at the heart of us. There is so much latent within us, and getting inspired, discovering what we are passionate about and becoming aware of the force of love within us are the ways that we access this power.

I like the idea that our mind is a goal-striving mechanism – it is always headed somewhere. Have you ever tried thinking about absolutely nothing? It's pretty hard to do, so why not aim your thoughts towards areas that inspire you? We have a relationship with our goals. Our goals are not isolated things: many will involve other people and other situations, so our goals also interconnect beautifully with the goals of others. If you want success it will be probably through a career, through offering your gifts and talents to an employer, colleagues and customers. You are part of their success as much as they are part of yours. True success is a win/win situation.

SOME IDEAS ON HOW TO SET GOALS

SHARPEN OUR FOCUS

He who wants to do everything will probably do nothing, so learn to be selective. Know what you truly want. Dig deep inside to find what really matters to you. Make choices about what you want, and what you don't want. When you are clear about your destination, you won't even notice some of the obstacles. Start writing lists of goals that are important to you.

This exercise was inspired by my friend Barbara Winter. Below are some ideas about how to set goals in a way that can capture your imagination, inspire you and motivate you. Cast your mind forward one year, and think about achievements, accomplishments and experiences that you would love to have in your life:

- *two things that you would like to have that you haven't got now: e.g. a new job, more money, a car, a new home, a CD player, a mobile phone;*
- *two things you'd like to experience more regularly in your life: e.g. love, fun, friendship, creativity;*
- *two things you'd like to have learned: e.g. a computer skill, a language;*
- *two spiritual goals: e.g. feel more at peace, more connected;*
- *two things you'd like to be: e.g. kinder, inspired;*
- *two places you'd love to visit;*
- *two people you'd like to meet;*
- *two things that you'd like to create;*
- *two things that you can start right now;*
- *two things that you can finish right now;*
- *two things that will make your work more exciting or interesting;*
- *two things you'd like to eliminate from your life: e.g. mess, energy-draining people;*
- *two things that you could do every day that would inspire you;*
- *two ways that you could explore and develop your spirituality;*
- *two things you used to love doing that you haven't done for a while.*

Do you get the idea? It's any way that you can light your inner spark, fan that flame inside you, and get your energy moving.

Now go through the list and:

- *put a star next to the three that you think are the most important to you;*
- *put an exclamation mark next to the ones that thrill and inspire you;*
- *put a line through those that you think are dull;*
- *note two that will need an investment of £100 or more;*

- *draw a circle around those that will add to the quality of your life;*
- *draw another circle around those that will also add to the quality of life for others.*

This will help you sharpen your focus.

SELLING OURSELVES FIRST ON OUR GOALS

A key both to the accomplishment and to our joy in accomplishment of our goals is first to ask ourselves why we want to achieve these goals. This is crucial to our success or failure. What will not sustain us is motivation that is based on either fear or guilt. If we only want to achieve something because we think we should, we are very likely to run out of fuel. So before we can even try involving others in our quest, we have to do the inner work of building self-belief. Only through self-belief can we build our dreams and ambitions on sure foundations. We also need to spend some 'down time' visualizing how our first steps on this journey to success will feel. This is an important dimension to goal setting which is often neglected, but imagining both the joys and the terrors of new and exciting ventures can inspire us – and can truly motivate us to move forward with our plans.

Here are some ways to focus attention, thoughts and action on the achievement of your goals:

- **Affirmations** *– positive presentation in the present tense of things you want to happen. 'I will, I can, I can have.' After a while it becomes natural. 'I can be a person who . . .'*
- **Creative visualization** *– create a mental picture of yourself doing what it is you want to do; see yourself being it. This adds the power of your subconscious mind to the power of your conscious mind.*
- **Treasure map** *or goal collage – things that visually represent your goals achieved. Look at it regularly, add to it.*

- Regular **reminders or symbols** – carry pictures, a talisman, something that often focuses your attention on your goals.
- **Celebrate every step** you take – don't wait for perfection or completion, but positively reinforce every positive step along the way. Build in the experience of success very early on, which builds motivation and momentum to continue.
- **Expand from where you are** with what you've got. It's easy to say if only . . . We need to see what we have, what our strengths are, our resources. It's another dimension of abundance to take an inventory of just what we already have. Who do you know? What contacts do you have? What money do you have? Who'd buy it? Who's a fan already? Who can you nurture relationships with?
- **Eliminate the non-essentials** – have you noticed how when you have something important to do, you suddenly feel an urge to clean the windows, or the filing backlog shouts out for attention? We need to clear the clutter in our life, begin to eliminate time-wasters, energy-draining distractions and unhelpful habits. It doesn't mean being harsh: it does mean being clear and focused.
- **Support that which supports you** – put time and energy into people and things that enhance you, bring out the best in you and raise your energy.
- **Change your attitude** – a small change in direction every day can make a huge difference to the trajectory of your life. Just imagine if a plane took off from Heathrow headed for New York, and its course was slightly less than a degree out to what it should be. Over the journey of 5,000 miles it could end up in Florida, several thousand miles away! This is the effect of a small change of attitude every day.

THE HIGHEST FORM OF GOAL SETTING – BE THE GOAL!

I had this theory when I set up my business. I decided that I would give just enough in order to achieve success. Then, when I got to be *really* successful and achieved all my goals I'd stop holding back, give it my all, and I'd then be inspired and creative. It sounded like a good idea, and seemed to be what much of the world does – give the minimum and withhold the rest.

About two years into running my own business I realized that the experience wasn't all I'd hoped it would be, and I was feeling a bit disillusioned. A conversation with a stranger held the key. He made me see that it wasn't about me reaching a goal one day, but about being inspired and creative. I needed to make *myself* the goal. If I wanted inspiration I could choose to be more inspiring; if I wanted more love I could choose to be more loving; if I wanted more friendship I could choose to be the best friend I could be; if I wanted more creativity I could choose to dig deep inside myself and bring my authentic self and ideas out more fully. If I didn't use all my creative gifts I was merely wasting them. This is a powerful lesson to learn. That day in the future when we can use all our latest abilities may never come. As Gandhi taught us, we can 'Be the change we want to see in the world.' I can identify this moment of awareness and am thankful for it because it became a turning point for me in my life and career, enabling a shift of focus from outer to inner, from getting to giving, from doing to being. Being the goal is about setting intention, choosing to be what we want to be.

Now, every day I set my intentions. I set the goal in my mind to be the most inspiring communicator I can be in my work; to be the most loving presence I can be in the world; to offer support to friends and clients and to be the best partner I can be to Helen. This shifts my attention from competitiveness and trying to be better, to consciousness and simply aiming to be the best I can.

Why wait for tomorrow? Why not go straight for the experience you want? Collapse time; choose what you want to be now! Everything you want will come as a by-product. This is setting your goal and unleashing the awesome power that is your intention. Being what we want is our highest function in life.

Commitment is another powerful friend. Very little is created without it. True commitment has very little to do with duty and sometimes not even very much to do with time. It has everything to do with quality and depth of giving and receiving: it is to do with giving ourselves completely in our work and in our relationships, it is about holding nothing back. True commitment could be for minutes or years. The crucial point is to be willing to commit wholeheartedly, without fear, guilt or any of the other barriers to our success.

THE POWER OF PERSONAL LEADERSHIP

Spiritual power – which comes from one's very being and is the capacity to influence others – knows no position. It is evident in both the poor and the wealthy, in people in high and low positions. Those who have it do not feel arrogant and self-satisfied, but rather gain a greater humility, realising that the true source of the power comes from a Higher Power, not from themselves.

DOROTHY MARCIC, author of *Managing with the Wisdom of Love*

We tend to think of power and leadership as having a job title and a position of authority, but actually leadership is our choice, not a position. Indira Gandhi once said, 'I suppose leadership at one time meant muscles; but today it means getting along with people.' Job titles may generate some following, but usually inspiration is only generated by people with hearts, not a job title. In the worlds of business and politics, we often speak of 'building power bases': we enrol other powerful people and build special relationships with them, protecting and rewarding each other but excluding outsiders. This is one way our ego sees power.

Our ego's prescription for personal power is built on defences. What is the greatest expenditure for most of the world's governments? Defence. Did you know that the world's defence expenditure is around £625 billion each year? Our ego is big on defence: the bigger the toys and guns I have, the safer I feel, it tells us. But bigger defences just create bigger fears. As we know, this just leads to escalation, and a situation where no-one can win.

Our ego has similar ideas about our personality. Wherever we have an emotional wound we put up a defence to protect ourselves. We want to defend against fear, doubt, anxiety and we want to protect our imagined weaknesses. But the more we defend, the more we seem to make what we defend real and fence ourselves off from our spirit, our freedom, inspiration and true power. Defences prevent true healing. The greatest problem with our defences is that eventually they don't work at all – they take us to the very place we wanted to avoid! What we run from, finally we end up running to! Fear just attracts more fear.

Blaming is one huge defence that robs us of our power. Through blame we make someone else wrong, rather than seek our inner power. When I was in the corporate world I blamed a lot. I blamed my boss, my upbringing, my company, the economy, and anyone else who came to mind. When I left to start my own business, I suddenly realized that I had no-one to blame, so I turned the spotlight on me for a while. It – whatever it was – had to be somebody's fault! Then I began to learn about taking more responsibility, about taking my power back and being the guiding force in my own life. Taking responsibility for our work and life is a courageous corner to turn for many of us.

Our defences do not make us strong; they disempower us. We can't be cynical and then expect to be inspired and creative; we can't build walls around ourselves and feel love and connection; we can't shut down and then shine radiantly. All true power comes from joining – both with the unconditional self within us and with other people.

Our true power base comes from *inside*, from the foundation of our identity where we will find serenity, guidance, inspiration and certainty. In silence we discover new things, are guided and comforted. We go to our own inner well and draw from it a greater sense of power, which we can then manifest in the world around us. When we know how to withdraw from the outer world, we can focus more keenly on the problems we face and in quiet contemplation discover new ways to resolve them.

True leadership is showing a way through problems, pain and difficulties, once we have discovered a way for ourselves, generated by our authentic self-expression. As a leader, instead of complaining that the world isn't how we want it to be, we take responsibility for that which is missing and try to bring the light to the dark.

THE FIVE ASPECTS OF PERSONAL LEADERSHIP

1. INNER DETERMINED

Our motivation is fired by our inspiration, guided by our intuition and is our calling. We listen to our inner voice, and have good self-knowledge. We know what our values are, and what we stand for. We are very connected to people and situations outside us, and our major motivation is from within, from alignment with our unconditional self.

2. AUTHENTICITY

We've relinquished our need to be perfect, and we are not content to play out roles. We are willing to be fully present in our lives, without inhibiting ourselves, sharing all our strengths, gifts and glories and all our weaknesses and vulnerabilities. We hide less. The truth is people see our shadow side anyway; we fool ourselves if we think we hide very much. We can be seen, warts and all. Those around us know intuitively what our Achilles' heel is. As leaders we are never fully prepared; we are always on the cusp ourselves, on the edge of our own learning, fear, growth and transformation.

3. SELF-EXPRESSION

As leaders we know what is really important to us and keep reminding ourselves. We have a strong sense of our purpose, and know and live our values to our greatest ability. We have learned many of our lessons in life, not just from textbooks and study but from the experiences of everyday life. We have our scars of battle. We have turned some of our most difficult life experiences into the compost and richness of our life now, and have awareness, compassion and understanding rather than judgement. We express our authentic emotions.

4. CREATE VALUE

We create results and add value to our life and the lives of people around us. Our successes inspire and nourish us and those around us. Through our own emotional and spiritual transformation we have realized that our purpose is to be servants to life. We are here to serve whoever we can, including ourselves. It is our joy and passion to serve – friends, family, strangers, even so-called enemies and competitors, as we know that love serves everyone equally. We find our niche where we are particularly called to serve and keep transforming. We know that up is not the only way; we also broaden and deepen ourselves, and our views on life. The *ups* we are interested in are the highs of joy, fulfilment and self-actualization.

5. OWNING OUR SHADOW PARTS

We are most powerful when we recognize that there are many aspects of ourselves we have hidden away. We can admit that we have dark and light within us, parts of us that we've neglected, because we have forgotten them, judged them, or denied them in ourselves. Our greatest power is acceptance, not judgement.

In *The Long Road to Freedom*, Nelson Mandela described how an officer who was leaving the prison on Robben Island came to Nelson's cell, shook his hand and wished him well.

He had been the most callous and barbaric commanding officer we had had on Robben Island. But that day in the office he had revealed that there was another side to his nature, a side that had been obscured but that still existed. It was a useful reminder that all men, even the most seemingly cold blooded, have a core of decency, and that if their hearts are touched, they are capable of changing. Ultimately, he was not evil; his inhumanity had been foisted upon him by an inhuman system. He behaved like a brute because he was rewarded for brutish behaviour.

That is true leadership: the ability to see beyond appearances with that X-ray vision, to forgive rather than hold on to grievances, and to find common ground and create understanding, not conflict; to believe in the essential goodness at the core of each human being. Long after Nelson Mandela has ceased to hold a position of political power, he has remained a leader. Leadership is our purpose, and is not sourced from any external position, but from alignment with our own heart and inner authority, our unconditional self. This is the ultimate power.

HONOURING POWER

Many of us are scared of power because we've seen it abused and used for purely personal gain, and may have experienced abuse of power in our own lives. We've seen the shadow side of power and have felt the pain. We may decide that we'll relegate our own power so that we don't become abusers or tyrants. But then we disown the very thing that we and the world needs – the ability to create what William Blake described as the good, the great and the holy.

THE ANSWER TO EXHAUSTION IS WHOLEHEARTEDNESS

Exhaustion is the natural result of not exercising our true and full power. Have you noticed that when you are exhausted even a full night's sleep doesn't fully restore you? That is because the antidote to exhaustion is not rest alone. Living your life with passion and inspiration is the answer – and when we combine these forces with those around us, we make connections that refresh and re-invigorate us each day. Can you identify people in your life who energize and refresh you? Are you able to reciprocate these gifts wholeheartedly and without reservation?

ASK FOR WHAT YOU WANT

Your problem is not that you ask for too much, but that you settle for too little.

A Course in Miracles

I had never met Richard but in his letter he explained that as part of his creative leadership programme at the Landmark Forum personal development course, he was creating a project entitled 'Loving Ourselves, Being Enough'. When we met, Richard explained that part of the programme was about building up self-belief, breaking through fears about asking for help and resisting the inner voice that says, 'Don't bother people – they are too busy/not interested.' I was impressed by his courage in asking for help, and shared some of my experience of organizing talks at Alternatives, the lecture series at St James's that I had run for four years. I wished him well and asked him to keep in touch.

I later heard that simply by stepping outside his comfort zone and asking the right people for what he wanted and needed, Richard received help from a church in Woking, Surrey. Not only did he get a really cheap rate for a room at the church but he received enormous help from friends and colleagues. When he asked me if I would be part of his special opening day, and give a two-hour presentation, I was honoured to accept. Again, simply by asking, he got coverage for the event and a big feature in the local newspaper. The local radio station also ran a 10-minute feature, and Richard persuaded the local bookshop to advertise and sell tickets. The local visitor centre agreed to publicize this special event for free. All this simply because he stepped through his fear and asked for what he wanted!

On the day itself there was a real atmosphere of co-operation, love and trust; all who came enjoyed themselves. Richard had inspired other people to be part of his vision; having decided to believe in himself, he created something that was a gift for many other people too.

We need to remind ourselves how much people love to help and that it's only our fear of rejection and lack of self-esteem that prevent us from reaching out to others.

Asking is still one of the best-kept secrets in life. How good are you at asking for what you want? It shouldn't be an unreasonable request, but something you want that you don't have now, right now.

When I was writing my first book, I thought I would like to ask some people if they would be willing to give me words of endorsement and praise for the book. I had met many of the people I had in mind through Alternatives, where I had been a director for a number of years, and had organized talks and events for most of them. But for me it was a challenge because they were my heroes, my inspiration. I looked up to them, and I certainly didn't see myself as their equal. To ask them meant putting myself up on the same level with them, and that was uncomfortable for me. Thoughts like 'Who do I think I am? They won't want to be bothered by me!' kept running through my mind.

I pushed through my resistance and wrote my dream list of people I would love to have words from, and it amounted to 22 names! I thought I'd play a numbers game, and if I got one or two I'd be thrilled. So I prepared a manuscript for each of the 22 people, said a prayer over them, and sent them off. I was amazed when within days I started to get some positive responses, and within a month I had 16 endorsements from people who had between them sold over 60 million books! I was blown away and thrilled, and learned a huge lesson about the power of asking.

WISDOM THOUGHTS

* If you knew you had all the support in the world, what would you begin and where?
* Think of three things that you would like and who you might ask to help you get them.
* Ask! Do it! Stretch yourself and actually ask for what you want.
* Get into the habit of asking every week for something that you find a little (or very) difficult to ask for. Establish some areas where you find it hard to ask for what you want. Here are some ideas:

* *Does anyone owe you money that you aren't asking for?*
* *Do you want a rise or more money for what you do?*
* *Do you want some appreciation from someone?*
* *Do you want less/more responsibility?*
* *Do you need help or support with a project?*
* *Is there someone you would love to meet?*
* *Is there someone you'd like to ask out on a date?*

THE POWER OF PEAK PERFORMANCE –
SUNDAY BEST *EVERY* DAY OF YOUR LIFE

To the Christian world, Sunday is a holy day, a sacred day set apart from the rest of the week as a day of thanksgiving. It used to be a day when we also donned our best clothes, were on our best behaviour, and generally presented our very best self to the world. Today, whilst we may not observe Sunday with quite the same enthusiasm as we once did, we still know the meaning of the term, 'Sunday best'. To me, it seems a shame that sometimes our best efforts, both in terms of behaviour and appearance, are reserved for special occasions only. If we can cast aside the cynicism that says 'why bother?', 'who cares?' we can shine every day of the week, and reach out for the unconditional success that is waiting for us. Cynicism is, after all, simply another negative defence mechanism that we use to protect ourselves from the possibility of failure and exclusion; it certainly doesn't fuel our motivation or lift us when we begin to doubt ourselves.

To perform at our highest energy, at our peak, motivation is essential. Every organization concerned about its place in the world is asking how it can get Sunday-best performances from its people. They are desperate for more adaptability, vitality and imagination, and the enthusiastic willingness to go the extra mile.

There is only one thing that will motivate and sustain us over the distance of our life and career, and that is to have a love and passion for our work. But motivation stems from our inner beliefs: no-one excels when threatened or pushed, at least not for very long. We inspire, celebrate, enthuse and love the best out of ourselves and others. Then we will keep raising our own bar, for the joy of seeing how high we can jump, how we can excel ourselves. The motivation that will get us there is not only to beat others, hit a target or keep our boss off our back, but to pull the genius out of the depths of ourselves, and share it with the world. We need to be curious about who we can become and what we can achieve, and let our work be the vehicle for the satisfaction of our curiosity. Indeed our work needs to become a vehicle for our lifelong learning, and lifelong self-discovery. When we have tapped into that inner motivation, and when it is genuinely supported from the outside, we are on track for a lifetime of peak performance.

We are all part of the one creation and our lives are about moving from a sense of isolation to a sense of greater connectedness.

•

Our sense of separation is at the root of all our problems in life.

•

Love's purpose is to undo this sense of separateness, and to recognize the unity of all that seems fragmented. We are powerful in love when we learn to partner in all areas of our life and work, rather than compete and fight.

•

We learn to access universal principles within each of us, rather than trying so hard to be different and special.

6

UNCONDITIONAL CONNECTION

A human being is a part of the whole called by us 'universe', a part limited in time and space. He experiences himself, his thoughts and feelings, as something separated from the rest, a kind of optical delusion of his consciousness. This delusion is a kind of prison for us, restricting us to our personal desires and to affection for a few persons next to us. Our task must be to free ourselves from this prison by widening our circle of compassion to embrace all living creatures and the whole of nature in its beauty.

ALBERT EINSTEIN,
1879–1955, theoretical physicist

Most of our problems in life come down to one basic issue – a sense of separation and lack of connection. Perhaps loneliness and isolation are the biggest diseases on the planet. The universe is one song, one creation in which everything is connected and part of the whole, yet in the rush and chaos of everyday life it is easy to forget this basic principle.

Ahmed was in his mid-thirties, single, and a successful business analyst. 'I'm *bored*,' he said, 'there is no flow in my life, I am just going through the motions. I don't feel appreciated. There is no buzz, no excitement. I want more.' Ahmed had tried some acting, and enjoyed it, had a dream about being a TV sports presenter, but no definite plans for what to do next. When I asked him what quality would underlie any next step for him, he thought for a moment and replied, 'Connecting with people.' His face changed, as the realization dawned on him. 'That's it,' he said, 'that's what's missing from my life. I have a great lack of connection with people. I tend to isolate myself and spend too much time alone.'

As we talked, it became clear that Ahmed felt defensive and was reluctant to fully express his need to relate more closely to his colleagues and acquaintances. He didn't give much of himself. 'It's my way of keeping myself safe,' he told me. He'd been very in-dependent much of his life and was doing well, but he'd reached a point where, although he had a lot of material things, he lacked the juice of life. He soon saw that his independence wouldn't get him further than he was now. To move forward he'd need to let down some of his barriers, be willing to show his true self more, and take some emotional risks. He began to realize that flow wouldn't just happen in his life, but he could initiate it by stepping out of his isolation. He needed to create it.

I asked Ahmed what he thought his greatest gifts were. 'Sensitivity and compassion, but I don't feel appreciated for them,' he replied. 'I guess it's hard to be appreciated for what you *don't* show to people!' I said, and he smiled. We worked on putting together a creative action plan, where he would connect with his creativity on a daily basis, and begin to take more emotional risks with people. As he started to move out of his comfort zone, he began to initiate that essential, creative flow that begins when we open ourselves to others. Before long, the new and rewarding relationships he had started to build created just the kind of energy and buzz that had been missing from his life. As he learned to trust, to share and to give, he experienced greater connections not only with his colleagues, but with the new business opportunities he was attracting.

Success based on fear will separate us because we are trying to defend ourselves, and many people find that success seems to isolate them from others. They need to compete at work and don't trust many people; they don't see friends and family as much as they'd like; they reach a plateau and try to draw up the ladder behind them so they can be safer. Once we've got what we thought we wanted, we need to keep other people away. Success based on love, creativity and abundance, however, will join us with others, will create partnerships, and will be a more fulfilling experience. It's time to redefine success as how connected we are.

Bola, a friend of mine from Alternatives who is African, told me once that in the tribe she grew up in nobody was allowed to do anything on their own. The spirit of co-operation was so strong that the tribe believed you should always be connected and supported by at least one person.

BECOME MORE UNIVERSAL AND LESS INDIVIDUAL

Ahmed, like so many of us, had created his own safe world where nobody could really get to him, or get *at* him. He'd thrived on his individuality until it became a straitjacket that hindered both inspiration and creativity. Too many of us live with the illusion that to be independent is to be strong. But, as the spiritual teacher Yasutani Roshi taught, 'The fundamental illusion of humanity is to suppose that I am here and you are out there.'

Separation, and the loneliness that it engenders, gives rise to depression, loneliness, struggle and conflict. It is a kind of hell that most of us at some time in our life will experience.

When we are tempted to fence off a piece of the whole, and call it our own, mine, self, our ego is gratified, but the price we can pay is estrangement and dissociation from the whole of creation. A healthier way to look at what we have is to see ourselves as stewards, temporary owners, looking after things on behalf on future generations. Think about it – everything that is ours now, won't be in 100 years' time.

Separation is at the core of any experience of lack and scarcity. We've believed it has been our safety, but it's actually been our downfall. The root of healing is joining, love, connection, reaching out, getting support, receiving, letting others help and being intimate. As we give up our defences and sense of separation, abundance will follow, as will inspiration and creativity. Love is inevitable, grace can flow in, aliveness can return. We are not separate and do not walk alone, it's just a trick of our mind. Every day say a little prayer, 'Today I am willing to give up the thought of separation, so that I can experience all the goodness of life.' My friend Robert Holden suggests affirming, 'All of heaven is in me, all of me is in heaven.' To be awake is to know that we are never separate.

BE YOUR SELF

It is important for us to understand the difference between being special, and being precious. Our unconditional self is absolutely amazing, powerful, precious, an expression of the whole of the universe. But it's nothing special, because that is within all of us. None of us are special: we are all equally endowed with this wonderfulness, we are all precious. But when we forget our true nature, we try to create something to make ourselves special. We try to fluff ourselves up, but nothing we can do can match what we already are. Our conditional self is anxious because its foundations are very shaky, in fact it has no true foundations at all. It's always trying to do something to prove itself. So it is always trying to make itself special – different from, better than, worse than or wiser than, sillier than, more important than, less important than, busier than, more successful than . . . The list can go on for ever. Do you recognize some of the ways you try to be special, different and separate from others?

In my coaching practice I find that many people I meet block their success by believing that they need to be special. They believe they need some special quality, something that they haven't got, some missing piece of the jigsaw. In fact, in order to succeed, we only need to be our natural self, and add love, self-belief, determination, and action.

Eugène Delacroix, the French painter and leader of the Romantic movement, expressed this concept beautifully when he said, 'What moves men of genius, or rather what inspires their work, is not new ideas, but their obsession with the idea that what has already been said is still not enough.' When you are inspired, it is not likely that you are going to come up with some brand new idea that no-one has ever thought of. But it may be a new idea for you, and it may be a new way of expressing an age-old universal idea. When I was writing my first book I thought, 'Why am I doing this? There are so many books out there already. Hasn't it all been said before anyway, perhaps better? Who needs my book?' Yet there are always new ways for us to express ideas. We need to value our way of doing, value our uniqueness, and know that there are people who enjoy and appreciate our way.

Dr Chuck Spezzano describes it this way, 'At the beginning of our spiritual journey, there is usually a lot of us (our ego) and very little of Heaven. As we travel along, there becomes less of us and more of Heaven.' Our sense of identity comes less from outer things, and more from our inner sense of knowing who we really are, and we root our identity in this. Best-selling author Dr Wayne Dyer said, 'All my life I wanted to be someone, and now I am, but it isn't me.' As we move along our path we can become personal embodiments of universal principles. The 12-step recovery programmes talk about principles, not personalities. There is nothing wrong with our individual personalities; this is merely a reminder also to focus on our universality, not just our individuality.

YOUR TRUE SPIRITUALITY IS ABOUT CONNECTING

Spirituality is not about withdrawing from the world and then coming back from the mountaintop to the boring world. It's about choosing to be authentic, joyful, alive and choosing to make connection in all areas of our life. It's about engagement and participation, not withdrawal.

WISDOM QUESTIONS

Think for a moment about a few of the happiest moments of your life. Haven't they involved a meaningful connection with someone or something?

* Who did you feel connected to?
* What was going on?
* What else contributed to this sense of connection?
* If you were on your own, did you have a precious connection with yourself?

EVERY ENCOUNTER IS A SPIRITUAL ENCOUNTER

In 1995 I went to India with my friends Robert, Miranda, Ben and Thérèse and for all of us it was both an adventure and a spiritual quest. We knew that India had been the birthplace of many religions and many gurus, so I think I expected the place to ooze with spirituality. Wrong! It did ooze with many things, but spirituality was only one of them! We got ripped off by Brahman priests, accosted by taxi drivers who wanted to take us to many places we didn't want to go to, we were all ill, and saw incredible poverty and incredible wealth. Call me naïve, but my initial reaction to this country was disappointment. And then moments of connection, kindness and love would happen out of the blue. Robert and I had taken to sitting down and drinking chai – Indian sweet tea – close to our hotel in Delhi. We loved watching the world go past, the colours, the smells, the sights. We got friendly with the chai seller, and what amazed me was that far from trying to rip us off, he wouldn't even take a tip from us. He was kind and gentle, and I saw more spirituality in him than in many of the priests we met.

I was reminded of the line in *A Course in Miracles* that reminds us 'Every encounter is a Holy encounter.' Whatever façade we are showing the world, whatever job we are doing, we are still God inside. In India they do recognize this. You have probably heard the word *namaste*, which is used as a greeting. Its literal meaning is: the place of divinity in me honours the place of divinity in you, and I honour the place where we are all One. Just imagine keeping that awareness every moment: that we are divine and everyone – literally everyone – is also divine. Mother Teresa said everyone she ministered to was Christ in another disguise.

True spirituality is about that place within us where we all are connected, we are part of one creation, and all differences, even religious differences, fade into insignificance. It's easy to look around at all religions, all attempts to be special, different and better, and be filled with despair. Gandhi captured this beautifully when he said, 'I believe that there is no religion in Heaven.'

HOW DO WE GET BACK INTO THE FLOW?

Flow is always there on the other side of stuckness. Our ego's agenda is always control, so when we are stuck it shows we are valuing control over our happiness.

- *Appreciation and gratitude* – find someone to appreciate, to thank and to give value to.
- *Inspiration* – ask your higher mind for an idea to move you forward.
- *Honest emotion* – don't deny how you feel, don't dump it on anyone, but be honest. Share your feelings with someone who you can trust to accept you and not judge you.
- *Taking risks* – do something that will stretch you emotionally, that may scare you but will get your emotion flowing again. Create intimacy with yourself or someone else.
- *Willingness to let a problem go* – be willing to make something else more important than the problem.
- *Asking for guidance* – our unconditional self will always tell us how to move forward, although we may not want to hear, or may censor what we hear.

THE POWER OF CONNECTING TO THE AUTHENTIC US

One of the challenging experiences in life is the dawning inner knowledge that the work you are doing and aspects of the life you are living are no longer *the true you*. We know then that we are being called to change, to be more authentic. This was David Whyte's experience. Born in Yorkshire, his life took him on a journey, via the Galapagos Islands as a marine biologist, to a life with his wife and child just outside Seattle. Later, working in an environmental organization, he gradually became more exhausted as he realized that he was not doing what he loved and that he wasn't really connected to himself and was only playing roles. He had lost himself and was asking himself that penetrating question *where's David?* A conversation with a friend helped him reconnect with his passion – poetry. It was the one thing that brought him alive and the only thing he was wholehearted about. Yet, understandably, he had always talked himself out of it. Poetry was not a career with which he could support a wife and family, he told himself. 'If ever I wanted to create a profound silence I would share with a friend my dream that I was thinking of becoming a full-time professional poet,' he said. But just because enough people agree with the rationalization of our fear, doesn't make it inevitable. There is always a power within us greater than any doubt or fear.

Over the coming months he began to rearrange his work around his own elemental waters as far as possible, doing all he could that was an expression of his truest self, and that connected him to himself. He did this knowing that he was creating the energy for a new trajectory, and to start a new conversation with and about the future. 'I decided two things. Firstly I would do at least one thing every day towards my future life as a poet. I calculated no matter how small a step I took every day, over a year that would come to a grand total of 365 actions towards the life I wanted. One thing a day is a powerful multiplier. Secondly, I told everyone I knew that I was moving towards becoming a full-time poet. I wanted them to hear it and hold me to what they heard. I was doing my damnedest to create a kind of gravitational field that would bring me increasingly to its centre. Three months later I found myself on a podium in front of 600 people at a conference, barely a quarter of the 365 actions completed. A speaker had cancelled, and one of my daily actions had brought me to the attention of a friend who ran the conference. From that infinitesimal but infinitely important connection, I and my work were catapulted into the visibility for which I had waited long years.'

ONE CONNECTION CAN TRULY CHANGE THE COURSE OF OUR LIFE

David has the ability to create connections between two apparently conflicting worlds – the world of soul and poetry, and the corporate world. He is a consultant to many Fortune 500 companies in America and businesses in Europe.

Today, David Whyte has had four books of poetry published and two books of non-fiction, *The Heart Aroused – Poetry and the Preservation of the Soul in Corporate America,* and *Crossing the Unknown Sea – Work as a Pilgrimage of Identity* which I helped to launch in 2001.

Whilst his outer achievement in the world is phenomenal, the greatest success has been his level of connection. Firstly there is the deep connection with his inner being, his unconditional self. Secondly, having made that inner connection, he made daily connections in the outer world, sharing his inner passion. In doing so he has connected with thousands of people in the soul-starved corporate world, and has helped them forge a deeper connection within themselves. Here is one of his poems:

The Opening of Eyes (after R.S. Thomas)

That day I saw beneath dark clouds
the passing light over the water
and I heard the voice of the world speak out,
I knew then, as I had before
life is no passing memory of what has been
nor the remaining pages in a great book
waiting to be read.

It is the opening of eyes long closed.
It is the vision of far off things

seen for the silence they hold.
It is the heart after years
of secret conversing
speaking out loud in the clear air.

It is Moses in the desert
fallen to his knees before the lit bush.
It is the man throwing away his shoes
as if to enter heaven
and finding himself astonished,
opened at last,
fallen in love with solid ground.

We should never, never, never underestimate the power of small beginnings. I was reminded of what the writer and advertising executive Bruce Barton said: 'Sometimes when I consider what tremendous consequences come from little things, I am tempted to think, there are no little things.'

OUR PURPOSE IS CONNECTION

A great problem we have is seeming to have many fragmented, conflicting and often opposing purposes, goals and beliefs. We want love but we want to be in control; we want to take risks but with the guarantee that they'll work out; we want to be in partnership but remain free. It can seem that many of our goals are irreconcilable. There is a way through – and that is through unity of purpose. The resolution of these conflicts can be found within our unconditional self. The love we are in essence has no conflict, and embraces everything, judging and excluding nothing. Our unconditional self sees that there are only two things going on – love or a call for love. It has X-ray vision that sees even what seems like an attack as a call for love.

'I was shocked,' Jean told me. 'Lena and I had been friends for ten years, we'd worked together for five and trusted each other enormously. Then she suddenly bawls me out, criticizes me for loads of things and storms out on me. I know she's pregnant, but I was so hurt. What should I do?' 'Sounds like she's in a lot of pain,' I said, trying to be as wise as I could! 'Can you sit down and talk with her and ask what is going on with her?'

A few days later Jean told me, 'We talked and Lena cried, telling me that for the first time in her working life she felt very vulnerable and scared. She is unsure how her pregnancy is going to affect her business and we are going through a tough time with one of our clients – so it was a culmination of lots of pressures. She acknowledges she is working too hard, but doesn't see any other way. We talked through a lot of stuff and in the end I felt much happier because we are communicating properly again and we have accepted each other's very different viewpoints and approaches to life. Funnily enough, we have ended up closer as a result of this.'

Often when we are scared, fearful and feeling vulnerable we lose the ability to communicate clearly. Suddenly those closest to us develop targets on their chests or backs with a sign saying 'Shoot here please!' Have you ever noticed that?

EMBRACE YOUR TRUE OCCUPATION – MIRACLE WORKER!

Knowing who you are and why you came here – that you are a child of God and that you came to heal and be healed – is more important than knowing what to do. What you want to do is not the important question. The question to ask is, 'when I do anything, how should I do it?' and the answer is 'kindly.' People don't normally associate business with kindness, because business has come to be regarded as simply a tool for making money. Miracle-workers are not in business only to make money; they are in business to inject love into the world.

MARIANNE WILLIAMSON, author of *A Return to Love*

Whatever job you do, your true occupation is invisible to our eyes. Your true occupation is that of a miracle worker – to bring love, joy, hope, vision and healing to a dark and fearful world. To be a miracle worker is to see everything – even violence, anger, pain, suffering, hatred or battles – as a cry for love. This is not an easy job! It calls us to develop that X-ray vision, seeing that only people in pain act in anti-social ways. We don't overlook their behaviour, but we understand the source of their motivation – pain and fear.

A *Course in Miracles* defines a miracle as 'a change in perception from fear to love'. To be a miracle worker does require seeing beyond appearances, seeing not what appears to be going on, but what is really going on. As we saw with Lena and Jean, Lena was very scared and anxious, so she went on the attack. Have you ever done that? Of course, I think we probably all have. Underneath, Lena was afraid, and needed love, support and understanding. This is not to condone bad behaviour, but to understand the motivation. All behaviour comes from feelings, which in turn come from our beliefs. A great question to ask ourselves when we don't like someone else's behaviour is, 'What must they be feeling in order to act in that way?' There are really only two things going on – perpetuation of the illusion of separation, resulting in pain, fear and guilt, or waking up to the truth of love. We are all here to wake up.

WISDOM QUESTIONS

When you attack someone, in your mind or in reality, or you yourself are attacked, ask yourself:

* How must you or they be feeling to act or want to act like that?
* What must they be believing about themselves to act in that way?

Attack, defence, counterattack, blame and condemnation are the currency of the ego. Think of any dispute in your work, in your life or in the world – in, say, Northern Ireland or the Middle East – and you'll find these dynamics at work. Nobody really listens to each other, nobody wants to truly understand; all they want to do deep down is unload their guilt by making the other person wrong. Our belief is that we are guilty, but we don't want to feel this guilt so we attempt to unload it by judging the other person. Often we don't even know that that is what we are doing. We know we feel bad, and believe it must be their fault. That's what enemies are for – to blame for our bad feelings.

Miracle workers know that guilt is not truth. They don't blame themselves, or anyone else, but know that there is another perspective, that of our unconditional self, which knows of no guilt, and sees no-one as being wrong. It just sees mistaken thinking and mistaken action that needs to be undone and healed in order to restore truth. We can't do this, it truly does need a miracle, but that is what is available when we ask for help of a higher power, and a higher perspective.

To become a miracle worker means to go beyond appearances and beyond the apparent laws and limitations of this world. *A Course in Miracles* teaches us that 'We are under no laws but God's'. We can and do dream we are subject to the world's laws of judgement, sin and condemnation. But there is another way of looking at this, and we can ask to be shown it. Our essential nature is not chained by the world, but is eternally free.

OUR FEAR OF CONNECTION

If feeling connected is so wonderful, why on earth do we resist it? Why do we create and maintain so many differences and conflicts, and keep ourselves separate? The answers are in our ego. The ego spins us all sorts of stories to try to convince us that separate is safe and connected is dangerous. One of the big fears it spreads is: get too close, and you'll lose yourself, you'll go into meltdown and disappear! And there is some truth in this. Our ego does need to die, but only to free us from the illusion of separateness.

The ego tries to offer us something that's a substitute for love, and that goes by several names – fusion and co-dependency are two of them. They are a form of closeness, but a form where we are really lost within a relationship, not knowing where we begin and someone else ends. Our boundaries are blurred. It's a bit like those three-legged races at school – we are emotionally tied to someone else, and we hold each other back through our dependency. Our past fusion with our family background can be very painful, so we end up running away from our pain by being very independent. We never want to have to go back there again. In order to create more intimacy in our lives, we may need to heal some of our old issues of fusion so that we can feel close without losing ourselves.

MAKING CONNECTIONS – SEND OUT SIGNALS

Are you letting people know who you really are, what you are really interested in and what you have to offer? My friend Karen, who used to work as a temporary secretary, often needed to be at different assignments every week. When she started a new assignment she would take a book with her, perhaps a popular personal development book of the time. Karen would deliberately leave the book in a conspicuous place, so that people who came to her desk would see it. She would notice how most of them would look at it; some would express interest or recognition and then she would strike up conversations with them, creating a level of interest and intimacy that was unusual in a workplace. Her books were her way of saying: 'This is who I am and what I am interested in', and sending out a signal which allowed her to connect with people in ever-changing environments.

> **WISDOM QUESTIONS**
>
> * What signals are you sending out to connect with people more?
>
> * Where could you go in order to meet more like-minded people, or connect with people more deeply?
>
> * Do you give people the opportunity to really know you? If not, why?

OUR LIFE EVOLVES THROUGH CONNECTIONS

Have you ever considered how your life has evolved? Who are the significant people you have met who have shaped the direction of your life? What were some of the defining moments of your life? Were there chance meetings, intuitions you followed through without knowing why? What connections have been significant in leading you to where you are? Sometimes we are so close to our life that we cannot see it clearly, but if we step back and look from a different perspective, beauty, magic and mystery are revealed.

Just after I moved into London from Essex in 1987, my father noticed that there was an evening event to launch an anthology of poetry. He thought I might be interested and so got me two tickets. The event was at St James's Church in Piccadilly, where I'd never been before. I went along and thoroughly enjoyed it, and while I was there, I heard about a programme called Turning Points that took place at the church, so I picked up a programme. I went along to Turning Points and met Malcolm Stern, the co-director. Immediately we became good friends, and he later invited me to become involved with the newly evolving Alternatives programme.

St James's has now been my spiritual home for the last 12 years, and my connection with Alternatives has been one of the most fundamentally transforming in my life, initially giving me the courage to quit the corporate world. I have made many friends from around the world, met teachers, run my talks and workshops, met my partner, promoted my book, and built a business, all through Alternatives. And it all happened because my father saw an advertisement in a paper for a book launch, and I chose to go.

WISDOM QUESTIONS

* Which people have been most influential in the evolution of your life?
* What books or events have been catalysts for your life moving in a new direction?
* What *chance* meetings or conversations have shaped the direction of your life?
* Trace back to the roots some of the major relationships in your life: what were the seeds?
* How have you been a catalyst for growth and change in others?
* What synchronicities or meaningful coincidences have been most important to you?

SEPARATENESS IS THE GREAT ILLUSION OF LIFE

In the Smithsonian Institution in Washington, DC, I experienced an extraordinary perceptual journey. On a film screen we were shown our planet – we could see it with our day-to-day perception. Then we were taken on a journey to the outer universe where we saw the galaxies, nebulae and black holes that we can't see with our eyes, but only with the help of radio telescopes. It was amazing. Then the journey took us to the subatomic world of electrons, protons and nuclei, and again this was phenomenal, revealing much that is normally hidden from us.

At the end of that experience, two things dawned on me. Firstly, how similar were the outer and inner universes. It was hard to know whether I was looking inwards or outwards. Secondly, wonderful as our perceptual apparatus, our eyes, ears and other senses are, they actually blind us to more than they reveal. There is so much more that we are not aware of. Our senses reveal a very thin slice of an enormous cake. I have heard both scientists and mystics describe how the universe is like a quantum soup, full of infinite possibilities, and it is how we are looking, and with what we are looking, that determines what we perceive and what we are aware of. Dr Deepak Chopra calls this the field of pure potentiality, and he teaches us that it is our perceptual apparatus that determines what and how we see. The world we think of as so solid and immutable looks totally different to an owl, a bee, a fish and a salamander, because each perceives differently. Literally, not just metaphorically, the world is not how it is, but how we are.

The mystic poet Jalaluddin Rumi described enlightenment as waking from a dream in which we live in a puddle, only to realize that we are part of the ocean, or discovering that we have been living in a tiny room within a vast and grand mansion. The mystic in you knows this already, it remembers the wholeness and inter-connectedness of all appearances. The mystic in us brings gifts from the other world to this one.

THE CORPORATE MYSTIC

I think many of us are corporate mystics, many more than we realize. Corporate mystics recognize the interconnectedness of everything behind the seeming diversity. They are spiritual leaders, inspired and inspiring, and visionaries. Intuitively they know what is true. Here are some thoughts about how to recognize the qualities of a corporate mystic:

- *Is your work about more than providing for your material needs and following your calling, or would you love it to be?*

- *Are intuition, inspiration, being creative, being authentic the driving forces in your work and life?*
- *Are you curious about what you can become?*
- *Do you want to bring out the best in yourself and others?*
- *Are you motivated to serve yourself and the world around you?*
- *Are you as interested in your being as your doing and achievements?*
- *Are you fascinated by ease and mastery rather than hard work, struggle and sacrifice?*

If any of these apply to you, then you are probably a corporate mystic! Whether we work for a company, are our own boss, or are even unemployed, as a mystic our work can be a vehicle for self-discovery and lifelong learning. This is what we yearn for. Corporate mystics are comfortable with their own spirituality, they come from a base of integrity and pursue their visions with passion and compassion, and in doing so evoke the full potential of themselves and those they come into contact with. They have managed either to maintain the sense of spiritual connection that they were born with, or to recover it later in life, having lost it in the world of work while providing for their material needs. They are comfortable with both commerce and spirituality, and have integrated them within themselves; they are their full and undivided selves. They are visionaries with their feet on the ground, with a broad view of life, valuing the switchboard operator as much as their biggest client, and seeing the innate value and humanity of every person.

OUR CALL TO SERVE

To serve means trusting the deeper movement of spirit in our lives. In the process of opening our hearts and minds, we discover an inseparable connection between ourselves and the world. Service expresses this connection, quickening the transformation of both character and community. For many of us it means choosing work imbued with the spirit of service, work that contributes to the healing of the world.

MICHAEL TOMS, author of *The Soul of Business*

What makes work meaningful? This is simple. It is recognition of our connectedness to each other in this world and that one of the biggest joys in life is when we lend a helping hand to another person. Meaningful work acknowledges our inherent desire to live an authentic life *and* make a positive contribution to the lives of others. We consciously want to do work that uplifts the hearts and minds of our clients, and true liberation comes when we understand that in serving our own needs we also can serve the needs of others.

Our work is our way of providing for ourselves and those we love, and when we dedicate it to love we are participating in the major task of the transformation of spiritual consciousness on this planet now. This is a reflection of our true spiritual power, the power of universal love within us. As Mahatma Gandhi said, 'If a single person achieves the highest kind of love, it will be sufficient to neutralize the hatred of millions.' This is how powerful we truly are. Transforming ourselves and serving the world are the same things.

At Alternatives we hosted a talk by author Peter Russell, who was talking at the launch of his latest book, *From Science to God*. Peter started his life with scientific training as a biologist and then developed an interest in spirituality and the study of consciousness.

He began by making a wonderful point: 'Science strives to answer the question *how did consciousness arise from the material world?* But it cannot answer that question, because it is the wrong question to ask. The true question to ask is *how did the physical world arise from consciousness?* Consciousness is the starting point, it came first.' In the West we are trained to believe in the material world as being the starting point, but in truth it isn't.

When Albert Einstein discovered that matter was actually energy in different form, he knew this heralded a complete overthrow of scientific thinking up to that point. But he knew that the old ways would take a long time to die and said, 'Everything has now changed except our thinking.' Dr Deepak Chopra has said that the discoveries of quantum physics and our understanding of consciousness herald 'The overthrow of the superstition of materialism'. *The Tibetan Book of Living and Dying* describes it this way: 'Matter is derived from mind, and not mind from matter.'

TRANSFORMING OUR MIND – OUR TOOLS OF PERSONAL ALCHEMY

One of the greatest discoveries of the last 100 years has been that we can, by conscious endeavour, change our mind and transform our thinking. Our being is fine – that is not the problem – it is our thinking that is the issue: how we think about ourselves and who we think we are. What we are trying to do is transform our mind so that we can think more with our spiritual mind, and less with our ego mind. We want to identify and weed out our fearful, guilty and wounded thoughts. We want to turn our lead into gold – this is personal alchemy. We have an unlimited power to evolve and blossom – to grow through life and not just go through life. It is lack of faith in our unconditional self that causes all our problems.

We grow naturally through our life experiences, life events, discussion, insights, books, talks, seminars, awareness. This is one level of change, while another is reached by counselling, coaching or some kind of cognitive therapy. Deeper levels of personal transformation are experienced through therapy, deeper emotional healing, loving and being loved. Some of my most profound shifts in consciousness have come through meditation, prayer, contemplation and miracles. I have found that some of my worst pain has dissolved through prayer, helping me find a peace that is not of this world and producing miracles in the outer world. Through prayer, love can transform us, shape us into what we truly are.

HANDLE WITH PRAYER

The ultimate success of your career will not be determined by credentials, backing or marketing techniques. It will be determined by your ability to access the spiritual Gulf Stream. Prayer makes that happen. Prayer is our way of signing up with the army of light and receiving its reinforcements on a regular basis . . . Our prayer is that excellence might come forth and serve the world. That is power. That is success.

MARIANNE WILLIAMSON, author of *Illuminata*

Prayer has been valued since the beginning of human history, and all traditions have their own ways of praying. It bridges the gap between separation and unity, and puts the power of creation behind all our efforts. Do you remember pictures from the early days of diving, showing the diver with air pipes that led up to the surface, where the air tanks were? That is how prayer works. It takes us from the state of separation and links us back to the state of unity. It puts us on the fast track of accelerated transformation.

Contemplation, meditation, quiet time and prayer seem to be making a comeback, if indeed they ever went away. They enable us to charge our spiritual batteries, transform our mind and develop our inner well-being, and they restore our connection to our unconditional self. We need to step back from the world regularly in order to function well in it. I was surprised to hear about the result of an employee survey in a large management consultancy in London. Employees were asked what changes would make their working environment a pleasanter place, and one of the answers was: a haven of peace, quiet and sanctuary! Accordingly, within their offices has been built a beautiful Zen garden, a place where no conversation or mobile telephones are allowed, just quiet. Here employees can recuperate, rest, think and be. Silence is restorative: it gives our activity and accomplishments greater depth and meaning, just as in farming fields need to lie fallow to be sustained and efficient – except that prayer is not passive, but active inner work. A symphony is made not by the notes alone, but by the silence between the notes. Our lives can become a cacophony of activity, and quiet can reconnect us to our roots and give us a new perspective.

A huge amount of scientific research demonstrates that when people learn to pray or meditate, and relax to a certain level, their state of consciousness actually has impact on their local environment: criminal activity goes down, economic activity increases, less people go to hospital for treatment. Isn't that amazing! Just as stress is contagious, so is peace and calm, and I would encourage all organizations to focus on this essential concept. If they did, productivity would increase, absenteeism would drop, and we'd be healthier and happier. If you are interested, one of the authorities on the subject is Dr Larry Dossy and two of his wonderful books are *Healing Words* and *Prayer is Good Medicine*. His scientific mind helps us truly understand the evidence.

Another study in a hospital covered 400 people who were admitted with suspected heart attacks. A group of people prayed for half of those who were admitted. The staff didn't know who was prayed for and who wasn't but the study showed that in the prayed-for group, fewer people died; they needed less medication and were able to leave hospital more quickly! Such studies show that our consciousness is connected to the consciousness of others, beyond time and beyond space. We are unconditionally connected.

We often use prayer as a last resort; when we are in trouble or when all our efforts haven't worked, we ask for help. We use prayer as an insurance policy to safeguard against something bad happening, or we're motivated by the fear of not praying. Yet more of us have grown up with an idea of prayer being like putting a coin in the cosmic slot machine. We try and strike a deal to get what we want. We are in a place of littleness, beseeching with the creator that we'll be good if we are given what we want. This is not a true understanding of prayer. We need to reclaim the gift of prayer for ourselves.

To truly pray is not just to ask for favours and dispensations from some capricious creator, but to remember our wholeness. In essence, we pray not for things but to see differently. True prayer asks for the blinkers to be removed from our perception and the light of truth to shine in, and it communicates from our separated mind to our wholeness. Our sense of ourselves mainly is of being separate from each other and from the creator. Prayer recognizes that this sense of separation is an illusion. Prayer doesn't bring us closer to God: it helps us remember we are already as close as we could ever be. It doesn't change God's mind, it changes our mind.

We may think that many areas of our life are inappropriate targets for prayer (the creator is far too busy to be concerned), or not spiritual enough to be worthy of prayer. One purpose of prayer can be to spiritualize – make a vehicle for love. There is no area of our life that can't have blessings bestowed upon it if we are willing to ask. What matters deeply to us matters deeply to God, with no exclusions.

WORK, REST AND PRAY

In the depths of the soul there is a profound desire which draws man from the visible to the invisible, to philosophy and the divine.

KAHLIL GIBRAN, author of *The Prophet*

One reason prayer is so important is that to think is to create, and to pray truly is to think with the thoughts of our creator rather than our separate ego. Whatever we think about regularly and consistently we create more of, and ultimately become, so prayer is about focusing on what is true about us, even if we are asleep to that truth. The thought that we are – in essence – totally lovable, whole, complete and lacking nothing will help us wake up to our true nature. We only really need prayer because we have forgotten or misunderstood the creator's will, and tried to replace it with our own will. The creator's will is already done – it is wholeness, love, joy, happiness, peace and truth. The purpose of prayer is to join with what already is, to replace our mistaken thoughts with true thoughts. Praying is simply thinking with the divine.

The greatest prayer of all is, 'Dear Creator, please let me realize that, in truth, there is nothing for me to pray for. Help me accept that through you I have all I need and lack for nothing.'

PRAYER IS BECOMING WILLING

Prayer is not the overcoming of God's reluctance, but the taking hold of God's willingness.

PHILLIP BROOKS,
1835–93, Protestant religious leader

The higher, universal power behind all life is the power that gives all to all; it is forever radiating, and doesn't know how to withhold or deny anybody anything. It doesn't play favourites, and only *we* can stop it, by standing in our own way. True prayer is a wonderful way to access this power. True prayer is affirming our willingness to receive and our own fullness.

Prayer is the medium of miracles. Prayer is the natural communication of the Created with the Creator.

A Course in Miracles

GRATITUDE – SEEING WHEN OUR PRAYERS HAVE BEEN ANSWERED

For many of us the problem is less about attracting to us what we need and want than about seeing it, wanting it and appreciating it when it is right in front of us! Our ego seems hard-wired for a kind of blindness, an ability to miss what is here, a failure to connect with and appreciate the blessings that exist right now in our lives. Our ego has an incredible ability to take our world and paint a picture of lack and scarcity, focus on what's missing, what's imperfect, who and what isn't enough. Rather than pray for things, we can pray for new spiritual eyes so that we can see what we already have. The choice to be grateful is a very powerful tool to change our perception.

We may have grown up with the attitude that if you are not grateful you will be punished and what you have will be taken away. Gratitude is a choice, not an obligation, and when we choose to see with the eyes of gratitude, we unfold an abundant world of gifts and love. It is less about what we have or don't have, and much more about how we view what we have. Gratitude is the choice to allow ourselves to feel the blessing of everything in our life now, and everything we have had – even everything we will have.

Getting and receiving are very different. Most of us are fed well, in the broadest sense – home, work, money and car. But often we don't receive the nourishment that is contained within what we have. We may suffer from the spiritual equivalent of a faulty digestive system. What should nourish us passes through us and we only get a fraction of its goodness. We need to learn to receive more deeply. Receiving accepts the essence of what we get and lets it nourish us.

When I left the corporate world, I rented my flat out, took a couple of months off and bought a round-the-world ticket before I fulfilled my dream of starting my own business. I had many adventures while travelling, and one that I didn't expect was the expanding sense of gratitude I felt on my travels across the USA, New Zealand, Australia, Singapore and Thailand. I had resigned from a high-flying job, given back my company BMW, left behind my lovely flat in Fulham, had no income, was burning up savings, and yet most days I felt content. Travelling on a Greyhound across America, with a backpack, a daypack, travel cheques, and some money in my pocket, I would feel incredible gratitude as I watched the world go by. I was happy. I felt a deep connection to myself.

I made a promise to myself that I have kept to varying degrees: that I would always remind myself of how little I actually needed to be happy. Much of my striving, I realized, had taken me away from happiness, not closer to it. I once saw a wonderful cartoon on this subject. It showed the entrances to two halls next to each other, with a sign above each door. The one saying WORKSHOP ON HAPPINESS had a long queue of people outside, while the other one, saying HAPPINESS, had no queue. It's strange how we often fool ourselves into believing that we have to keep working hard to earn and deserve things. I was fortunate that I could arrange my life to take that time out, but we must give ourselves the opportunity to remember that happiness is inside us all.

I made a decision that as much as I could I would keep my life simple by always focusing on what was important to me – my family, my friends, loving my work, having fun, healing, being a force for love and inspiration wherever I could. All else, as Princess Diana once said, is the froth. When seven years later I travelled to India, again I was reminded just how much I had to be grateful for. Again I vowed I would always count my blessings and remember just how privileged I was, living in the West.

VISIONARY LEADERSHIP

The rational leader has got business where it is – they will not be able to take it where it needs to go tomorrow. The leaders of tomorrow will need to be ordinary human beings with extraordinary talents. The new leader will be both inspired and inspiring. They will be able to find and hold a vision while enthusing others to share that vision.

RICHARD OLIVIER,
author of *Inspirational Leadership – Henry V and the Muse of Fire*

The word *manager* is derived from the old Italian word *maneggiare* and the French word *manège*, both meaning the training, handling and riding of a horse. It's interesting to think that the whole spirit of modern management is derived from the concept of getting on the back of a horse, digging your knees in and heading it in the right direction! It implies domination, control, command and the taming of wild energy. It implies that those being managed don't want to be managed, and have to be coerced. This is brilliant for riding a horse, but most people I know don't respond with the passionate and creative participation we are looking for when the boss climbs on top and shouts 'giddy up'! Of course we need people with management skills – we need managers to efficiently run finished cathedrals, but we also need inspired, imaginative and courageous leaders who can see the finished cathedral in the rock pile.

I was astonished to read an article in the *Harvard Business Review*, the bastion of tough business, which reported the results of a long-term study of leadership in a sample of outstanding organizations. What the researchers discovered they called *Level 5 Leadership*. Far from being the tough sterotypes of leaders we often have in mind, the leaders that achieved such incredible business results in the long term were described as 'building enduring greatness through a paradoxical mixture of humility and professional will . . . both shy and fearless'. We often think of being either strong or weak, defended or vulnerable, but we need to embrace and integrate all aspects of ourselves, knowing when each quality is appropriate.

Often the honest and real expression of what we think or feel is an enormous gift, and honest communication can be refreshing and even transforming. When we are honest, people can relate to us and connect with us. In a world obsessed with appearance and image, honesty can be like an oasis in a desert, and very disarming. It can inspire, give hope and courage to others, even bring ideas back to life and move lives forward. And it can take great courage to speak from our heart: our vulnerability when we do it connects us to others. The real beauty of being a visionary is that in a state of vision nobody loses, everybody is included. Here is some of Martin Luther King Jnr's famous speech, 'I Have A Dream':

I have a dream,
That one day on the red hills of Georgia,
The sons of former slaves and the sons of former slave owners,
Will be able to sit down at the table of brotherhood,
I have a dream.

I have a dream.

Just as I have a dream
My poor little children will one day live in a nation,
Where they will not be judged by the color of their skin,
But by their conscience and their character,
I have a dream today.

I have a dream

We will be able to speed that day,
When all of God's children, Black men, white men,
Jews and Gentiles, Protestants and Catholics,
Will be able to join hands and sing the words of the old Negro spiritual:
'Free at last! Free at last! Thank God almighty! We are free at last!'

That is a state of vision, that is connectedness, and it speaks to that part of us where we are all one.

We are fed up with boring work, and we can only live spiritless lives for so long. We want work that reconnects us with our heart, spirit and soul. We want leaders who care about profit, but aren't just interested in shareholder value, money, efficiency. We want people who care about the most important things in life – love, inspiration, caring, creativity, spirit, soul and energy. These things aren't measurable in any conventional way, but are crucial to the spirit of all work.

Personal responsibility and leadership is not about waiting for someone else to change and make the first move, but about being the change you want to see. It doesn't mean that you have to do it all, but you could kick-start the process, get things going. We are those leaders. Each of us is a leader in our own life, whether we know it or not. We all have the capacity for creativity within us. All we need is a place of safety, a place where we are truly encouraged to bring out our best, not just go through the motions – a place that allows us all to be leaders.

WHAT MAKES PEOPLE WANT TO SUPPORT A VISION?

People don't care how much you know, until they know how much you care.

ANON

The simplest answer is, 'When it comes from someone's heart, and we feel we are part of it, and when we sense a genuineness and honesty.' Companies come up with initiatives and vision statements, and then try to cascade them throughout an organization. Most people just smile politely, file them away and think no more of them; they know that within a few weeks or months there will be a new one, and nothing much really changes.

We want to have our heart touched, our imagination awakened. We want apathy and cynicism not to be the ultimate truth. We want something to truly believe in, something good. We want to be shown possibilities of courage and love.

How much of your life have you spent trying to be someone? A big part of the journey to unconditional success is our willingness to give up trying to be someone special, recognize that who we already are is more than enough, and simply be who we are in essence. When we are inspired, it is our universal spirit at work, not our ego, although our ego may soon kick in. Inspiration calls us to transcend our sense of smallness and separateness. Our ego tells us we need to regularly bolster up our sense of our self by gaining the approval and recognition of others. With our ego, everything is about *us*, our needs and our safety. Our ego's main questions are 'Who is my enemy?' 'How can I prevent myself getting hurt here?' 'Will they like me?' 'Will I get what I need?' 'What's in it for me?' 'How can I be right here?' 'How can I win?' Our unconditional self needs little or none of this. It simply is, and knows itself to be precious, without conditions.

WORKPLACE AS A COMMUNITY WHERE WE CAN GIVE AND RECEIVE GIFTS

Where productivity becomes god, each individual is reduced to a function. It would be wonderful if the workplace were a place of real inspiration with the work engaging your creativity. Your gift would be welcomed there, your contribution seen. Everyone has a special gift. Your life becomes happier when your gift can grow and come to expression in your place of work . . . There is no reason why every workplace could not begin to develop such creativity.

JOHN O'DONOHUE, author of *Anam Ċara*

At Alternatives we invited Thomas Moore, author of best-selling books including *Care of the Soul* and *Soul Mates*, to give a talk. He explained that he is often invited into organizations and asked for quick pointers and 'fix its' on how to bring soul into the workplace. There is no short answer but he knows he has to say something. His usual reply, he told us, is 'Friendship'. He explained that this answer usually meets a silence for a few seconds, and then a response like 'Is there anything else we can do to bring soul into work?'

Like the example I gave of the chickpea evening at Atsitsa in Chapter 3, we love to bring out our gifts, share them, and enjoy the gifts of others; it is one of our greatest joys. Wouldn't it be wonderful to have the workplace as a place of friendship, rather than of competition and control? A place of appreciation rather than belittling; celebration rather than appraisal; belonging rather than isolation; encouragement rather than withholding; trust rather than defensiveness; a place to see and be seen, rather than ignored?

ADDING ANOTHER DIMENSION TO THE FOCUS OF OUR WORK

For many of us, the focus of our work may have been one of the following:

- *doing the right thing, not making mistakes*
- *carrying on procedure*
- *being a yes person and sucking up to the right people*
- *putting up with being treated badly for the financial, material or status rewards*
- *being tough and scaring or belittling people into doing things that otherwise they wouldn't have done*
- *climbing a ladder to get to the top of something or somewhere*

Seeing the workplace as a community involves a shift in the purpose we give our work, away from the predominantly financial to embrace creative, personal and spiritual development. It involves the realization that results and achievements alone won't fulfil our heart; that it is the quality of relationships, how we learn and grow and how we see ourselves and others, that will lead to our ultimate fulfilment.

THE LEADERSHIP SHIFT – FROM ME TO WE

The frontier we are standing at is the opportunity to move from *me* to *we*. This is the new paradigm. Unconditional success is not about one or some of us winning individually at the expense of others. It's not about reaching the summit of a mountain and leaving the pack behind, but all of us reaching the mountaintop, the summit of higher spiritual consciousness, together. As we reach it, we want to help others; as others reach it, they help us up.

The ego says that when we hit a formula for success we should immediately copyright it, protect it, withhold it unless we get something in return, sue anyone who copies it and look after our own interests above all others. Our unconditional self has another take. Its natural response is: share it! let everyone have it, let as many people as possible benefit, serve the greatest good. Our ego immediately translates this into sacrifice, putting others first and leaving ourselves out of the question. But what we are really talking about here is the truest win/win, true abundance.

There needn't be a conflict between whether I look after my interests or the interests of others. Unconditional success is looking after both. Creating what we need and serving the greater good is the unity beyond the seeming conflict. This is one of the greatest secrets our ego keeps from us – what we accept first for ourselves and share with others is what we truly receive. True giving and true receiving are both love's expression. Starving people have a hard time sharing, so we must look after our own needs first in order to see beyond ourselves. We must, of course, recognize that we will never be fully fed; we are partially fed, but the partially fed can serve admirably. But the more we receive, the more we share, the more the doors of Heaven will open to share the abundance with us. Start sharing whatever you have now: not just money, but ideas, love, appreciation, humour, and your dozens of other gifts.

WISDOM QUESTIONS

* What are you withholding that you'd love to share more of now?
* How could you share it more?
* Why wouldn't you?
* Why will you?

Our desire to serve, to give beyond ourselves, is our most common and natural response. One of the biggest joys in life is when we lend a helping hand to another person, even in the tiniest way. When we see a beautiful sunset we don't say, 'Nobody look!!' Our response is to say, 'Wow, look at that, everybody. Isn't it beautiful?' We want to share what we've found that is beautiful, and what is precious within us. But love demands no sacrifice. We don't have to set up a stall saying 'Everything free, please help yourself, take whatever you need and don't worry about me.' Martyrdom is not required, that is the old paradigm.

Only those who have learned the power of sincere and selfless contribution experience life's deepest joy – true fulfilment. We all respect those who consistently give of themselves, and we all have that capacity. Life is a gift, and we have the responsibility to give something back. We can demonstrate our unlimited capacity to care. We can all make a difference in the world. Whatever it says on our desk or door, part of our spiritual job title is to give.

OUR DESTINIES ARE INTERCONNECTED

When I started out on the path of loving my work and teaching on the subject, I hit a huge layer of guilt within me: how can I be happy in work when so many people *aren't* happy? I thought. My deepest fear was people saying to me: it's all right for you, you don't know my boss/haven't got my responsibilities/haven't got my problems. But I began to realize that my best gift was not to suffer.

I knew enough about suffering in my work, I'd never forget that! My gift was to find happiness for myself, and to want to inspire and help others find their happiness too.

Our success can be an inspiration because when we fulfil our destiny, it helps other people find theirs. The light that we shine in our lives can illuminate the lives of dozens or even thousands of others. Another way of viewing our journey of unconditional success is to describe our universe as a big jigsaw puzzle, with a unique shape cut out for each and every one of us, a little space in the cosmos that only we can fill. The miracle comes when, as we find our place in the jigsaw puzzle, we form the pattern for others to find theirs. When one person's success in living authentically can make such a difference to the planet, what could we create when many more of us achieve unconditional success? Fulfilling our own destiny is not selfish.

When we find and follow our calling, it has a profound impact on many other people, often in ways that we will never even be aware of. It all starts with us saying 'yes!' and keeping going through our resistance. In many stories, when the King or Queen is asleep, everyone in the kingdom is asleep too. When the King or Queen awakens, those around them awake. The buck starts here, with each one of us. The author Saul Bellow says that the hardest thing in life is waking up and staying awake, but we owe it to ourselves and to each other to be awake, and to be authentic. I love the poem 'A Ritual to Read to Each Other', by William Stafford:

> *If you don't know the kind of person I am*
> *And I don't know the kind of person you are*
> *A pattern that others made may prevail in the world*
> *And following the wrong god home we may miss our star.*

For there is many a small betrayal in the mind,
A shrug that lets the fragile sequence break
Sending with shouts the horrible errors of childhood
Storming out to play through the broken dyke.

And as elephants parade holding elephants' tails,
But if one wanders the circus won't find the park,
I call it cruel and maybe the root of all cruelty
To know what occurs but not recognise the fact.

And so I appeal to a voice, to somewhere shadowy,
A remote important region in all who talk:
Though we could fool each other, we should consider –
Lest the parade of our mutual life get lost in the dark.

For it is important that awake people be awake,
Or a breaking line may discourage them back to sleep;
The signals we give yes or no, or maybe –
Should be clear: the darkness around us is deep.

We need each other!

Our destiny is to choose love over fear, and to have courage in the face of all our fears and doubts.

•

One of our great joys is the joy of growth, being at the cutting edge of our life by daily moving into a greater expression of our authentic self.

•

We can bring home the parts of ourselves that we have judged and buried, and integrate their power into our life, and in doing so move from hard work alone into mastery and even miracles.

•

Enough love will undo all limits, all pain and all suffering, and there is a spiritual solution to every problem in our life.

7

UNCONDITIONAL LOVE

Though the human body is born complete in one moment, the human heart is never completely born. It is birthed in every experience of your life. Everything that happens has the potential to deepen you. It brings birth to new territories of your heart.

JOHN O'DONOHUE, author of *Anam Cara*

You and I are destined to choose love over fear; whether we know it or not, that's why we are here; it is our purpose and our destiny. It's not a one-off decision, but a daily, hourly and moment-by-moment choice. When we choose to put the mystical power of love at the centre of our work, success and career, we have put our self on the spiritual fast track. We have aligned our self with the universe's great power and life's greatest mystery. When we invite love to be at the centre of our life, we have invited the mystical third to be present, and all Heaven will be let loose! It is revolutionary. It allows us to step outside our personal identity, culture and religion to experience more directly the great mystery. We have asked that we be transformed and pulled on to the path of courage and trust.

BEING AT THE CUTTING EDGE OF OUR LIFE

I had been invited to make a presentation to a group of chief executive officers of multimillion-pound companies on the subject of fulfilment at work. I was terrified! I hardly slept the night before for worry. All my fears had risen to the surface. I told myself I was naïve, stupid, I should never have got involved, who am I to think I can do it, they are only interested in money . . . do you know that kind of inner dialogue? The chairman hosting the session had suggested that the group would respond well to being challenged so I asked my intuition what a suitable challenge would be. The answer came, 'Give them some soul. Read them some poetry!' and a particular piece came to mind. I had one of those moments where I wanted to ask, 'Is there another intuition I can talk to?' Reading poetry to millionaire businessmen? Still, I thought to myself, I do teach that we should trust intuition, perhaps I had better practise it!

When I reached that part of my presentation where I was going to read the poem, I had another of those inner dialogues which went something like 'You don't have to read that poem. They never knew you were going to, so if you don't, you won't have to face that fear and they will be none the wiser! If I blow it then they'll tell every other CEO in the UK and I'll never work again . . . But I want to be true to myself and not wimp out . . .' When I asked the voice of trust to guide me, it said 'Just read it!' I had what I have come to call a near-life moment – when I am scared to be really authentic, yet excited, all in one moment. A cutting-edge, love or fear moment. So I explained what I was going to do, took a deep breath and started to read the poem. As I began, my fear subsided a little. As I connected with the words I was reading, my self-consciousness gradually disappeared. It took about two minutes and at the end I looked up and – they were still there! Many asked what the poem was and I told them it was from a book by Oriah Mountain Dreamer called *The Invitation*. Several asked if they could have a copy, and as I had brought some with me, each of the 10 men took one. We had another hour together after that, and the quality of our time shifted several gears. We became much more honest, discussing some of the joys and challenges that they were facing, and what really gave their lives meaning and purpose.

On the train home I felt exhausted and happy, having stretched myself. Within a couple of hours I'd had a telephone call from the chairman of the group, thanking me for the presentation, telling me that he had initiated dialogues with several of the men that he hadn't been able to up to now. Here is the poem.

The Invitation

It doesn't interest me what you do for a living.
I want to know what you ache for, and if you dare to dream of meeting
your heart's longing.

It doesn't matter to me how old you are.
I want to know if you will risk looking like a fool for love, for your
dream, for the adventure of being alive.

It doesn't interest me what planets are squaring your moon.
I want to know if you have touched the centre of your own sorrow, if
you have been opened by life's betrayals or have become shrivelled and
closed by fear of further pain.
I want to know if you can be with joy, mine or your own, if you can
dance with wildness and let the ecstasy fill you to the tips of your
fingers and toes without cautioning us to be careful, to be realistic,
to remember the limitations of being human.

It doesn't interest me if the story you are telling is true.
I want to know if you disappoint another to be true to yourself; if you
can bear the accusation of betrayal and not betray your own soul; if you
can be faithless and therefore trustworthy.

I want to know if you can see beauty, even when it's not pretty, every
day, and if you can source your own life from its presence.

I want to know if you can live with failure, yours and mine, and still
stand on the edge of the lake and shout to the silver moon, 'Yes!'

It doesn't interest me where you live or how much money you have.
I want to know if you can get up, after a night of grief and despair,
weary and bruised to the bone, and do what needs to be done to feed
the children.

It doesn't matter to me who you know or how you came to be here.
I want to know if you can stand in the centre of the fire with me and
not shrink back.

It doesn't interest me where or with whom you have studied.
I want to know what sustains you, from the inside, when all
else falls away.

I want to know if you can be alone with yourself and truly like the
company you keep in empty moments.

When we experience that genuinely exciting, cutting-edge moment in our life, we can never be bored. It's not just adrenalin, but the joy of true growth. It's the daily and hourly opportunity to bring our authentic self to life. When we choose our authentic self we're taken on an upward spiral, we're in the flow, we're evolving *and* transforming in love and consciousness, and having fun. This is available to all of us, when we listen and honour those inner promptings and the call of our heart. This is a life of courage. As Eleanor Roosevelt said, 'You gain strength, experience, and confidence by every experience where you really stop to look fear in the face . . . You must do the thing you cannot do.'

Courage is not the absence of fear – courage is acting in the face of fear. Those of us who do less with their lives are just as scared as those of us who take major risks. It's just that the first group get scared over smaller things. Why not get scared over something significant? We all get afraid, but each of us is afraid of different things. To most of us, walking outside our home is natural; to an agoraphobic this could be an act of supreme courage. Some of us are scared of success, to others it is natural; some of us are scared of being alone, and others love it. We can learn not to judge our fear, but simply recognize and accept that we all have our own fears, and have the courage to move beyond it.

We can become warriors of the spirit, and it has nothing to do with waging war against others. Being a warrior means having the courage to know who we are, through and through. As authentic warriors we recognize around us the inherent basic goodness of life that is more profound and more enduring than all the ephemeral ups and downs. As warriors we never give up on anything, including ourselves.

Perhaps one of the most courageous things we can learn to do is live life as fully as possible in a world of uncertainty. We can never eliminate uncertainty, we just need to learn to live with it and develop our sense of courage. In fact, whether we know it or not, we all live in faith and courage every day, navigating uncertain waters and unconsciously trusting our inner knowing, our intuitions.

WISDOM QUESTIONS

﹡ Where are you aware that you are allowing your fear to shrink your life?

﹡ Where are you being called to be a warrior of the spirit right now; what big fear are you facing?

﹡ Intuitively, what gift is on the other side of this? What joy and freedom are you being offered if you have the courage to reach out beyond your fear?

SUCCESS IS A CHOICE AND THE CHOICE TO KEEP CHOOSING!

Success is available in every moment. But success is also the choice to face, accept and embrace our feelings of failure, of competitiveness, of guilt, of scarcity, of unworthiness. We can feel guilty but choose our innocence; feel angry yet choose peace; we can feel unworthy, and choose to love ourselves; we can feel there isn't enough and still choose abundance. That is success: choosing and choosing again. Sometimes those choices feel like the hardest thing in the world to make, and often we can feel they are impossible to make.

GET SPECIFIC!

Write a list of your specific fears of what might happen. Write as many as you can think of: losing a partner, losing a job, a limb, being childless, getting married, getting divorced, and so on. Naming them diffuses some of their power. They are brought from the darkness of our unconscious to the light of our awareness. Some of our fears are deeply buried, and throwing light on them weakens them.

BUILD YOUR 'FEAR-DISSOLVING' MUSCLE

It's so easy to put off facing a fear until 'one day' arrives. Make today the day – every day – that you set a little goal that will stretch you, that will involve you going through a fear and coming out the other side. Be kind to your fear: don't fight it, but move with it.

Decide what you will choose instead or fear. By focusing on what is on the other side of fear, we have something to aim at, to make more important than the fear itself. It is love, faith, it is the creative power behind the whole of life. Remember that your unconditional self knows nothing of fear. This part of us is always there for us. We always have a choice, and we can choose our way back to peace.

We all feel fear and anxiety, and the greatest courage is to choose love when we are not feeling powerful. Don't wait until you are not afraid – you could still be waiting on your deathbed – but act while you are doubting or afraid.

We may need to remind ourselves of this. We may have developed habits, strong grooves in our mind that are well worn. We may be used to listening to our conditional self, but less so to our unconditional self. We can start asking ourselves, is this my ego or my higher mind talking? In any situation where we feel conflict or doubt, a good technique to practise is to ask ourselves: what would love say? What does love want to happen here? This means developing a new habit, and breaking an old one.

Our life shrinks or expands in proportion to our courage in facing and dispelling our fears. We cannot escape fear. We can only transform it into a compassion that accompanies us on all our adventures. We can take our fear and turn it into growth and into maturity. We gain strength and confidence every time when we really stop to look fear in the face, when we do the thing we thought we could not do. This is not to do with being macho or tough – just being true to our heart.

The path of unconditional success is the expanding realization that we are safe, that ultimately there is nothing to fear. As Franklin Roosevelt reminded us, 'The only thing we have to fear is fear itself', but to most of us fear feels very real. We are not talking about denying fear, but recognizing that fear is never the only option; there is always another choice. There is always that holy and whole place inside us where peace and certainty abide, and where everything is OK. It's there even when we aren't aware of it. The peace inside us never goes away, even if we can't feel it.

HOW CAN WE STAY SUCCESSFUL AND EVOLVE?

I was invited to be part of the BBC Radio 4 *In Business* programme on career change and work satisfaction. I thoroughly enjoyed giving a 30-minute interview to the presenter, which when broadcast turned out to be reduced to two 45-second soundbites! What stunned me was that over the following weeks and even months a considerable number of people contacted me, although the BBC had not broadcast any contact details. I met a number of them, and was astonished at how a few words had had so much impact. When I asked them what it was that had struck them they mostly responded, 'Your description of helping someone plan their escape route.' I had told of a coaching session I'd had with someone who wouldn't give me any information before we met. When we met he said, 'I am the MD of a successful merchant bank, and I want out. Can you help me plan my escape route?' and we spent a couple of hours doing just that.

The people I met after the BBC broadcast were mostly professional and successful in the world's eyes, but wanted a major course adjustment, or even a new course. I really started to think about success and why so many people want to escape from it when they have achieved it. How can we be successful *and* retain personal freedom?

Success can be strange: once it arrives it can alter us. We may have been creative and taken risks in order to become successful, but once we are, we stop being creative and stop taking risks, not wanting to jeopardize what we have achieved, even though it worked for us in the past. Our success then becomes our prison.

Over 10 years, Jim had built up a global trading division within a bank from 20 people to over 800, and his next step would have been to the board of the bank. 'I don't want to go on the board,' he said. 'Most of my work is now ceremonial – being seen in the right places, by the right people, and doing the right things, and I am quite bored and unfulfilled. I miss the days when we were starting out.' The pioneering spirit that had created his success had got lost in the routine of running what he'd created. He was hoping to give it all up to join a smaller bank, to start a new division and rekindle his creative spirit. He wanted to get back on his evolutionary trail, and experience adventure again.

THE COURAGE TO MOVE FROM HARD WORK TO MASTERY AND EVEN MIRACLES

There are South Sea islanders who can navigate for 1,000 miles with no sun, moon or stars, under totally overcast skies. They know their position at any moment by the size, shape and formation of the waves. That's mastery, and it stems from a deep connection with ourselves and our environment.

Our culture is dominated by the belief, which so many of us have inherited, that life is a struggle, and that nothing is, or should be, easy. If it's easy, we've cheated. We need to be constantly vigilant, constantly busy and pushing ourselves; we can't relax, and if we aren't pushing all the time, nothing, or at least not much, will happen. We believe that anything worthwhile must have involved lots of struggle to make it happen. Struggle makes us valuable human beings and earns us merit points. This gives rise to a type of consciousness that many of us live with, a consciousness based on fear.

This is not the complete truth, but it can take courage to realize this when it is so ingrained. The work ethic is a smokescreen to cover our true power. It hides the fact that our greatest power is not in hard work, but in mastery, and even ease and miracles. Mastery starts within, and the more we are aware of the power of love and the vast possibilities that exist within us right now, the more we are able to manifest greater things in our life. We allow success to happen, rather than tire ourselves trying to make it happen. In mastery, one decision made from the centre of our being can move our life in a whole new direction; one decision can bring about a whole new level of success, creating new opportunities and greater abundance. In mastery we create success even when we are taking time out.

HEALING THE STRUGGLING ETHIC – FROM EFFORT TO ALLOWING

Our struggle is actually resistance, and is not the only option. When we struggle so much we are almost too tired to enjoy the fruits of our success, so a major motivation is being able to retire, give up doing what we've had to do to be successful. Life can be easy, but it will take all our faith and trust to let it be; it might mean stepping through lots of inner voices of fear and doubt. It means we will need to stop trying so hard to do it all ourselves, and let it be done *through* us and not *by* us. Our struggle covers old wounds, old pain, old distrust, and is reminding us that there is another way.

SUCCESS IS NOT JUST HARD WORK

Life is always flowing, creating is always creating, abundance is always bringing forth new life. That is the natural order of things. Grass doesn't struggle to grow, it just grows; the sun doesn't try to shine, it just shines. Mostly we have become accustomed to pushing against this kind of natural order. We have learned to strive and make life difficult for ourselves. Once we learn to trust in ourselves and others we see that we don't have to be in charge of the flow of life – life itself takes care of that. Our purpose is to move ourselves back into alignment with the flow.

Why do we push ourselves so hard? I believe this stems from our survival instincts and our fear that, if we don't work hard, then

- *nothing will happen for us*
- *we'll be found out to be lazy or be seen as a failure*
- *life will overwhelm us*
- *we won't be employable*
- *we can't succeed*

The Protestant work ethic has enshrined the idea that we are not good enough. That slothfulness is a sin. Old sayings such as 'The Devil makes work for idle hands' also encourage us to keep working hard, and to feel guilty if we don't. Add this to family, societal and employers' messages and we may soon believe that our value is intrinsically linked to our willingness and capacity to work hard and achieve. But however well we have been conditioned, success is not about how hard we work. Success is about being fulfilled, creative and authentic. It is about experiencing joy and happiness.

So much success is about having great expectations of ourselves. Then when we succeed we succeed in becoming good people. But true and unconditional success is about being authentic; with authenticity comes greater honesty with ourselves and others, and the abandonment of fear.

In a consciousness of fear, we are always fighting to get; in a consciousness of love, we are always cultivating our willingness to receive. We don't push to make things happen, we get clear on our intention, remove resistance and move forward with confidence. We move from chasing success to attracting and being success.

DEEP DOWN, WE MAY BE TERRIFIED OF GREATER SUCCESS

Although success is a gift and a joy, many of us are terrified of it, sometimes without even realizing it. There are deeper and usually hidden parts of our mind that equate greater success with being overwhelmed, becoming greedy, not being able to trust people, losing freedom, time, integrity or other forms of loss. Without thinking, but intuitively, ask yourself the following questions:

1. *Why wouldn't you want to be more successful?*

2. *What are you scared you would lose if you were more successful?*

3. *What pain might you suffer if you were more successful?*

4. *Who might you have to take care of if you were more successful?*

5. *Who would you have to stop blaming in order to be more successful?* ·

6. *What problem would you have to let go of in order to be more successful?*

7. *What control would you have to relinquish?*

8. *What do you believe you'd turn into if you became more successful?*

THE VOICE OF 'NO!' TO SUCCESS

All of us have the voice of 'No!' in us, and each of us has our own wounds and anxieties. In all of us there is a belief that more success will somehow mean more pain or the loss of something that we hold precious. Of course we want to save ourselves from pain, so we resist greater success. Below are some of the most common fears that I have discovered:

- *I'll look stupid*
- *I'll lose money*
- *No-one will come along*
- *I'll be betrayed*
- *I'll be attacked and criticized*
- *It will all fall apart*
- *I'll have no support*
- *I'll be overwhelmed*
- *I'm fooling myself*
- *I'll get it wrong, it will never work*
- *I won't be enough*
- *I'll fail*
- *It'll be too good*
- *Why bother?*
- *I need to be more special than I am*
- *There'll be a price*
- *I couldn't cope*
- *I won't be taken seriously*
- *Who do I think I am?*
- *I'll lose everything*
- *Are you crazy, are you out of your mind?*
- *I'm being naïve*
- *I won't really help*

Add the voice of your own specific 'Noes!' here too.

THE VOICE OF 'YES!' TO SUCCESS

Sometimes the voice of 'No!' is so loud that we can easily forget the voice of 'Yes' that is always speaking to us too. We give less attention to what can go right, to the joy and fulfilment being offered to us, to the deep sense of satisfaction, to the simple peace available. We neglect the mental, emotional, spiritual, financial and other material benefits being offered to us.

Here are some offerings from the voice of 'Yes':

- *I'll be fulfilled*
- *I'll make money*
- *I'll help so many people*
- *It will be fun*
- *I'll grow creatively*
- *So many more good things will happen*
- *I'll be in the flow*
- *I'll fulfil my destiny*
- *I'll know love and true success*
- *I'll be inspired*
- *I'll be able to have a better life*
- *It's what I've always wanted*
- *I'll be so proud*
- *I can do it*
- *Go for it*
- *I'll grow in self-belief and self-respect*
- *It'll be so true*
- *It's who I am already*
- *It'll bring colour to my life*
- *It's OK to shine*
- *I need a purpose*
- *It will release my life's creativity*
- *I'll be free*
- *I can travel all over the world*
- *There'll be new adventures*
- *There'll be so much love*

Write down your unique 'Yeses!'

I think our focus is often biased towards listening to the voice of 'No' rather than the voice of 'Yes'. Then our thinking and feeling become skewed, we don't give our attention to the possibility of joy, happiness and the deep fulfilment of our destiny. When we also focus on those we are more likely to compel ourselves forward.

DISCERNING OUR TWO TYPES OF RESISTANCE TO WHAT IS TRUE FOR US

We have two types of resistance running within us:

- *The resistance that arises because something really isn't us. We are pushing ourselves to do something we think we ought, must or should do.*
- *The resistance that arises because something is so true for us, and then our ego kicks in to try to stop us going there.*

It's crucial that we learn the difference between the two. Often I meet people who say 'I'd love to do that, but it's so scary that it can't be right.' An important question to ask is: 'If I wasn't feeling scared, would I want to do this?' Invariably the answer is 'Yes' – a strong indicator that you simply need to learn to raise the courage to deal with the fear.

THE COURAGE TO TRUST

Trust is such a big lesson because it involves us being willing to relinquish control, but not responsibility. Trust is allowing our life to unfold and evolve on a daily basis, for our path to reveal itself moment by moment, for insights to emerge at each step of the way. When we trust we set our sails in a particular direction and move forward. Trust usually involves us letting go of something.

Trust is not naïvety. You may have heard the story of the man who has complete faith. When his neighbourhood is flooded he doesn't worry, he simply prays for help and deliverance. Rescuers in a boat come by and ask if he wants help. 'No thanks, I have faith.' The flood waters rise, and the boat comes by again, but he still refuses help. Eventually he has to go to the roof to rise above the water, but when a helicopter flies over offering to help, he refuses it too, and a few hours later drowns. When he gets to Heaven, God meets him and the man is furious. 'I had complete faith in you, and you let me drown. How could you do that?' God responds with complete love and says, 'But I sent two boats and a helicopter. What more did you want!' Trust is knowing that we are constantly surrounded by help and support, visible and unseen. It's just that we may not see it or be willing to receive it.

What are we really doing when we truly trust?

- *We are letting life support us rather than controlling life.*
- *We are letting down our defences.*
- *We are listening to our inner guidance system and following what we are called to be, say and do.*

We often have a list of requirements that we demand be met before we will trust. Which of these can you identify with?

- *I'll trust soon.*
- *I'll trust when this situation resolves itself.*
- *I'll trust when I am sure.*
- *I will trust when they demonstrate they are trustworthy.*
- *I'll trust when I have sorted out my money.*
- *I'll trust when I feel more secure.*

WISDOM-ACCESSING QUESTIONS

By now I imagine you are ripe for greater change. I've always liked the idea that questions are the answer, and the answers you need for your next step into unconditional success are within you right now. Questions are a key to unlocking your innate potential. Below I set out a list of wonderful questions that will get your mind and heart focused on your next steps.

YOUR CALLING:

- *What do you want next?*
- *What is your dream?*
- *What wonders are ahead for you?*
- *What has to happen for you to take the next step?*
- *When will you take that next step?*

YOUR CREATIVITY:

- *What gift are you being called to embrace next?*
- *What do you most need to receive now?*
- *What is your next step of creativity about?*
- *In what way are you being called to shine?*
- *What would make you most happy now?*

YOUR COURAGE:

- *What are you most afraid of having next?*
- *What are you most afraid of losing?*
- *What is it costing you not to move on?*
- *What would make the most difference for you now?*
- *What is true for you right now?*

YOUR SUPPORT AND ENCOURAGEMENT:

- *What support do you need now?*
- *Who can you get that from?*
- *What decisions do you need to make?*

LETTING GO:

- *What are you willing to give up?*
- *What do you need to complete?*
- *What do you want to release and let go of?*

EMBRACING SUCCESS:

- *What is the best that could happen now to fulfil your needs?*
- *What would delight you and make you feel truly blessed?*
- *What are you willing to receive now?*

SELF-BELIEF:

- *What do you need to believe about yourself now?*
- *What are you being called to believe about life?*
- *What limiting belief has outgrown its usefulness?*

ACTION:

- *What can you no longer put off doing?*
- *What small step do you want to take now?*
- *What action could you take in the next 10 days that would most enhance your self-esteem and self-worth?*

These questions will help you shape your perception of precisely where you are and what is next for you to do and be. Capture the answers that come to you in your journal and perhaps take on a few questions as a new project.

INNER SUCCESSES

When you were a child, you got report cards filled by teachers to tell you how you were doing in school. It's difficult to make the transition from external judgement to internal acceptance, but it's a journey we all must make to reach our essential selves as adults.

SARA BAN BREATHNACH, author of *Simple Abundance*

Much of our history of success is based on external recognition, judgement or approval – what others say about us, tell us about ourselves, or the way they evaluate us. Our ego is preoccupied with 'What have I got to show for my life?' and needs material things to support its sense of self. A large part of the journey of un-conditional success is the shift to inner acceptance and knowing we are aligned with ourselves and only *we* can know that. If success is about more than certificates, money in the bank, elevation up the ladder, what is it about? How does our heart, soul or spirit define success? Sometimes it is the inner and core work that we do, the shifting of attitudes, the emotional healing, the releasing of fear, that are our truest successes. The world doesn't often see those, and doesn't give us a certificate or a fanfare. Yet those inner shifts are precious and *we* need to learn to recognize them and be willing to value them. We can learn to appreciate *ourselves* for our courage, appreciate ourselves for who we are and who we become, and the contribution we make to life.

When we are fulfilled, we feel a kind of blessing, that there is nothing higher that we could ask for. Curiously, this begets a desire to go deeper into our inner well and pull up more pails of creativity and inspiration; it is regenerative. Like a comet, each fulfilled idea leaves a trail of other ideas in its wake.

A WORLD BEYOND FEAR – GO TO WORK AND SPREAD LOVE

Do what you love. Do what makes your heart sing. **And never do it for the money.** *Don't go to work to make money, go to work to spread joy. Seek ye first the kingdom of Heaven, and the Maserati will get here when it is supposed to.*

MARIANNE WILLIAMSON, author of *A Return to Love*

M. Scott Peck, author of *The Road Less Travelled*, wrote a follow-up book called *A World Waiting To Be Born*. Inside all of us, he suggests, there is another world, in embryo. It is a world based on love, inspiration and vision, not fear or guilt. But for many of us the major purpose of work has been material survival – earning the money that we need to live and providing for others. For many generations, that may well have been the aim of work – we work or we starve. Today we still need to provide for ourselves, but we have so much more opportunity to work in ways that we'd find fulfilling if only we could leave behind our inherited negative conditioning and lack of self-belief. In many of my workshops I ask, 'What are the most unhelpful beliefs that we have grown up with around work?' and earning money is the only major purpose of work that is always a top belief. We often don't even allow ourselves to think that there could be another purpose. Or we tell ourselves that when we have sacrificed and been successful, then we'll do something creative, loving or wonderful.

Our spiritual renaissance is calling us to a higher purpose in our work – not to sacrifice anything, not to give up material comfort, but to create even more material comfort, through doing work that we love to do. Love gives us energy. It is our spiritual fuel. As Dick Richards wrote in *Artful Work*, 'All work is spiritual work. All work has meaning beyond the surface realities of a job, a production schedule or a pay cheque. All work concerns spirit and soul and involves our ability to connect them with surface realities.' It all comes back to whose purpose we have given to our work and earthly activities.

Our unconditional self has only one agenda and one purpose – to extend, spread and share love in the form of our many gifts. Joan Borysenko, the writer and spiritual healthcare expert, reminds us that 'Spiritual attainment is not ascending a ladder into heaven and hobnobbing with the angels. It's being able to function with clarity and love right here on earth.'

When we work with love we draw others to us; when we work with love people know it and feel it, they are helped by it and want to keep returning to it. It's a positive vibration of passion that draws people naturally into its sphere, consciously and unconsciously. That's why love and passion are the best marketing tools around.

IF YOU CAN'T DO WHAT YOU LOVE, CHOOSE TO LOVE WHAT YOU DO

Peter was beginning his new career as an actor when we met. After giving up sales and marketing, he'd signed on with a number of agencies and one day he received a call offering him a day's work handing out information packs at an exhibition. The money wasn't brilliant, and he had to dress as a rabbit! His heart sank, but he needed the money, so he said yes to the work. He arrived at the exhibition venue and felt a bit resentful that he had to do this. But then it dawned on him that he had a choice – he could either feel resentful, or he could decide to be grateful that he had the opportunity to work, and aim to enjoy himself as much as he could.

He made the decision to give himself to the day, to enjoy connecting with people and have fun. He found by the end of the day that he had really enjoyed himself, met some interesting people, and realized that his power of choice was more powerful than he'd thought. That power of choice is there for all of us in each moment. Sometimes it takes us years to exercise it, but it is always there.

In Buddhism one of the most powerful images is that of the laughing Buddha. Buddha left his wealthy family and his privilege to seek spiritual enlightenment, which he eventually discovered after meditating beneath a bodhi tree. He laughed and laughed, because his blinkered awareness had been removed and he could see through all the suffering, judgement and pain; he saw how ridiculous it was, and that it was all based on misunderstanding. Other people describe enlightenment, the knowledge and experience of their divinity, as being surrounded by peace, others as taking off an ill-fitting and constricting suit of clothes and then feeling free. Whatever it is, one characteristic I have seen in many spiritual masters over the years is a lightness, a playfulness that challenges our perceptions of what we think it means to be spiritual.

IT'S NOT WHAT YOU DO, BUT THE SPIRIT IN WHICH YOU DO IT

I learned that courage was not the absence of fear, but the triumph over it. I felt fear myself more times than I remember, but I did it behind a mask of boldness. The brave man is not he who does not feel afraid, but he who conquers fear.

NELSON MANDELA, in *Long Road to Freedom*

On one of my trips to Dublin, my friend Michael arranged for me to spend a day with the drugs unit he managed in one of the poorest areas of the city. This unit provided support and counselling for cocaine and heroin addicts despite some opposition from the local community, who either wanted to sweep the drugs issue under the carpet or refused to acknowledge and support close family members who were suffering from drug dependency.

Although the team was housed in just two Portakabins, they managed to offer support and practical help to many of the 20,000 local residents and, in fact, because of the success they had achieved, were beginning to attract people from outside the area. This led to further action, with separate men's and women's groups being set up in the local area.

On what became a very special day for me, I was soon aware of the tremendous energy, love and enthusiasm that this unit offered its clients – particularly the young teenagers who were struggling to deal with severe problems of low self-esteem. These young people had written themselves off as hopeless cases and much of the unit's work involved helping them to believe in themselves. They were there every step of the way, mending broken spirits and hearts when they slipped back and offering practical support to rebuild sad lives.

We talked about how it felt to be a giver rather than a receiver – how hard we found it to value ourselves. Towards the end of the day I told them I felt their work was sacred; there was something very precious about what they had created, which was in essence a place of acceptance and nurturing. They all enjoyed working there; the clients enjoyed coming there, even to the extent of wanting to keep coming well beyond giving up their dependency on drugs. At the heart of this unit was great honesty and authenticity, a true grittiness, and everyone was fed from this resource. Whilst they didn't condone the habits of their clients, they always honoured the intrinsic worth of people, and saw their value beyond their behaviour. They knew they couldn't help through judgement, but only through acceptance. One of the team, Michelle, described how they had to be brutally honest with the children. 'It's not a question of telling them that drugs are terrible and they won't like them. When they try them they probably *will* enjoy them, so we have to be honest and make them really clear about the *consequences* of drugs, not the experience of them. We also need to help them reach highs and escape their problems through other means.'

My day at the unit helped me realize that it wasn't what they did that was important so much as the spirit in which they did their work. Even in the most difficult of situations, the human spirit could prevail – there could be love, laughter, caring and acceptance. There could be a true richness of spirit.

THE COURAGE TO CREATE A VEHICLE FOR OUR LOVE AND PASSION

The vehicle for our unconditional success may not exist; we may be called to create our own path. That's where the excitement and the challenge can lie. In both our relationships and our work we must create a vehicle through which we can channel our love into the world. In work, it has always taken courage to follow an individual path, exactly because making our own path takes us in directions which can sometimes be profoundly unsafe. Finding the form of our work is also very important. Do we want to work for an employer? Would we love to work for ourselves? Would we like a combination of employment and self-employment? Some people thrive in organizations, others crave the freedom that self-employment can offer. It's important to know what shape of work supports the shape that we are.

WISDOM QUESTIONS

Answer these questions with no thought of *how* you could create the work, but answer honestly about what most appeals to you:

* What structure of work would best suit you?
* If you could create your work any way you liked, what would it look like?
* Whose working life and style do you most admire and envy?

THE COURAGE TO DO WHAT YOU LOVE – THE HEARTFELT ENTREPRENEUR

The word entrepreneur brings to mind Bill Gates or some other techno-wizard seeking to build a multimillion or billion dollar firm. I seek to work passionately on a variety of projects in my small back porch office. I want to make a reasonable living, keep control over my working conditions, enjoy what I do, follow an honourable path and spend some time in the Greek Islands. Funny as it may seem now, I did not quite know this was an acceptable dream.

WENDY NEMITZ, business owner

A largely neglected area in the UK economy, and perhaps throughout the Western world, is the rapidly growing group of people who are looking to work for themselves, perhaps even working from home. They don't necessarily want to make millions, they simply want to turn one or several skills, talents and passions into small businesses. Some people have called this downshifting or portfolio working, but neither label captures the positive essence of why people are choosing this route.

In Britain we have rather skewed ideas of what it takes to be an entrepreneur. Images of tycoons, Arthur Daley from *Minder* or Del Boy Trotter from *Only Fools and Horses* spring to mind – slightly (or very) dodgy, taking whatever opportunities they can to rip people off, whilst remaining likeable rogues. Somehow it's not quite a respectable job, not a proper way of working. This could be echoed in what we see going on in Russia right now, with entrepreneurialism meaning those who have power and influence dominating those who don't. This is not the kind of entrepreneur I am talking about.

There are two types of entrepreneurial spirit:

1. *Those who love business for the sake of business. These people are not neces-sarily interested in what the business is about but they love growing it and making money.*

2. *Those who have a passion and a love for something, and want to discover ways of turning that which they love and enjoy into an income for themselves. They have an inner calling, are curious and motivated to create an authentic life.*

I am particularly interested in the latter group, because that is where the potential for huge fulfilment, creativity and pleasure lies. These are the heartfelt entrepreneurs. Here are a few very different and much more positive descriptions of entrepreneurs:

- *They are the principal instigators of social change.*
- *They are those who gets out of bed fastest and go to work happiest.*
- *They have a vision of the world, being both dreamers and doers.*
- *Their primary motivation is psychological, emotional or even spiritual rather than financial.*
- *They hit the floor running because they express themselves through their work.*
- *What drives them more than anything is their need to make a creative statement.*

Entrepreneurs are enterprising; where others see problems, in-justices and unfilled needs, they see opportunities to serve, contribute, and fulfil themselves and others. Heartfelt entre-preneurs do not see the world through pound-sign glasses; they see it as full of unmet human needs and aspirations that they would love to help people achieve. They know that because of their motivation to serve, their positive sense of purpose and their creativity, they will never be redundant. Indeed they know that the world can only offer them growing opportunity during their life. They are on their own path of self-discovery, and know this is a journey that will unfold and evolve throughout their lives. Often they want to combine their work with the *big* work of transforming the planet. Ultimately we are all Self-employed. Our highest work is to radiate our unconditional self throughout whatever work we do, whoever pays our salary. We work for our self, the love within us that promises to make our work a beacon.

According to the Global Entrepreneurship Monitor, at any moment in the UK, around 1.5 million people (3 per cent of the adult population, which represents about 7 per cent of the working population) are actively considering starting their own business. Barclays Business Banking calculate that every year, one in three of these people – approximately 500,000 people – actually start their own enterprises. This is a very considerable trend. The idea of earning our income without the tedium, drudgery and office politics seems like a dream – and by working for ourselves we have the chance to achieve this. By learning inspirational and practical strategies for making working for ourselves a reality, we can gain greater fulfilment, creative self-expression, a better work/life balance and personal freedom, as well as an abundant income.

HEARTFELT ENTREPRENEURS CAN HAVE MULTIPLE INCOME SOURCES FROM MULTIPLE PASSIONS

Ironically, when doing work we are passionate about, we end up making more money.

BARBARA WINTER, author of *Making a Living without a Job*

Many of us harbour a sneaking suspicion that we could actually be good and successful at more than one thing, but mostly we have been encouraged to consider only one form of work. We usually end up trying to conform and squeeze ourselves into that job or career, squashing our authentic self, distorting ourselves out of shape and shoehorning ourselves into something that no longer fits. A bit like taking scissors to a large picture of ourselves to cut off parts so that it fits in the frame, we repress and deny other creative and passionate parts of ourselves, in order, we believe, to satisfy our obligations.

THE RENAISSANCE OF RENAISSANCE IDEAS

Many of us are multi-talented, creative, enterprising and natural adventurers, enjoying change and evolution. We have a synergy of gifts and talents. Just imagine being told every day as a child, 'There are many things that you can love and be good at.' My young friend Ellie goes to Millfield School near Glastonbury, and their education ethic is 'We believe that each child can excel at one and often many things. So we provide as many activities as possible so that each child can find their natural gifts and affinities.' Each day they offer Ellie and the other children over 150 activities for them to choose from! But most of us grow up with a work ethic that says we should find that one thing and stick with it, even though we have many talents, passions, gifts and skills.

In the Renaissance period, in the 1500s, there was a belief that everybody was multi-talented and skilled. People could understand many things and had diverse interests. Leonardo da Vinci was the archetypical Renaissance man – painter, sculptor, inventor, engineer, architect. He truly was a genius, but he was not unusual for his time. Nobody told him, 'Get a job!' Yet some time during the Industrial Revolution, with the creation of factory and office working, we moved away from this multi-faceted ethic. Today we judge people who are good at a number of things – calling them 'dabblers', or jacks of all trades but masters of none. We seem instead to aim for jobs, even if they are repetitive and unrewarding. The word *job* actually derives from the middle English word *gobet*, which means a small piece or a lump. Isn't that how much of our work can feel? A lump we carry around! I think we are having a renaissance of the Renaissance idea – that we are richer and more diverse, multi-talented and many-faceted, and want our work to be a reflection and expression of our skills and talents. Many of us want to be portfolio workers – to do several things – either consecutively or simultaneously. Perhaps the drift into jobs was a temporary diversion, a fossilized belief that is now being undone by the human spirit. We are reinventing jobs and work.

Ever since I started to run my own business, I have had many passions. Now I earn a living from a number of different sources – I give public talks, run public workshops, train with companies, consult, coach, speak at conferences, write books and articles, broadcast, develop products, sell products and promote other speakers. These are all passions of mine, and whilst no one area could support me, together they give me an adequate income.

WISDOM THOUGHTS

✳ Write down six different ways that you could earn money, right now, if you wanted to and needed to.

✳ Write down the six ways that you would most love to earn money.

SIX MOST ·USEFUL ATTITUDES FOR LOVE AND MONEY

1. *When you focus on your love and passion, you can make money as a result.*

2. *You deserve all the money you want.*

3. *Having money and making money can be easy.*

4. *Money is holy and spiritual.*

5. *Doing what we love, have passion for and are inspired by can be the major*

focus of work. It needn't be money alone.

6. *Money can come from multiple sources.*

SIX MOST UNHELPFUL ATTITUDES FOR LOVE AND MONEY

1. *Money only comes through difficulty and struggle.*

2. *Money is bad, unspiritual and unholy.*

3. *I don't deserve money.*

4. *Money is the only real purpose for work.*

5. *You have to sell your soul to make money.*

6. *You can't make money doing what you love.*

BECOME FASCINATED BY LOVE AND MONEY

Who do you know who is most passionate about their work and earns a good living? Who do you know who has most integrated their love and money in their life?

Spend time focusing on how you could turn your passions into income.

THE COURAGE TO HAVE OUR LIFE BE REALLY GOOD

Our ego labels everything really good as terrifying.

Anon

We have to remember that our ego takes everything that is truly good, and somehow puts a spin on it and tells us that it's bad. Then it offers a substitute in its place, something that glitters but isn't the true gold. We can surround ourselves with objects of beauty, but unless we've found the beauty in our own soul, there will always be something missing from our lives. Our greatest pains in life come from playing too small, from trying to squeeze our spirits into jobs, work or job titles that are too small for us, and hiding or denying our grandeur. Success is being more of who we already are.

The journey of unconditional success is the journey into our good feelings – our love, joy, fulfilment, peace and happiness. The question is: how good will we let it be? How much joy and happiness will we allow ourselves to receive? We need our heart to allow us to feel deeply, to enjoy the fruits of our achievements, otherwise we are just collecting trophies, going through the motions with lots of ticks in boxes but without the deep feelings of gratitude. This is not about being smug or self-satisfied, but about experiencing the greatest gifts and blessings of the spirit. When we are truly content we want to share with others – smug is just for us; true fulfilment is a blessing we want to share.

LOVE SHINES ITS LIGHT INTO OUR DARK PLACES

In 2000, a year after my first book was published by Element Books, I was told that they were in trouble financially and were looking for someone to buy them outright. I didn't realize the extent of their difficulties until I had a telephone call informing me that Element had gone into receivership. I was devastated. My book had been selling brilliantly, but was suddenly unavailable just as it was about to be reprinted. They owed me money, and I felt that I had lost a support system in my life. I felt shaken to my core, and certainly couldn't see how this was ever going to be for my highest good.

It wasn't until a month or two later that I had an awareness of what this had triggered for me. It was as if a depth charge had gone off deep inside, and its repercussions were still resonating. My book represented to me a large part of my success in the world. Deep down there was still a part of me that felt I was a failure, but my book proved I was a success. Without my book, I was left again with my own feelings of being a failure. I knew this was an old feeling, not really to do with the current situation, but triggered by it. I felt depressed and unhappy.

I hit a real low, and when I feel like that I often want to hide away and not talk to people. This time I made a new choice and decided not to hide, but to be honest and ask for help. I called my friend Jeff Allen, a very skilled therapist and healer and someone I knew I could trust when I was feeling so vulnerable. The only mutually convenient time when we could both talk was when I was on my way to a meeting, so I stopped off in a garden centre Alexandra Palace in north London, and called him from my mobile phone. It was around Christmas time and it felt very bizarre to be sitting in my car crying my eyes out, while people around me were carrying their Christmas trees. Jeff helped me to understand that the real source of this pain stemmed from my childhood, when I felt I had failed to make my family happy, and judged myself for not being good enough. But Jeff suggested it was time to get myself off the cross! What I'd been running away from, I ended up running to. As I allowed myself fully to feel this pain, it was awful. But without an awareness of our feelings, we cannot experience compassion. I realized that I can only truly share the sufferings and the joys of others when I've truly experienced my own.

Over the next week I spent time with that young boy in me who felt so awful, and I poured love and acceptance into him within my mind, bringing him back to life. I felt as if a deep healing was taking place within me, as if my circuitry was being rewired, and my foundations rebuilt. What was even more amazing was that within a month I had appointed an agent to represent me and he got an incredible two-book deal with a new publisher. Another publisher took over my first book, which went back into print. The coming months saw new and higher levels of success and personal well-being. The wound in me was poorly healed, but in ripping off the bandage and allowing proper healing, I let a new strength come through. Love wanted me to have this healing; I had been resisting it. This is the core work we sometimes need to do, the facing and melting of our old fear and pain, the inner healing and the restoration of love within our minds. In many spiritual traditions the transformation of attitudes and old emotional patterns is daily work. But it needn't be hard work.

To open to greater love we must first recognize that we have to pierce the armour that we've spent our whole lives building up as our defence, and that process is very uncomfortable. It's as if we need to go through an emotional detox in order to travel on this road to liberation. Rivers of tears may have to flow from us to melt our hardened hearts, but this is not weakness or failure, it is part of the journey. As Kahlil Gibran wrote so eloquently in *The Prophet*, this is the pain that 'Breaks the shell of our understanding'. So first we experience pain, and then out of that is born a new sense of power. We understand that we've created a sense of our self built on fear, which only love can dismantle.

RECLAIMING WHAT WE'VE HIDDEN AWAY

We all have our hidden shadows, the parts of us that are imperfect, that are controlling, that are co-dependent, that are angry and vulnerable. The real courage comes from making your life an act of courage, from being willing to keep moving to your own edge and into more authentic expression. Go to the edge and take another step, rather than stop. This is self-acceptance – recognizing and embracing our multi-faceted nature.

Unconditional success is the courage to reclaim the lost and neglected parts of our selves.

REDEEMING OUR NEGLECTED ASPECTS RESTORES OUR POWER

Do you ever get bored? I think boredom begins when

- *we stop taking risks*
- *we stop giving or receiving*
- *we need to choose to stretch ourselves*

Another message that boredom is trying to get across to us is that we are being called to reclaim some aspect of ourselves that we've neglected. We can bring ourselves back to life by reclaiming something of what we've denied or are hiding about ourselves.

Andrea came to see me. She described how she was bored in her job as a teacher. She wanted to know how she could have more fun and excitement in her work and life. As we talked, it became clear to me that Andrea was actually a very creative soul. She had a gift for painting, played the cello, sang, loved gardening, but currently wasn't pursuing any of her creative passions. She'd travelled extensively and loved outdoor projects and adventures, and had lived in the heart of Africa. Her father had been in the armed forces and had led an interesting, diverse, eclectic life and she felt envious of what he'd carved out for himself. 'It seems to me that you are a creative adventurer, trying to squeeze yourself into a job,' I said to her. Andrea's face lit up, and she replied, 'I hadn't really thought of myself that way, but I suppose I am.' I said, 'I can't see you being happy unless you are being more adventurous.'

Andrea had been trying to sideline her passions, creativity and adventurous spirit in order to be sensible and earn her living. In doing so she had repressed much of her energy. What she had relegated to the shadows, she needed to bring out into the light. Her father had. Yet, he had given her a gift that she hadn't fully accepted yet – an example of how to live a life of creativity and passion. Andrea needed to find her own brilliance and this is true for many of us. By trying to squeeze ourselves into jobs and careers, we have cut ourselves out of a picture that we thought didn't really fit our needs.

One view of success is that it is staying in control of our feelings and behaviour. The big problem is that we can't close down on just *some* feelings. We either choose to feel or not feel, we can't choose what feelings to feel. Feelings have only one purpose – to be felt! What we don't feel doesn't go away, it just gets stuck.

We may think success is escaping some feelings that we know are there, and if we can only get far enough away, they'll disappear. But without our heart, without the many hues and shades of our true feelings, I don't think we can ever experience real success.

Twelve years ago when I was still involved in sales I read a book called *Iron John*, by American poet Robert Bly, and found some of his ideas very interesting. A friend who had done some work with Robert suggested I meet him. I was terrified at the prospect of being with 100 other men just like me on a country weekend, and had heard all the jokes about banging drums and dancing around fires. The weekend was on the subject of 'The Wild Man', that part of man that is passionate, alive, creative, spontaneous, emotional and unpredictable, very unlike the good boy I had tried so hard to be. (There were also 'Wild Women' workshops, run by and for women.)

I found the experience very scary and very powerful. I realized that I loved being involved with other men, and talking about male things. It enabled me to get in touch with feelings that I had buried away – like anger, grief, joy and creativity – and that weekend helped me to reconnect with a sense of what I can only call my true hidden self, my soul.

I felt I'd been running away from a lot, without really knowing why and when Robert read a poem called 'The Wind One Brilliant Day', it touched me deeply. It still does.

The wind, one brilliant day, called
To my soul with an odour of jasmine.

'In return for the odour of my jasmine,
I'd like all the odour of your roses.'

'I have no roses; all the flowers
in my garden are dead.'

'Well then, I'll take the withered petals
and the yellow leaves and the waters of the fountain.'

The wind left. And I wept. And I said to myself:
'What have you done with the garden that was entrusted to you?'

ANTONIO MACHADO, *translated by Robert Bly*

SPIRITUAL WORK IS NOT RUNNING AWAY FROM PAIN, BUT HEALING IT

As I heard this poem I was filled with a terrible sadness because I realized how much of myself I had thrown away, disowned and tried to run away from. In an attempt to be loved and liked by everybody, I had tried to make myself into what I thought they wanted me to be. My denial resulted in a life of depression, boredom and even a large degree of cynicism. As I started allowing myself to feel again I started to look for my lost self and to experience the kind of joy and creativity I thought were lost for ever.

Today, I think healing is a lifelong journey, a pilgrimage to the lost and neglected parts of ourselves, and we can achieve this little by little, every day. Unconditional success is much more than a defence, and an attempt to escape from feelings of failure and not being good enough. It is joy itself.

I saw grief drinking a cup of sorrow, and called out, 'It tastes good, does it not?' 'You've caught me,' grief answered, 'and you've ruined my business, how can I sell sorrow when you know it's a blessing?'

JALALUDDIN RUMI, mystic poet

Our work is not to deny pain, nor is it to indulge in it, but to be willing to honestly feel that we can become free of it. As we have discovered, a large part of this journey is to be willing to stop blaming and take responsibility: much of our pain is caused by our *thinking*, not by other people. Unconditional success is about digging deeper into ourselves to find greater gifts and greater joy. Sometimes we hit a bedrock of old stuff, but as we've discovered, we are never alone; a loving presence is always with us and can give us incredible comfort and support. *A Course in Miracles* re-assures us that, 'If you knew Who walked beside you on the way that you have chosen, fear would be impossible.' We experience fear only because we have forgotten how loved and supported we are. As we practise remembering and becoming aware of this constant presence, our fear begins to dissolve.

SELF-ACCEPTANCE – THE RICHNESS THAT WE ARE

The only devils in the world are those running around in our own hearts, and that is where all our battles should be fought.

MOHANDAS (MAHATMA) GANDHI

Conventional ideas of success are about trying to eliminate experiences and aspects of ourselves we don't like and find unacceptable as well as about trying to create what we do want. Success can be a getting away from this and a way of never having to go back there again. But whatever we find unacceptable about ourselves or life doesn't disappear – we simply see it out there, and fight it out there rather than embrace it, in here. Carl Jung, the Swiss psychiatrist, put it beautifully when he wrote: 'That which we do not bring to consciousness appears as fate in our lives.' What we don't recognize within ourselves, and either bury or deny, we end up feeling a victim of.

Unconditional success is concerned with moving on beyond victimhood, to true power. True power is found in acceptance, not in judgement. When we judge, we are always battling and defending against what we have judged as bad. To accept is not necessarily to condone, but to acknowledge that something exists and to find an alternative.

EVERY SHADOW HIDES A GIFT – ALWAYS AND/AND

Perhaps all the dragons of our lives
are princesses who are only waiting to
see us once, beautiful and brave.
Perhaps everything terrible is in
its deepest being something
that needs our love.

RAINER MARIA RILKE, Austrian poet

If I were to ask you to write a very honest list of what you find unacceptable about yourself, how long would the list be? Blank? A few items? Dozens? Pages? In my experience most of us have lots of things we find unacceptable about ourselves, things that we dislike and despise or even hate. We may think our very survival depends on us never allowing these sides of us to be seen, although on this journey to unconditional success we have learned that we can embrace all aspects of our nature. As we do, we melt our shadows and see the light that shines in each of us. It is the light of unconditional love. Human existence is half light and half dark, and our possibilities seem strangely linked to those parts of us we keep in the dark. What is hidden always holds a treasure. We think we are chained to our shadow, but it is only a dream. When we awaken we will see that we are free.

We need to differentiate between a person and their behaviour. Of course, there is a lot of behaviour that is unloving, unkind and cruel. But the person is not their behaviour. Unloving actions and behaviour are only created by unloving thoughts and ideas – by the ego. However horrible the ego looks, behind it is still the un-conditional self. It hasn't gone anywhere. The person is still responsible for their behaviour, but the solution is correction, not punishment, forgiveness, not revenge. When we are able to love and accept what we find to be unlovable and unacceptable – when we forgive – the behaviour will begin to disappear.

PERSONAL DEVELOPMENT, SELF-IMPROVEMENT AND SELF-ACCEPTANCE

Much of the world of self-improvement has as its starting point: you are not good enough, there is something wrong with you, you need fixing and there are undesirable elements about you that need eliminating. We can easily spend years 'working' on ourselves, and trying to get rid of what we've judged to be unacceptable traits. But at the heart of it, and why self-improvement can only ever have limited effectiveness, is that whatever we judge in ourselves, we can never get away from. It just goes underground psychically, meaning it is alive and well and living in our unconscious and subconscious minds. The only way we get to see our judgements is in the people around us. The world is our mirror – we see the content of our mind played out every moment of every day. We end up trying to change the mirror, rather than what is reflected in the mirror.

SELF-ATTACK IS THE WORST DISEASE IN THE WORLD

Have you ever thought that you have become like something or someone you used to really dislike? I often laugh now as I recognize I am becoming more like people I used to really hate! Two friends of mine told me that they used to be Marxist socialists, and are both now property-owning landlords! I think there are two prerequisites we need in order to search out our shadow side – great courage, and a great sense of humour. What we believe about ourselves in the darkest places in our minds is often so horrible, so nasty, that we bury those parts of us and overcompensate by being very nice and by doing all the right things. It is as if we are playing a role to prove that we are not as horrible as we think we are.

WISDOM QUESTIONS

* What do you judge most in yourself? What do you attack yourself for being and doing, or not being or not doing? Get specific, and write a list.

* What do you find most acceptable in yourself?

* What do you find most unacceptable in others?

    *

* Which are you better at seeing – your apparent faults, flaws and deficiencies or your strengths, your brilliance?

* Are you better at seeing what is right with you, or what is wrong with you? Or do you see them pretty equally?

LOVE IS TRANSFORMATIONAL

Love is the spiritual spotlight that will shine a light into all our dark places, into our vulnerabilities, but will also fully allow us to heal them and release them. When love shines its light on us and starts bestowing its gifts on us, we may find it too bright, and shrink back. Like a prisoner kept in the dark too long, our eyes need time to adjust. Or we may not feel worthy, thinking: You've got the wrong person, I don't deserve this. This is another of love's functions, to identify and stimulate old feelings of unworthiness so that we can release them and be available to receive. In Chapter 4 I wrote about my first introduction to St James's in Piccadilly, where I went along to the launch of a poetry anthology. A poem that touched me deeply was 'Love' by George Herbert, who lived in the seventeenth century:

> *Love bade me welcome; yet my soul drew back,*
> *Guiltie of dust and sinne.*
> *But quick-ey'd Love, observing me grow slack*
> *From my first entrance in,*
> *Drew nearer to me, sweetly questioning,*
> *If I lack'd any thing.*

> *A guest, I answer'd, worthy to be here:*
> *Love said, You shall be he.*
> *I the unkinde, ungratefull? Ah my deare,*
> *I cannot look on thee.*
> *Love took my hand, and smiling did reply,*
> *Who made the eyes but I?*

> *Truth Lord, but I have marr'd them; let my shame*
> *Go where it doth deserve.*
> *And know you not, sayes Love, who bore the blame?*

My deare, then I will serve.
You must sit down, sayes Love, and taste my meat:
So I did sit and did eat.

The words 'a guest . . . worthy to be here' resonated with me. I suddenly saw that I had felt unworthy and undeserving. I had closed the door to so many good things because of these feelings. I now know that we are all worthy of gifts of love and abundance and that love is always calling us to shed our false ideas, to nourish and fulfil ourselves.

Even from a medical perspective, we are discovering the healing power of love. Dr Dean Ornish, in his book *Love and Survival*, collected evidence from around the world on the part that love, connection and community play in the healing process. He concluded,

If a new drug had the same impact, virtually every doctor in the country would be recommending it for their patients. It would be malpractice not to prescribe it – yet, with few exceptions, we doctors do not learn much about the healing power of love, intimacy and transformation in our medical training. Rather these ideas are often ignored or even denigrated. Love and intimacy are at the root of what makes us sick and what makes us well, what causes us sadness and what brings happiness, what makes us suffer and leads to healing.

It is love that sees the spirit in others, sees their gifts, sees their beauty, their loveliness and their preciousness. It is love that nurtures the spiritual growth of another. And we need to start by loving ourselves. We can more truly help others when we have helped ourselves first. Loving ourselves is our first great lesson, and one that we will be attending classes in for the remainder of our lives. Not a narcissistic love, but a deep knowing of our own intrinsic worth, that we are lovable by the nature of our very existence. This is the unconditional love in which we are always held, but are unable to see.

OUR SUCCESS IS OUR PEACE AND HAPPINESS

Sometimes when we are standing at what feels like a cliff edge in our lives, we don't know whether we will be dashed against the rocks below, or will sprout wings and take off into flight. Maybe we're scared to fly, so familiar are we with our land legs. We can sit on the cliff edge speculating for ever. The only way we'll discover is by jumping. Perhaps the whole purpose of our life is to face and gradually melt all our fears, and to begin to remember that we are eternally safe within the mind of our creator. We are free to imagine death, loss, pain and tragedy, and we all do. But the purpose of the journey of unconditional success is to shine away all our illusions about ourselves, and remember that we are eternally safe. We are returning home to the place we never left.

EPILOGUE

ONLY THE LOVE IS REAL

Our affections and loves will not be denied but must find a home by being expressed in the world. Work is the ground of their arrival, and ours too. Our work is to make ourselves visible in the world. This is the soul's individual journey, and the soul would much rather fail at its own journey than succeed at someone else's.

DAVID WHYTE, author of *Crossing the Unknown Sea*

Through continuing to follow our inspiration, we bring new territories of our heart and new regions of our soul into being. We find our way home to ourselves, and our true nature. We talk about outer space being the final frontier of knowledge and understanding, but the true frontier we stand at now, personally and globally, is the frontier of inner space. We need to remember and discover the incredible human capacity for creativity, for laughter and joy, for wonder and growth, for forgiveness and inventiveness, for the daily celebration of all the good things we *do* have. Love is what we have to give each other, to give ourselves and give the world. It conquers all. Nothing else is real.

Love is at the centre of absolutely everybody. We are here to remember that together.

God bless.

CLOSING MEDITATION

To be a true success in whatever way you want, is a true blessing:

To choose abundance rather than scarcity and lack is a gift and is success

To choose love rather than fear is a gift and is success

To choose creativity over cynicism is a gift and is success

To shine rather than hide away is a gift and is success

To give our gifts to the world rather than go through the motions is a gift and is success

To join with others rather than judge them is a gift and is success

To form a team rather than be a lone ranger is a gift and is success

To fulfil your destiny is a gift and is success

To play big rather than diminish ourselves is a gift and is success

To hold ourselves innocent rather than condemn ourselves is a gift and is success

To know our true value rather than think we aren't worth much is a gift and is success

To know that we are love in essence is a gift and is success.

BIBLIOGRAPHY

I can personally recommend all the books and tapes below to inspire and uplift you on your journey of unconditional success.

A Course in Miracles, Penguin Arkana, 1975.

Autry, James A., *Love and Profit*, William Morrow, 1991.

Barks, Coleman, *The Essential Rumi*, HarperCollins, 1995.

Berke, Diane, *Love Always Answers*, Crossroads, 1994.

Bly, Robert, *Iron John*, Element, 1990.

Bly, Robert, *The Kabir Book*, Beacon Press, 1977.

Boldt, Laurence G., *How to Find the Work You Love*, Arkana, 1996.

Breathnach, Sara Ban, *Simple Abundance*, Bantam Books, 1997.

Caddy, Eileen, *Opening Doors Within*, Findhorn Press, 1987.

Cameron, Julia, *The Artist's Way*, Pan Books, 1994.

Carpenter, Tom, *Dialogue on Awakening*, Carpenter Press, 1992.

Chopra, Deepak, *The Seven Spiritual Laws of Success*, New World Library, 1994.

Cohen, Alan, *Handle with Prayer*, Hay House, 1999.

Cohen, Alan, *I Had It All The Time*, Hay House, 1994.

Cohen, Alan, *Lifestyles of the Rich in Spirit*, Hay House, 1996.

Covey, Stephen, *The Seven Habits of Highly Effective People*, Simon and Schuster, 1989.

Dossy, Dr Larry, *Healing Words*, HarperCollins, 1997.

Dossy, Dr Larry, *Prayer is Good Medicine*, HarperCollins, 1997.

Dyer, Wayne, *You'll See It When You Believe It*, Arrow, 1989.

Dyer, Wayne, *Your Sacred Self*, HarperCollins, 1995.

Gibran, Kahlil, *The Prophet*, Heinemann, 1993.

Gray, John, *Men are from Mars, Women are from Venus*, HarperCollins, 1993.

Handy, Charles, *The New Alchemists*, Hutchinson, 1999.

Hansen, Mark Victor, and Canfield, Jack, *Chicken Soup for the Soul*, Vermilion, 1998.

Haskell, Brent, *Journey without Distance*, De Vorss, 1994.

Hendricks, Gay and Luderman, Kate, *The Corporate Mystic*, Bantam Books, 1996.

Holden, Robert, *Happiness NOW!*, Hodder and Stoughton, 1998.

Holden, Robert, *Shift Happens*, Hodder and Stoughton, 2000.

Hotchkiss, Burt, *Have Miracles, Will Travel*, Greensleeves, 1990.

Jampolsky, Gerald, *Love Is Letting Go of Fear*, Celestial Arts, 1979.

Jampolsky, Gerald, *Wake Up Calls*, Hay House, 1992.

Jeffers, Susan, *End the Struggle and Dance with Life*, Hodder and Stoughton, 1996.

Jeffers, Susan, *Feel the Fear and Do It Anyway*, Rider, 1991.

Levoy, Gregg, *Callings*, HarperCollins, 1997.

Mandela, Nelson, *Long Walk to Freedom*, Abacus, 1995.

Marcic, Dorothy, *Managing with the Wisdom of Love*, Jossey Bass Wiley, 1997.

Matthews, Andrew, *Follow Your Heart*, Seashell Publishing, 1997.

Moore, Thomas, *Care of the Soul*, Piatkus, 1992.

Mountain Dreamer, Oriah, *The Invitation*, HarperCollins, 2000.

O'Donohue, John, *Anam Ċara*, Bantam Press, 1997.

Olivier, Richard, *Inspirational Leadership – Henry V and the Muse of Fire*, Industrial Society, 2001.

Ornish, Dr Dean, *Love and Survival*, HarperCollins, 1999.

Peck, M. Scott, *The Road Less Travelled*, Arrow, 1990.

Pilser, Paul Zane, *Unlimited Wealth*, Simon and Schuster, 1995.

Price, John Randolph, *The Abundance Book*, Hay House, 1987.

Renshaw, Ben, *Successful, but Something Missing*, Rider, 2000.

Renshaw, Ben, *Together, but Something Missing*, Rider, 2001.

Richards, Dick, *Artful Work*, Berrett-Koehler, 1995.

Rinpoche, Sogyal, *The Tibetan Book of Living and Dying*, Rider, 1992.

Russell, Peter, *From Science to God*, Peter Russell, 2000.

Schulz, Mona Lisa, *Awakening Intuition*, Bantam Books, 1999.

Siegel, Bernie, *Love, Medicine and Miracles*, Rider, 1986.

Sinetar, Marsha, *To Build the Life You Want, Create the Work You Love*, St Martin's Press, 1996.

Spezzano, Chuck, *If It Hurts, It Isn't Love*, Hodder and Stoughton, 1999.

Toms, Michael, *The Soul of Business*, Hay House, 1995.

Whyte, David, *Crossing the Unknown Sea*, Penguin, 2001.

Whyte, David, *The Heart Aroused*, Industrial Society, 1999.

Williams, Nick, *The Work We Were Born to Do*, Element, 1999.

Williams, Nick, *The 12 Principles of the Work We Were Born to Do*, Element, 2002.

Williamson, Marianne, *A Return to Love*, HarperCollins, 1992.

Williamson, Marianne, *Enchanted Love*, Rider, 1999.

Williamson, Marianne, *Illuminata*, Rider, 1994.

Winter, Barbara, *Making a Living without a Job*, Bantam Books, 1994.

Wright, Joel, *The Mirror on Still Water*, Mind and Miracles, 1997.

Yogananda, Paramahansa, *The Law of Success*, Self Realization, 1998.

CONTACT DETAILS AND RESOURCES

UK

Nick Williams
The Heart at Work
PO Box 2236
London W1A 5UA
07000 781922
success@heartatwork.net
www.unconditionalsuccess.com and www.heartatwork.net

ORGANIZATIONS MENTIONED IN THE BOOK:

Alternatives
St James's
197 Piccadilly
London W1J 9FF
020 7287 6711
post@alternatives.org.uk
www.alternatives.org.uk
Where Nick was director for many years and is now a trustee

Findhorn Foundation
The Park
Findhorn
Scotland IV36 3TZ
01309 690311
reception@findhorn.org.uk
www.findhorn.org.uk

Happiness Project
Elms Court
Chapel Way
Botley
Oxford OX2 9LP
01865 244414
hello@happiness.co.uk
www.happiness.co.uk
Runs the work of Nick's friends Robert Holden and Ben Renshaw

The Miracle Network
12a Barness Court
6–8 Westbourne Terrace
London W2 3UW
020 7262 0209
info@miracles.org.uk
www.miracles.org.uk
Supports students of *A Course in Miracles*

Psychology of Vision
France Farm
Pewsey
Wiltshire SN9 6DR
01980 635199
www.psychology-of-vision.com
Supports the work of Chuck Spezzano and Jeff Allen

HEART AT WORK SUPPORT PRODUCTS AND SERVICES

Heart at Work, founded by Nick Williams, aims to serve the needs of three key groups:

1. *Individuals seeking career inspiration and guidance.*

2. *Individuals considering or already running their own small businesses, based on their passions.*

3. *Organizations in the public, private and voluntary sectors who want to inspire the best from their staff.*

Here are some ways we do this:

- *Heart at Work runs regular events around the UK, and we'll happily send you a programme; or look at our web site.*
- *One-to-one coaching with Nick Williams or a skilled colleague.*
- *We run a 'Heart at Work' programme to help you lay the foundations for your work and success.*
- *We offer a free monthly e-newsletter with inspiration and ideas.*
- *We offer a year-long e-mail coaching programme. Every week for 52 weeks you will receive e-mail coaching direct from Nick Williams to help you create unconditional success and the work you were born to do. This costs only £35 for a whole year.*
- *Contact us for full information on how we can work with your company or conference, from a 60-minute presentation to a year-long programme.*

For information on these contact us at:

Nick Williams
The Heart at Work
PO Box 2236
London W1A 5UA
07000 781922
success@heartatwork.net
www.heartatwork.net

PARTNER ORGANIZATIONS AROUND THE GLOBE:

Australia
Ian Hutchinson
Life by Design
Suite 19
88 Helen Street
Lane Cove
NSW 2066
Australia
00 61 2 9420 8280
Fax: 00 61 2 9418 7747
info@lifebydesign.com.au
www.lifebydesign.com.au

Ireland
Michael Daly
The Barnabas Project
152 Willow Park Drive
Glasnevin
Dublin 11
Ireland

00 353 1 842 0544
barnabas@gofree.indigo.ie

New Zealand
Liz Constable
Life Coach
12 Hollywood Avenue
Titirangi
Auckland
New Zealand
00 649 817 5189
goddess@planet.gen.nz

South Africa
Helen Burton
Cape Town
South Africa
00 27 21 (0)825777772
burton@intekom.co.za

USA
Barbara Winter
Winning Ways
PO Box 390412
Minneapolis
MN 55439
USA
001 952 835 5647
babswinter@yahoo.com

International Association of Career Management Professionals
(IACMP)
204 E Street

Washington
DC 20002
USA
001 202 547 6377
www.iacmp.org
Has chapters worldwide. Nick is a member and has presented at their conferences.

INDEX